South
of Dust

Scott Michael Bowers

To Mom:
with all of my love

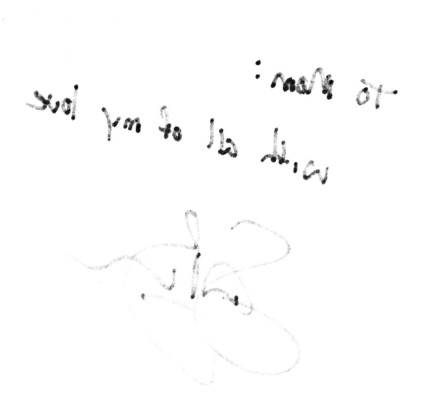

DEDICATION

For Emily, always pushing, believing and loving.

For Fiona, Gideon & Rio, the dreams to come.

For Three Amigos, that laughed in the nights of youth.

For Mom, for everything else.

CONTENTS

ACKNOWLEDGMENTS

Special thanks to my wife, Emily for coming up with the title one night and
then designing the cover art.
Thanks to Ello for creating a social media space that inspired me to simply
sit down and write.
Thanks to Google Maps for saving me countless expense in physical
research.
Thanks to those that believed, encouraged and supported.
I'm going to assume you know who you are.

"Men are haunted by the vastness of eternity. And so we ask ourselves:
will our actions echo across the centuries?
Will strangers hear our names long after we are gone and wonder who we were,
how bravely we fought, how fiercely we loved?"

Odysseus

CHAPTER 1

The highway turned back south. The soft lights of the interstate were dancing across my shoulders and chest as I drove. I reached out for the radio dial and turned it down just a little as it went to commercial break. A jingle about some kind of soft drink, or strip club, or cleaning product — who the hell knows. My mind was tuning out, or maybe just tuning to something different. I adjusted in my seat, sitting a little straighter. I still had another 200 miles to drive.

Jilly shifted in the seat next to me, her blonde hair falling at different angles across her peaceful, sleeping face. Roan slept in the backseat, softly snoring, his chest rising and falling in slumber. Three amigos, three pals. Three fools, most likely, wandering across the highways of the southern United States. Waste of gasoline and purpose. I was gonna keep driving.

In the 10 years since the three of us had graduated from Alexander Central High, we had made this same Spring Break trip to the Gulf of Mexico each year. It was actually 13 years in a row, counting three years in high school, but now the trip was beginning to feel like a sad reminder of bygone days. Most of the people we would now encounter over the next 8 days were 21 or younger. Last year, Roan had 'accidentally' slept with some 17 year old from Birmingham. His defense was pointless and pale, and for a while there I thought Jilly may finally want to end her friendship with him, and me. She didn't speak to me again until my birthday in mid June. Our friendships were based on less and less in common each and every year. Roan had been kicked out of four colleges — from the university level all the way down to a recent community college — while Jilly breezed through four years of college, grabbed her Bachelor's Degree and went to work one week after her college graduation.

Not sure we could have been three more different people riding in one car with a common past but equally uncertain futures. At least we had a shared short-term future; a future that would include beer, mixed drinks, loud music, fast food, too many cigarettes, not enough sleep, sand and sea air clinging to every part of our bodies and our clothes, and eight days to make some additional, and traditional, at least for us, memories.

Jilly kept an honest to God scrap book on the annual trip. A book filled with pictures of drunken fools, topless girls and random stolen objects that Jilly had collected as a memento of every trip to the Gulf. She even had ashtrays in her apartment from the various hotels, motels, or rental homes we had stayed at over 13 years — and she didn't even smoke in her apartment. I had loved her since I was 8 years old, and we had shared just about everything over the last 20 years, from a sloppy first kiss to an awkward first time, to remorse over the changes that pull people in different ways. Now, I guess I loved her more like some kind of sister or cousin. I remained fiercely protective, maybe a touch possessive, but I wasn't *in* love. I honestly didn't know, as I sat staring out of the windshield, steering the car on the straight path to the Gulf on this April night, if she was in love with me or not. I doubt she knew.

Jilly turned towards me in her sleep, and perhaps consciously or not, reached out and placed her hand on my thigh. She wore a pink tank top with the the word, 'PINK,' displayed across her breasts (she found that funny) and tan shorts. Her hair, which more than one female friend had labeled as 'perfect,' seemed far from it as strands floated in the night air, while others continued to lay, haphazardly, across her face and head. I could just see the tip of her butterfly tattoo on her right hip and as the streetlights of the interstate danced and receded, again and again on her face, she looked as beautiful as ever. More so. She was now in the fullness of her beauty; a woman grown.

She and Roan had started drinking at 5 p.m. Jilly had taken a half-day off from work to get her final packing done for the nine-day break from reality, eight of which would be spent in the Florida sun. Roan had clocked out from the shipping company at 4 p.m., tossed clothes into an old duffel bag and parked his piece of shit Ford outside Jilly's apartment. It had fallen on me to drive this year in our rotation and that allowed the two of them to drink heavily. I hadn't finally turned in my last assignment until nearly 10 o'clock and by the time I pulled into Jilly's complex it was after 11 and the pair were nicely buzzed in their alcohol-fueled party kick off.

"Time to turn it up," Roan had said loudly into my ear as we had merged onto the interstate. Roughly twenty minutes later, Roan was already turned down for the night. To be fair, he had been up since 4 a.m. I was thankful for the silence; which spoke to how different I was in just five years. Maybe just the last three.

At the start of this trip five years ago, I was on the verge of graduating college and I thought it was to be our last spring break trip together. It was on the return that Jilly, looking out the window at the vast nothingness that is Alabama, decided we weren't done.

3

"We need to do this every year," she said then. "Every year, try and all get together and just keep the tradition alive."

Five years later, it was already getting tougher to do that and I wondered if this might be the last of our trips to the Gulf.

The trips had contained so much of what is right and wrong about youth. Stupid decisions made after midnight, but decisions that have to be made. Choices. Learning. There had been lines of coke, and too many beers to ever count. Sex with strangers. Sex with friends. Sometimes both. Swimming. Parasailing. Countless pictures from Jilly's cameras — most of them disposable; the cameras and the pictures. But some of those pictures caught something. Showed us something. From tenderness to cruel personal pranks of kids. Even when we had reached an age when the word 'kid' no longer really applied. It somehow still did. We were older, but not wiser. Educated, but not smart. We had standards, but no morals. We had opinions, but no beliefs. We ran along the beach under the sun, and walked along the beach under the moon. We had forever, and we were running out of time.

The bright lights of a service station appeared on the horizon and I knew the further we got into Lower Alabama the odds for fuel would decrease this late at night. I hit the exit ramp and turned onto the two lane state road that ran east to west and turned left across the bridge. I pulled into the station and was happy to see that the station was actually still open — too many of these stations left lights on for advertising purposes, but would in fact be shuttered at nightfall. I drove to the pump, shut the engine off and got out to fuel. Three dogs stood about two hundred feet from me, barking into the night seemingly at a fence-lined field.

I finished fueling and headed into pay for the gas.

"Hey," the attendant named Roger said.

"How ya doing," I asked back.

"Not bad," Roger said with a grin. "What them dogs barking at?"

"I'm not sure."

"You ain't from 'round here, is ya?"

"No."

"Heading to the beach, huh?"

"Yep."

"Yeah, we get that a lot."

"I imagine you do."

"Ain't never been to the beach."

"It's impressive. You should go."

"Naw, too much sin down there. The devil goes walking after midnight. Least, that is what mama said."

"Did she?"

"Yeah, she was a good Christian woman. You'd a liked her."

"Well, it was twenty on gas and let me get a carton of those Camels."

"That'll be $38.42. These cigarettes are getting more expensive all the time. I smoke Winston myself."

"Here's forty." I said as I pulled two twenties from my faded blue jeans.

"You drive safe, now."

"Will do. You take care ... Roger."

"I'll do that."

I stepped back into the cool night air of Alabama and looked back towards the trio of hounds barking into the field.

I could see just enough of them under the street light to make out the color of their coats. One dog had a black coat, while one was dark brown and the last, tan. They looked like three different cups of coffee standing there, with various shades of creamer having been added or omitted. The biggest of the three, the black one, turned towards me and gave a playful bark as if to say that all was okay on that end of the road and whatever it might have been had tucked tail and run off.

I lit up a cigarette, got back behind the wheel, fired the engine back up and turned back to the Interstate. I'd have to get off the Interstate for good and get on the state road that would drop us down south into Florida and eventually Panama City Beach. I turned the radio back on and left the volume down as Robert Plant wailed over Jimmy Page's Gibson guitar. A Black Dog indeed.

The next hour seemed to zip by and somehow remain stagnant. Such is the burden of driving in a car with two sleeping people at 4 a.m. The silence in my mind was only broken by the occasional recognition that the radio was still on. A snippet of a song would catch my thought and hold it for a minute or so before I drifted back into the reaches of my own thoughts. Many of those centered on Jilly. What was happening between us? Were we a couple on this trip? Two old friends out for a good vacation? Would we sleep together? Would I regret it? Would she?

We hadn't seen each other in roughly three months, well, since New Year's when we all meet in Atlanta to watch the Giant Peach drop. There'd been 12 of us that night, all huddled around a couple of bottles of Jack Daniels and one bottle of cheap champagne waiting in the cold for a silly jeweled peach to descend a rope and declare the arrival of a new year. The highlight was watching Megan throw up on the sidewalk. She had two kids and a husband named Peter, who was a lawyer. Real estate law as I recall. He was 32 or 33 and the oldest of the group that night.

"Hey, if you get arrested, I know a good lawyer," he quipped.

Yeah.

Jilly and I had kissed at midnight. But it was forced and insincere.

"Three more years, and it'll be 2000," she said, as I held her close after the kiss.

"Imagine that."

"Maybe, I'll get married before the turn of the century."

"Really. Who are you gonna marry?"

"There's no shortage of assholes in Atlanta. I'll find one of them."

"Be careful what you ask for," I said, maybe a little too sharply.

"I always have been."

I rubbed my tired eyes and the memory from my mind as Elton John began "Goodbye Yellow Brick Road." I turned the radio off.

"I like that song," a sleepy Jilly said from the passenger seat. I liked the song as well, but it always filled me with sadness.

She reached up and turned the radio back on, boosting the volume two clicks. The song filled the car and the air. It filled my soul as the wind blew through my open window and against my face.

"What time is it?" asked Jilly, as she stretched in the seat.

"Just past four. About four-ten or so."

"Where the fuck are we?"

"Lower Alabama."

"Son of a bitch. I was hoping to sleep into Florida and miss all of ... this," she said.

Jilly pulled my pack of Camels from the center console, lifted one, lit it, rolled her window down a little and sat back.

"You okay," she asked with genuine concern in her voice.

"Oh, yeah, I'm good. I slept until eleven and got to the paper around one or so."

"You newspaper guys. Easiest job in the world."

"Yeah, right."

"Please. You all sit around drinking and bullshitting about women you've fucked for three hours before you do anything."

"Yes, of course we do. That's hard work. You know what kind of liver you have to have for a job like mine? Not for the weak, chick." I said with a smile.

"Yeah, okay. Besides even when you guys get people bitching, y'all always get the last word in."

"Mark Twain, baby, Mark Twain."

"What the fuck does Mark Twain have to do with it?"

"Never pick a fight with a man who buys ink by the barrel. Mark Fucking Twain."

"Interesting. See, even then a bunch of drunk ass reporters sitting around, bitching about women."

I was glad she was awake.

We rode in silence for awhile with Roan continuing to sleep in the backseat.

Jilly took sips off a lukewarm Coke, and smoked my Camels.

"You cold?" I asked.

"No, I'm fine. I am gonna get that blanket from the backseat, though." Jilly reached around and pulled out a fleece blanket from a bag in the floor boards.

"Did you hear Michelle and Paul broke up?" She half-asked, half-exclaimed as she returned to the front seat, adjusted her body and her blanket and curled up in the passenger seat. But she wasn't cold.

"No, what happened?"

"Well Ronnie's cousin, what's his name? Phil? Yeah, Phil. He said he heard Michelle caught Paul cheating with some stripper he meet at a club. Did you know Phil has a thing for Michelle? So, yeah, I don't know. Maybe Paul cheated on her."

I took a drag off my own cigarette before responding, "Now, didn't Paul work at the airport?"

"Yeah, I think he's a baggage handler for Delta Airlines."

"I never really knew Phil. I know Ronnie pretty well. His mom lives next to my parents now in Madison."

"Really? I didn't know she had moved out there."

"She moved in about a year ago, I guess. My dad cuts her grass."

"How are your parents doing?"

"I don't know," I started. "My mom seems good, but quieter somehow since the surgery. Dad is still Dad. But I can tell he's worried about her."

"They are the cutest couple. I'll never understand how they ended up with such a shit-head for a son," Jilly flashed her eyes at me quickly, and even if she hadn't I would have known she was joking.

"Hey, maybe the milk man had something to do with it."

"Whatever you need to tell yourself, stud," Jilly said before continuing her story. "I heard from Rhonda that Michelle is heartbroken. But she told a different story from Phil's so I don't know."

"Does it matter," I asked. I honestly didn't care what the answer was.

"No, I guess it doesn't," Jilly said, annoyed, turning towards the window and blowing smoke into the now very early morning air. The sun was still over an hour away and the darkness seemed to engulf the car from all angles.

9

"You know, Chaz, you are lacking in empathy," Jilly said.

"I am working on it," I said. I knew nothing I said was going to climb me out of this hole.

"Working on it. Yep. You're working on it," Jilly said, with obvious frustration in her voice.

"Look, I haven't seen Paul in what? Eight years, maybe. And you know I was never Michelle's favorite person," I began in my defense.

"You took her virginity and then acted like an asshole, and you're not her favorite person. Boy, that is a surprise."

"Hey, wait up, now. We've been over that field of grass before. She made sure that happened," I said.

"You poor defenseless man," Jilly said sarcastically.

"Fuck. Okay, yeah, that's exactly what I was saying."

I reached down and picked up the Camels, pulled one and lit it. I needed a drink.

"Why do you always take this route," Jilly asked, abruptly changing the subject.

"I stay on the interstate for as long as possible because I can drive 80 out here. As soon as we drop onto 231 the speed limit is gonna drop," I explained.

"God, 231 must be the most desolate road on Earth."

"I am sure it is high up there in the ranks of desolate highways," I said.

Jilly pulled open the box of cassettes laying at her feet.

"They have these things now called, 'CDs,' you should really look into those," she said.

"I don't have a CD player in the car."

Jilly pulled out Billie Holiday's Greatest Hits.

"This is new," she said. "You listen to the strangest music of anyone I have ever known."

She slid the cassette into the player and turned the volume up another notch. Holiday's voice took over as "Lover Man," played from the speakers.

"She had a beautiful voice," Jilly said.

"Yes, yes she did."

CHAPTER 2

The plan was to meet Sarah Hopper, Kaelyn Peters and their boyfriends, who I had never met before, at the Days Inn in Panama City Beach. Before that, however, we were supposed to meet Roan's cousin, Rich in the Pretty Bayou area of Panama City, on Grant Ave., off of West 23rd. Rich was a good guy, who knew the town and the beach as well as anyone having spent his whole life in Panama City.

When we were all 15 or 16, we were all jealous of Rich thinking he had a great life just living at or near the beach. It probably took us until we were 25 to realize Rich's life wasn't all swimming and partying.

The eight of us were going to stay at the Days Inn, but odds were Roan and Rich wouldn't be around much and unless I figured out what was going on between Jilly and I, well, I wasn't going to be around much either.

"Can we find a place to stop for coffee," Jilly asked.

"Yeah, we need to get Roan up anyway. Maybe grab some breakfast and switch out drivers," I replied.

"You getting sleepy?"

"Yeah, but I am hungry now."

Jilly spun around and punched Roan twice in the rib cage.

"Hey, loser! Wake up," Jilly was only kind of kidding. There was still some tension between them.

"Damn. Okay, okay. Shit, I'm up," Roan sat up and ran his hands through his thick black hair, scratched his scalp a couple of times and began to cough. "Hand me a cigarette."

Jilly tossed a pack and a lighter back at him in the general direction of the backseat. Roan lit up and again tried to clear his throat.

"Where are we? What time is it," He asked.

"Comin' up on Samson, Alabama, and it's almost five-thirty now," I said.

"Making good time, then?"

"Yeah, no cops." I said with a smirk.

"Where y'all want to eat," Roan asked.

"I saw a sign for the Sunrise Cafe. We might as well try there," Jilly said.

"Not a whole lot of choices down this way," I said.

We made the right onto Main Street in Samson and pulled into the dusty lot that served for parking. All three of us were weary, even if it was in different stages. The sky was beginning to shift to a purplish hue as somewhere further east the Sun was making its climb.

The Sunrise Cafe was like countless other Southern dinners that featured plastic chairs with red and black checker patterns across the seat cushions and plastic table cloths sealed in some nasty combination of polyurethane and wax; the kind of table that never feels clean no matter how many times you washed it down. It was the kind of place that always felt greasy and dirty and the kind of place that just might have a cockroach crawling around in the kitchen. But it was also the kind of place where the food was good and inexpensive. The eggs and bacon were listed at $1.75.

The restaurant was probably approaching its morning rush as four of the sixteen tables were filled. All of the customers were either truckers, or plumbers, or lumber yard employees, or painters. There was not a white collar to be seen. Probably not until the mayor showed up for eggs and ham.

We took a booth close to the door and Jilly quickly asked the waitress, who was laying down napkins and utensils on our table, for the ladies room. As she walked towards the bathroom, I saw one heavy set fellow give his friend a slight jab in the ribs and he whispered, but loud enough for me to hear, "Damn, look at the tits on her."

The guy code on behavior like that is kind of loosely written. And seeing as how there were some fourteen fine and classy men, who probably all called Samson home, and were probably all cousins to the town's sheriff or deputy or whatever, I decided I was gonna let that one slide. It wasn't loud enough where it was obviously meant for Jilly or me to hear it. It was just something said to a friend. And if I opened up that can ... well, I was never scared to fight, but I didn't want to fight the whole place and in a town this size that was a real possibility.

I quickly shifted to the other side of the booth so that when Jilly returned I could let her sit next to the wall. I would have to act as a buffer.

My plan only had one kink.

"Did you hear that motherfucker?"

Roan.

I met Roan when we were both eight and going into the third grade at Alexander Elementary. His father worked for Southern Bell and they had moved into the neighborhood of about sixty or seventy ranch style homes that dotted the rolling land about two miles outside of Alexander in the summer before school started back. We were both into G.I. Joe, Superman, KISS, football and baseball cards, and riding our bikes as fast as our little legs would allow at a time long before bicycle helmets. Our cuts, scrapes, bruises, gashes, wounds, tears, bandages and excuses to mothers would all heal into beautiful scars that told a wonderful story of a youth well-spent. We both got the chicken pox in fourth grade and it was then that we discovered telephones. I'd call his house or he'd call mine and we'd talk about whatever nine year old boys with chicken pox might think to talk about; usually it involved Bugs Bunny or the Road Runner or some show our parents had let us stay up late to watch.

From the age of eight until we were eighteen we'd been in exactly five fights — with each other. It was always over something stupid. The first was over this blue Hot Wheels car I had and the last was over some red-haired girl from Putnam High that he had had. In addition, we'd found ourselves in three fights in which we had to defend each other or step up and brother up for our friend. All three were his fault.

I loved Roan dearly, but he could be a jackass at the wrong time and over the wrong thing. This was one of those 'right things,' but it was clearly at the wrong place and at the wrong time.

"Hey," I hissed between my teeth. "This is trouble we don't need. Let it go."

"That fat ass needs to watch his fucking mouth," Roan hissed back.

"Yes, I know. But he wasn't trying to start shit, he's just an ass," I replied. "If he says something, then we do something — but let's not start it over some shit no one really heard. We can't back that up and he'll just deny he said shit."

The waitress was back at our table.

15

"What'cha y'all be wantin,'" She asked with her distinctive Alabama drawl.

"Can you bring us three cups of coffee and creamer to start," I asked.

"Sure thing, honey."

She spun and headed to the counter along the far wall to retrieve our coffees. Jilly returned and I stood up and let her slide across the booth to the wall. I stared back at the rude fat man, who had made the earlier comment, but his face was buried in his plate of eggs, hash browns and sausage patties.

"Did y'all order yet?" Jilly asked.

"Just coffee," Roan replied. I eye-balled him in that 'don't say a word,' kind of way. He smirked back in an affirmative non-verbal reply.

The waitress returned and sat three coffees down in front of each of us, pulled a small note pad and a pen from her smock and wrote down "coffee," before clearing her throat.

"Okay, well, what can I get y'all to eat?"

Roan immediately ordered, followed by Jilly and I went last. All three of us ordered the basic combination of eggs with hash browns or home-style potatoes, and a range of breakfast meats. The waitress again took off for the counter and I could hear her voice over my right shoulder as she called in the order to a short order cook hidden behind a wall and a wide range of kitchen appliances.

"What has Rich been doing," Jilly asked of Roan.

"My mom said he was working with the railroad. Not sure what he does, though. He's got one more year of probation, I think," Roan said.

"How old is he now, twenty-nine? Or thirty?"

"Thirty."

"That's right. He's two years older than us," Jilly recalled.

"What happened with that body shop job," I asked.

"I guess they fired him," Roan stated.

All three of us lit up cigarettes as we awaited our food.

Just then two additional men entered the cafe — both in white collars. The first was a portly man of about sixty, who was clearly the mayor of Samson as several hands shot into the air and voices rose in greeting. The second of the two was a tall, pale man with a sweater vest, who clearly had to be some kind of minister or funeral director.

The mayor went and clapped his hand down on the fat man's shoulder.

"Did you call mama, Vern?" He asked.

"Not yet, damn. I'll do it tonight," the fat man, who was now identified as Vern said. Vern was clearly the mayor's younger brother. They probably came from a family of six or more based on the age difference from the mayor to the fat ass named Vern.

"Well, she is doing well. The doc said the surgery cleaned up her eyes real good like and she should be out and about any day now," the mayor reported to basically anyone within ear shot. Which, met with the approval of the entire cafe as they collectively offered some kind of Amens, praise to Jesus, or general well wishes.

The mayor then set his eyes on us.

"Well, look at that. Is it that time of the year already," the mayor asked of anyone and everyone.

"Now, Walden, you leave my young customers alone. They are good tippers and I know I ain't gonna get anything out of this miserly bunch in here."

"I got something for ya, Valerie," called a voice from behind me and the room erupted into laughter and guffaws.

"Hush your ugly mouth," Valerie called over her shoulder, balancing the trays with our breakfast on it as she approached our table. "If I want tiny sausages, I can get those here for free."

Again laughter rolled lightly through the cafe, along with a whistle or two. These were people that had known each other their whole lives, and they seemed to have a jovial spirit.

"Where you folks heading," asked the mayor in a pleasant voice. "Y'all going to the beach or heading home?"

The three of us sat silent for a split second as we mentally tried to decide who to nominate as group spokesperson. I believe it was assumed since I was driving that I had to do the talking as well.

"We're heading down to Panama City, sir," I offered.

"Beach. Panama City Beach, son, they are two separate towns," he seemed to offer condescendingly.

"Yes, sir, I am aware of that. We're heading into Panama City. Gotta meet a relative of my friend here," I replied with a wave of the hand toward Roan.

"Hm. I see," the mayor said. "I was actually born in Panama City. My momma and daddy came this way when I was about five or six. Course my daddy was from Samson and my momma was originally from Southport in the Fanning Bayou. Now her family goes all the way back to those Indians that lived down there during the days of that Columbus and that de Leon fellow."

He let out a small laugh to himself and continued.

"Funny thing is that my daddy's family was kind of notorious Indian fighters. Which my Mama Jenkins said always explained why my momma and daddy fought so damn often."

And with that punchline he fell into a hysterical fit of laughter at his own joke. Roan, smart ass that he is, joined in with huge gasps of air — and although his laughter would have appeared genuine to those unfamiliar with him, I knew him well enough to know when he was full of shit.

"So, say, where you folks from," the mayor asked.

"Georgia," I said.

"I see. And what brings you this way again? Going down for Spring Break or just visiting family and friends down there? Because the beaches are gonna be real filled up over the next few days and I imagine thousands of college and high school age kids are there already, and no offense, but y'all don't look high school age ... maybe, y'all are still in college then?"

"No, sir," Jilly spoke up. "This is kind of an annual tradition amongst a group of friends. We still meet up, as many of us as can make it, down in Panama City and Panama City Beach."

"I see. An annual tradition, you say? Now that is interesting. Yes, that is something else," the mayor's eyes dropped onto the word 'PINK' on Jilly's shirt more than once, but I knew he wasn't trying to read the word, nor understand it. "Now, I went to the University of Alabama, and I'm just guessing here, but y'all look like Bulldogs to me. You just don't strike me as any namby-pamby Yellow Jackets."

All three of us chuckled at that.

"Yes sir, Chaz here and I are both Bulldogs ... we're not quite sure what Roan is," Jilly said with a smile.

"Go War Eagles," said Roan. "Er, the Georgia Southern ones."

"Georgia Southern? Did you even make it through a semester there," Jilly asked.

"I do not recall," Roan said with a grin.

"Okay, so you're Chaz," the mayor said gesturing in my direction. "What are y'alls names?"

"I am Jilly. It's short for Jillian. Long story, but family nickname," Jilly explained. "And that is Roan. It's short for pain in the ass."

The mayor nearly fell off his chair in laughter. I don't think he'd ever heard a woman speak quite like Jilly was known to speak, or in the manner. She could be as matter of fact as anyone I'd ever known.

"Oh, doll, you are such a peach," the mayor said, wiping away a tear of laughter from his eye.

Valerie, our waitress, and the only waitress present in the Sunrise Cafe, came and topped off our coffee cups, placed more creamer tubs on the table and headed off to look in on the other customers. The cafe was now around twenty customers when the door opened and a thin, pixie-haired girl with a nose piercing came through the door.

"About damn time," Valerie said to the 20-something, obviously late to work waitress.

"Sorry, the damn truck wouldn't start, so I had to grab a ride from Vince," she said.

"Take tables one through eight," Valerie said. "And table seven wants some more pancakes."

The mayor was conversing with Jilly as I looked at the new waitress, who had almost purplish eyes. Or at least it seemed that way in the light. She had her dirty blonde hair, with a purple streak on the right side of her head, cut in a way that reminded of Winona Ryder or maybe Jennifer Anniston; one of the movie or TV stars had a similar cut, but I couldn't recall which one.

I scooped up some hash browns on my fork, took a bite and turned toward Jilly and knew she had seen me looking at the waitress just from the look on her face.

"Yes," she said to the mayor. "I did like Birmingham. I thought it was a pretty town, but I have to say that I liked Huntsville better. No reason why, maybe it was my age and all."

"Never made it as far north as Huntsville, but I've heard tell that it is a nice place," the mayor responded. "And you son? What's been your favorite place to visit?"

It took me a moment to realize he was addressing me.

"Hmm, I guess I'd say Costa Rica," I offered.

"Costa Rica? You been all the way to Africa?" the mayor exclaimed.

I thought Roan was going to choke on his sausage patty, and Jilly let out a little laugh before politely stepping in.

"Oh, no sir. Costa Rica is in Central America. Below Mexico, basically," she said.

"Well, bless my heart. I am sorry. I was certain that was an African nation. Learn something every day. Thankful for that as well. I recall being in school, but well, back then, well, schooling was just different. We didn't have too many books at our little school up here then. In fact, the school I went to is shuttered. They built the new elementary off 87 in 1984. This town used to be nicknamed, 'Snuff City, USA,' after a folly with a snuff car during the Great Depression, and I'll bet y'all didn't know that? See, what I mean, ya learn something new each and every day. Each and every day.

"Well, I best be getting over to my table. It has been real nice talking with you young folks and I hope you have a pleasant journey to Panama City and maybe y'all will stop back in on your way home," the mayor said as he shook each of our hands.

21

I thought he might have been campaigning with the vigorous nature of his handshake and his million dollar smile, but he did seem genuine enough, and he was certainly friendly.

The new waitress took his place alongside our table. Her name tag read, Lexie.

"Y'all need anything," she asked.

"I'm good," I quickly offered.

"I'd like some more coffee," Roan stated.

"I'm fine," Jilly said cooly.

"I love your top. That looks really nice on you," Lexie said to Jilly.

"Thank you. Got it at the Gap," Jilly said.

"Oh, I think they have one of those stores up in Auburn," Lexie said. "Maybe next time I go up that way I'll look for one. It is very cute. I'll be right back with your coffee."

And like that she was gone.

"Nice girl," Roan said. "Not as nice as the mayor. I may vote for him."

"You can't vote for him, you idiot," Jilly said.

"Sure, I can. I can write his name in for President in three years," Roan said, and then stuck out his tongue at Jilly.

He was 10 years old all over again. Jilly took a small fork-load of hash browns and sent it flying across the table at Roan. And she was suddenly 10 years old all over again. The Great Jilly Bean, she had called herself back then. She'd wanted to be a magician for a while and made all her friends and her younger brother Toby, plus two cats and one dog her various assistants and part of her magic tricks. She once made an egg disappear in a trick at her friend Maggie's birthday party. Everyone had been impressed by that.

Lexie was back at the table to top off Roan's coffee cup.

"Anything else, or are y'all ready for the check," she asked.

"Yeah, go ahead and leave the check," I said.

"So, y'all heading to Panama City then," she asked.

"Yes, we are. Care to join us?" Roan said with a grin.

Lexie lightly laughed.

"I'll be down there on Wednesday I think," she stated. "Gonna tag along with my friend Grace. Her momma lives there and we're gonna go clubbing at PCB next Friday night."

"We're staying the week at the Days Inn. Drop by and have a drink with us," Roan offered. Always smooth.

She looked down at me and said, "I might just do that."

She reached into her smock, pulled the ticket she must have gotten from Valerie and placed it on the table.

I pulled my wallet out, pulled out a $20 bill and handed it to her. Without really thinking, I said, "Just keep the change."

The bill was only about $12 and I had just given this girl an $8 tip.

I could feel Jilly's eyeballs drilling a hole through the back of my skull.

CHAPTER 3

We stepped out of the Sunrise Cafe and back onto Main Street. The sky was softening as 6:30 a.m., quickly approached, and a single streak of reddish-orange danced along the tops of the pines. Jilly made a beeline for the car.

"Can you unlock the trunk? I want to get a shirt out."

"Sure." I said, catching up to her and popping the lock to the trunk.

She pulled the medium sized suitcase of the three she had brought with her and unzipped the top compartment. A new shirt actually sounded like a good idea, and I even thought of perhaps running back inside the cafe to the bathroom so as to change my jeans. Riding in the same jeans for roughly six hours gets uncomfortable and I felt dingy from the overnight ride.

Jilly pulled her PINK tank top over her head to reveal a pink bra. She tossed the shirt on top of her suitcase and pulled a long sleeve shirt over her head.

"You cold?"

"Not really, just chilly," she said. "Do you want me to drive?"

"That would be great," I said. "I'm thinking of taking the back seat and napping for a little bit. Well, until we get into the city."

"That sounds like a plan," she said. "Roan can ride shotgun and help navigate."

If she was pissed off at me for looking at the waitress she didn't say, but her mood seemed to suggest she was.

Ultimately, I just swapped out one t-shirt for another, a simple dark blue tee. I zipped up my suitcase, helped align Jilly's suitcase back in the trunk, and slammed the lid down.

"Everybody ready," I asked.

The passenger door to my 1977 Chevy Camaro would stick at times, but the car was in great shape overall for 20 years old. My oldest brother Jack had taken good care of it and gave me a pretty good deal when I bought it off of him in 1993. There were one or two chips in the black paint job, and one or two snags on the black vinyl interior, but the engine hummed and the car still had good top end speed. Although my days of pushing the boundaries of the speed limit were by-and-large over, it was nice to have the extra speed when battling Atlanta's interstate traffic.

I climbed into the back seat and pulled the passenger seat down behind me. Roan's soft duffle had acted as his pillow during the first part of the trek and I planned on using it in the same way. I pulled Jilly's red and black University of Georgia blanket into the back seat with me and tried to get as comfortable as I could in the small back seat area. I was not as tall as my three older brothers, and at 6-foot-2, I had heard my share of 'short' jokes from my brothers who all stood 6-foot-4 and above. Jack, the eldest, was actually shorter than brother number two, Sage, who was 6-foot-6 and still meaner than a Texas rattlesnake; even at 32 years old. He was on wife number two, as was Jack.

Brother number three, Arlo was, like myself, still unmarried and so the holidays could be quite interesting as the two twice-married older brothers threw the usually insults, name-calling and jabs at the two youngest, never-married brothers. Nothing they said could be as biting as my mother's often sarcastic remarks about our seeming lack of interest in what my mother still called, 'holy matrimony.'

Arlo often got it much, much worse than I did, however, since he was now 30 and I was still the 'baby.'

Roan climbed into the passenger seat and immediately began going through my box of cassettes, which I had left in the floorboards.

"Did you bring any Metallica?"

"I don't know," I said. "I just kind of tossed a lot of different things in there."

"Billie Holiday?" Roan looked back over his shoulder. "You going gay on me, bro?"

"Fuck off."

"Man, what is all this weak ass shit ... The Cure. The Police. Men At Work. You are aware that there is good music in the world, right?"

"Enlighten me, Roan. What is the good music?"

"Dude, seriously? C'mon bro, you have like no Slayer. No Megadeth. Are you sure you didn't grab some chicks cassettes by mistake? This is like all post-break up, cry me a river bullshit you got in here."

"Put the radio on then. I'm going to sleep so listen to whatever you want," I curled up and pulled the soft blanket over my head. We only had about an hour until we got to Panama City and I could tell it was going to be a long, restless hour.

Jilly buckled in and fired up the Camaro.

"Alright, let's get this done," Jilly remarked to no one in particular as she adjusted the mirrors and pulled back onto 87.

The steady rhythm of the tires on the asphalt, and the radio's low volume, helped me to doze off quickly. It was a soft sleep as I recall the ever brightening sun bouncing its light off a myriad of objects and sources and onto my face. My eyes would force tight, and I could feel myself tugging the blanket over my face again and again.

I felt snippets of dream roll over me; gently touching the front of my mind and fading as quickly and as softly as they had arrived. Snapshots of my mom, a long dead dog named Flip, and unwrapping presents on a Christmas morning filled my head in one dream that had that millionth of a second time frame to it. In another, a house boat at Lake Lanier, grilled hot dogs and the sounds of Braves baseball. A play-by-play voice seemed to be stuck, repeating the same phrase over and over; a phrase I couldn't recall. In yet another, traffic lights lined up one after the other as far as the eye could see in a desert — all the lights were red. I'd never been to the desert, although I continued to promise myself that I would go. Maybe this summer. I still had one week of vacation of the two the company gave me.

I could hear Jilly and Roan talking at times in the front seat, but like my dreams, only snippets and clips of words entered my consciousness. The rest was like some kind of free form jazz, just bouncing loosely off my skull and sticking to nothing.

Somewhere in that twilight, somewhere in that dim place between sleep and what passes for awake and alive, I wondered what I was doing here. Why this need to be with these people; to cling to some past that was filled with my whole life. Every meaningful event in my life had taken place between the two people now seated in the front of my car.

From my truest friend to my first, and in so many ways only, love of my life. They meant everything to me, and somehow they meant so little. Could I go forward into adulthood clinging to the two people who seemed most inclined to cling to our collective past? Where was I in my life? 28 years and drunken, hazy memories were the best I could pull up? That was the best of who I was. That? Was I to be doomed to that beer gut guy who talks loud at parties, so that his story was most remembered and the soonest forgotten?

Somewhere in that twilight, somewhere in the gloom of my tilting mind, I wanted to be someone like those in generations of lore that had left marks, histories, impacts, created legacy — and I felt like the biggest fool of all for wanting something. For feeling the need to want something. How could I not be happy to have two friends who actually cared how my day went, what crazy thing happened, where my keys were, why I liked mustard on my eggs and not ketchup and I had these people in a world where friends, true friends, should be held as gold.

And yet, I felt like they were this weight that would keep me trapped in a childhood and in a teenage dream that I could not escape.

Thirty would be on me soon and I was trapped somewhere in the twilight.

Deeper slumber took me again; back to some memory of Michelle Whisnant and the backseat of a 1980 Chevy Nova. Night Ranger blasted from the speakers as I fumbled with a bra clasp, our tongues darting and dancing.

"Hmm, baby, I want to feel you in me so bad," she whispered. "God. Please, baby."

I was 16. The male mind at 16 has basically three functions — breathing, eating and trying to get laid. She wasn't going to have to ask again.

She pulled her jeans and panties down in one motion and tossed them into the front seat, laid herself on her back and tossed her legs in opposite directions. I guided myself in and she bite her lip. We rolled in the usual manner for several minutes and when I pulled away there was blood on my dick. The third time in a year I had had sex that ended with blood on my dick. I wondered, in my simple, inexperienced mind, if that would always be the case. It didn't take long to get the answer.

Less than 24 hours later, I was in Jilly's bedroom, sipping on a beer, her parents in Savannah for a friend's son's wedding.

"What'cha wanna do hot stuff," She asked playfully.

"I don't know," I replied. "Wanna go see a movie?"

"You're such a dumbass," Jilly said as she climbed onto my lap. She pulled her shirt over her head and tossed it to the floor. Her breasts pressed hard into my chest as her hands wrapped my face and she forced her tongue into my mouth. My beer slipped from my hand and spilled on the carpet. Neither one of us noticed.

The night was ours. Our bodies seemed without beginning or end. Fingers laced, clasped and released again and again. I could breathe her. She was intoxicating. Color was lost and all seemed black and white in the moonlit bedroom, filled with stuffed animals and white furniture with red hearts painted at the corner of each drawer face and flat surface. In that colorless world, our bodies looked vintage and timeless, like two naked people in some 1920s pornographic photos. Nothing seemed to be of the moment. And everything was. I rose above her, our hips grinding to a soundless beat; I took her left leg in my hand and lifted it from the back of the knee. My left hand holding me aloft above her body and face, bathed in soft light. She moaned.

The night was ours. We spun and turned, shifted and churned in a sea of sheets, sweat and semen. I pinned her arms to the small of her back, her face buried down between pillows as her ass rose to meet me with her legs bent at the knee. Our skin smacked and popped, the bed squeaked in protest. My breathing was harder now, her moans louder; cries muffled into the pillows. We collapsed. Sunlight found our naked bodies draped across the bed, a lone sheet covered her lower body, but I was exposed to the world.

I stood up, slowly, and inspected my flaccid penis.

"You okay?" her soft morning voice asked from behind me.

"Yes, I was expecting to find blood."

"You're such an idiot," she giggled. "The first time, I was a virgin, dumbass. The second time I was on my period. Does that make sense?"

"Oh."

High school is always one degree of separation and it took until 2nd period for Jilly to find out that I'd fucked Michelle.

"You motherfucker!" Jilly screamed as she hurled her book bag at me in B hallway.

In the years that would pass, the story had changed depending on who told it. People who never witnessed the fight claimed Jilly punched me in the mouth, which did not happen. But that story stuck. So much so that four years later while home from college on a summer break I found myself listening as Reggie Bennett told his friend that I was the guy that Jilly had punched in the mouth. I told them both that had never happened. They seemed unconvinced.

What really happened was mostly tears and curses hurled at me by Jilly, who tossed the ring I had bought her at a mall in Decatur into the trash. Never did get the ring back.

It took until Halloween of our senior year, some three months later, for Jilly to forgive me and take me back as her boyfriend. During those three months, I basically ruined Michelle's reputation with anyone I could. I spread horrible stories about her, all in a misguided attempt to get Jilly's forgiveness and understanding. Jilly and I broke off for good the following Christmas during our freshman year in college. If we were actually broken up was another question altogether different all these years later.

The real punch in the mouth came just before Thanksgiving break at a party at Maddie Craig's house. Michelle's two older brothers, David and Michael jumped me in the front yard.

"Calling our sister a whore, you faggot," David said as he kicked me while I was on the ground.

"Look at this bitch, David," Michael yelled. "Fuck you, you pussy."

I got 12 stitches and a concussion.

David and Michael got it much worse.

Sage was one of the first in the hospital emergency room that night as they stitched my head. How he had found out so quickly I had no idea.

"Who did it," he asked, and there was a look on his face that said you best tell me or I'll find out from someone else.

"Sage, let it be," said my momma, sitting beside the bed, looking pale.

"Who did it?" Sage said again, pretending not to hear mom.

"David and Michael Whisnant," I said.

Within 48 hours, David had a broken collarbone, a fractured orbit bone, a broken ankle and a concussion, while Michael had four broken ribs, a broken jaw and a fractured skull. Sage spent the next week in jail before Jack got back to town from Oklahoma City to bail him out. My parents had refused to pay his bail.

I was lucky at 28 to not have many regrets in life, but I did regret the way I acted towards Michelle. She didn't deserve the things that I had said about her. But I was too young to know how to really make up for such a huge personal mistake — except make additional personal mistakes, like drag a girl's name through the mud. We'd only ended up in that car after she had broken up with Paul, her boyfriend since she'd been 12 years old, the Wednesday before fucking me. The same Paul that she had dumped or been dumped by again according to Jilly's extensive rumor circle.

I felt bad that David and Michael had needed to defend her honor, such as it was, and that they had taken such an incredible beating at the hands of the meanest of the Wilson brothers, Sage.

I felt bad that I'd never really told Jilly the truth, that I'd only fucked Michelle so that I could have more experience with women. That I needed that kind of experience spoke volumes about my insecurities as a young man of 16. That I didn't know whether or not I was 'good in bed,' and the only way to get good was to practice. I really didn't know that Jilly was going to throw herself at me the next night. But I suspected she was going to. She had repeatedly said all week that her parents were going to be gone that Saturday night and that we needed to hang out at her place. She said that despite three or four different invitations to go and do other things.

I felt bad that Sage ended up spending six months in the county lock up and the next two years on probation. He never felt bad about it, but I did.

I felt the car lurch to a stop. The feeling of a jolt, sat me upright in the backseat.

"We're here," Jilly said excitedly.

Pretty Bayou.

Rich, Roan's cousin, lived in a typical Florida trailer park. Hundreds of the same white trailers lined up in pretty little rows, all with the same sandy yards and palm trees standing next to white mailboxes. Dozens of them even had the same yard ornaments — combinations of pink flamingos and yard gnomes or roosters standing at attention.

I rubbed the little bit of actual sleep I had had from my eyes and combed out my longish, brown-blondish hair with my fingers. I stifled a yawn in my mouth and shoved the passenger seat forward to climb out into the early morning Florida air.

Roan was knocking at the front door.

"Rich. Rich, it's us, man. Open up,"

The door swung open and a woman in a tattered bathrobe with tattoos on both arms and both legs stepped into the open doorway.

"Hey, y'all Rich's kin folk," she asked.

"Yes, I'm Rich's cousin, Roan."

"Oh, yeah, Rich was telling me that y'all was coming for a spell," she said before turning halfway into the trailer. "Rich! Get yer lazy ass up! Your cousins are out here."

"Well, I'm the only cousin," Roan tried to explain. "These are my friends, Jilly and Chaz."

"Jilly?" she asked with a look of bewilderment on her face. "That's an unusually handle you have there, hunny."

"Yes. It's a family thing," Jilly said with a smile.

"Well, y'all grab your bags and come on in. I'm sure Rich will be excited to see all of ya."

CHAPTER 4

We walked into Rich's trailer and dropped our bags on the living room floor. We were supposed to stay the night with Rich so as to save a night's expense at the Day's Inn, which suddenly looked a lot better compared to the inside of the dimly-lit trailer.

"So, my name is Hope, but everyone calls me Dallas," she said as she dumped three or four glasses down the sink, dropped them and moved back to clear the makeshift kitchen table; which also stood in the living room.

"Dallas? Why do they call you Dallas," asked Jilly.

"Oh, that's just my stage name down at the Toy Box. It's a gentleman's club in town," Dallas said, kind of proudly.

"I see. So you're an exotic dancer then," Jilly asked.

"Um, not really. Just a stripper," Dallas said. I was certain she had never heard the word, 'exotic' until that moment.

"Nice. So, how did you and Rich meet," Jilly asked, taking a seat at one of the faulty-looking kitchen chairs.

"Oh, he was a regular customer for a while there and when his old lady moved out, well, I kinda moved in," Dallas said. Hardly the stuff of romance novels.

There was a stumbling sound from the back of the trailer and then a loud curse.

"Goddammit woman, don't you pick up a goddamn thing? Fuck me. Goddamn all this bullshit," Rich yelled loudly from the back of the trailer.

"Oh, for god's sake, just step over it you dumbass and get out here. You got family visiting," Dallas yelled back.

Rich walked out of the dark hallway and into the kitchen and living room area in a pair of red boxer shorts and nothing else. He looked much like the kid I once knew, save the larger belly and the thinning hairline.

"Son of a bitch. Is today Friday? I thought y'all weren't coming until tomorrow," Rich said as he suddenly scooped up Roan and gave him a bear hug.

"Holy shit. Is that Jilly-Bean? Damn, woman you look so fucking fine," Rich exclaimed before bending over to give Jilly a big hug. His penis slipped out from the crotch of the boxers and he quickly pushed his member back into his shorts.

"Well, goddamn, sorry about that. You know they have a mind of their own after all," he said without a trace of embarrassment.

It was my turn for a hug. I moved off the wall and threw my arms, loosely, around his back trying to avoid touching too much of his skin.

"Chaz, you bulked up dude," Rich said. He then patted my belly which was at least six inches smaller than his own and made a joke about drinking beer being the downfall of all good men.

"So, what'cha y'all want to do tonight? I thought we'd run over to the Toy Box and catch Dallas' show around 9 or so and then maybe head over to momma's for a bonfire," Rich suggested, but it sounded like a firm plan to me. Rich's mother was Roan's aunt on his mother's side. The two women were not very close as Tammy had moved Rich to Panama City with her second husband when Rich was just a little over a year old. Roan's mother Denise had very little good to say about her sister, Roan's aunt.

"Yeah, man, that'd be cool," Roan said.

"Y'all want some breakfast? Dallas, did you offer'em somethin' to eat yet?"

"No ..."

"Naw, man, we ate already," Roan interrupted. I think all three of us sensed some kind of argument brewing between the two lovebirds of trailer 67.

"Oh, all right then. Well, hell, y'all wanna beer," Rich asked.

"If it's just the same to you, Rich, I'd like to sleep for a little bit. If that's okay," Jilly asked.

"Sure, no problem. I forgot y'all drove all night," Rich said.

"Chaz, you wanna crash with me for a bit? You slept less than any of us?" Jilly said, it wasn't really a question. I could tell by the sound of her voice she didn't want to sleep alone in a strange trailer.

"Yes, I need some sleep. A few hours should do me," I said.

"Good enough. The guest room is the first door on the right. The second door is the bathroom, so help yourself if you need a shower or whatever. The water never gets real hot, but it is pretty strong water pressure in there, so be warned," Rich instructed.

Jilly and I each picked up our bags and headed for the spare room. It was sparsely decorated. A queen size bed took up most of the floor space and the mattress simply laid on top of a box spring. No headboard, footboard or rails of any kind supported the set. There was a dresser along the left hand wall, opposite of the bed and a Van Halen poster above the dresser.

"Awesome room," Jilly shouted back into the kitchen, her sarcasm lost on her intended targets. "Let's get some sleep, okay?"

I wasn't sure if that was a reference to 'no sex,' or simply her way of explaining why she wanted company in bed.

Jilly closed the door behind us and I stripped naked, opened my suitcase and grabbed a fresh pair of boxers. Jilly pulled off her shorts and climbed into bed. I climbed in behind her and put my arms around her.

"Oh, fuck it," she said.

She spun around in my arms and thrust her left hand below the waistband of my boxers, grabbing my cock and squeezing it firmly, yet gently. She threw her open mouth on mine and we were suddenly on fire. The grip of passion grabbed our weary bodies; but bodies young enough to shake off weariness for passion in seconds. I was erect and enflamed as her tongue danced over my nipples and chest. She quickly sat up, pulled her shirt over her head, tossed it onto the dresser, unhooked her bra and tossed it to the floor. She laid back and peeled her pink panties off. I removed my boxers and went to climb on top of her, but she forced my shoulder back down and climbed on top of me instead.

She guided me into her wetness and began to slowly rock her hips back and forth. Her breasts were tipped by two hard, dark pink nipples. I sat up just a little and took one of her nipples into my mouth. She fell forward onto me, pushing my head back down, but her nipple remained in my mouth. Her motion sped, her breathing became heavy. She looked down into my face, her blue eyes shining. I reached up and grabbed a handful of her hair at the base of her skull and forced my mouth onto hers.

She moaned loudly.

"Fuck," she whispered. Obviously upset at herself for making what she must have felt was too much noise.

We continued until we rose and fell in mutual orgasm.

"So, wanna be my boyfriend for the week," she asked jokingly.

We talked for a short time, in hushed tones, mostly about her family or mine. The various goings on in our worlds. Her job. My job. Her roommate and her roommate's mean cat, Virgo. We talked about paying bills and credit cards and taxes and 401Ks and whether or not we should quit smoking.

We eventually fell asleep.

It was mid-afternoon, sometime around 2 or 3, when we finally woke up. I walked to the bathroom, pissed and went back into the bedroom. I pulled on a pair of jeans and a gray Rolling Stones t-shirt.

"I'm gonna try out the shower," Jilly said as she covered her nakedness with a pale pink bathrobe. I leaned over and kissed her forehead gently.

"I'm gonna go see what Roan and Rich are doing. I'll take a shower later."

"Okay," she said, her mouth open as if she was going to say something more.

"What?" I asked instinctively.

"Nothing. I'm fine," she smiled.

I walked down the hall and found the kitchen and living area empty, so I pushed open the front door to find Rich and Roan sitting in lawn chairs in the front yard.

"Fuck that Sammy Hagar, man," Rich said loudly.

"Yeah, man, that muthafucker sucks ass," Roan agreed as he took a long hit off the joint the two appeared to be sharing.

"Hey, bitch. What's up," Rich asked as he noticed my presence. "Naw, man, I mean Van Halen was so fucking good with David Lee Roth. I just don't understand why those muthafuckers can't just get along. I mean, c'mon, Van Halen I, Van Halen II, Fair Warning, Women and Children First, Diver Down ... yes, 1984 sucked ass, that pussy shit they tried with the keyboards and all that shit; but those first five albums man, those were like the best fucking albums ever recorded. What do you think, Chaz?"

"Don't ask his pussy ass. He listens to like Billie Holiday and shit," Roan said hitting the joint again before passing it back to Rich, who offered it to me. I took a hit and handed it back.

"What are we talking about," I asked.

"Van Halen, man. Is Sammy Hagar better than David Lee Roth," Rich asked.

"No, I guess not," I replied.

"Fucking-A. See what I mean? Everyone knows Sammy Hagar sucks like donkey balls or something," Rich said.

"Okay, okay, I got one — best rock band ever," Roan asked looking at me for a response first.

"I don't know. I like a lot of them. Maybe, Zeppelin," I offered. "Probably the Rolling Stones, though."

"Fucking Led Zeppelin. That was the mother fucking shit right there," Rich agreed.

I felt like we'd had this conversation before, only we'd been teens then.

"Can't argue Zeppelin, man." Roan stated to no one in particular.

"The Who. Those were some bad motherfuckers also," Rich said hitting the joint hard. He offered and I passed, so he handed the joint to Roan.

"Man, right now, Metallica is the best band in the world," Roan said, before taking a hit.

"I can't argue that shit. But if Roth rejoins Van Halen, man. Fuck, they will ass fuck Metallica like a bitch," Rich said enthusiastically.

"Oh, no doubt," Roan said.

"Which part," I asked.

"What'da ya mean, which part," Roan asked.

"I mean will Roth rejoin Van Halen, or will they literally ass fuck Metallica like a bitch?"

"What the fuck man. We're just talking here. Fuck," Roan looked away disgusted.

"I'm just wondering if Lars Ulrich will let Alex Van Halen ass fuck him. And if he does, does that make Van Halen a better band?"

"What the fuck you been smoking, Chaz," Rich asked. "I mean, you're not on crack or anything, are you?"

"No, Rich. Just fucking with y'all," I said.

Rich started laughing, but Roan was smart enough to know that I was being a smart ass. But he wasn't gonna call me on it.

"I'm hungry. Anywhere to eat around here," I asked.

"There's a McDonald's about a mile that way and a Hardee's just a little further down," Rich offered.

"I'm gonna run to Mickie D's ... anybody want anything," I asked.

"Yeah, man. Get me a couple of double cheeseburgers and some fries. I got lots of beer in the fridge so we're good there."

Rich worked for the railroad and he worked in seven day shifts. He'd report back to the railroad on Monday, and although I was unsure why, he said he wasn't going to be able to join us at the Day's Inn. The combination of "too many days off" and his "fucking parole" meant he couldn't go. He made good money at the railroad, or so he said, and probably could have been out of the trailer park if it weren't for his love of beer and marijuana, which he smoked in copious amounts. How he'd managed to stay on parole and out of jail was a mystery for the ages.

I went back into the trailer and grabbed my keys and then knocked on the bathroom door. Jilly cracked the door and I asked her if she wanted anything from McDonald's, which she agreed would be a good afternoon snack, and she placed basically the same order as Rich had.

As Jilly closed the bathroom door, Dallas opened her door and was standing naked in the bedroom.

"You going to McDonald's," she asked.

"Yes."

"Cool. Get me a double cheeseburger and a chocolate shake. Hang on, let me get my purse."

"It's okay, I'll pay for the food."

But she brushed past me and into the living room. She bent over the sofa and looked for her purse, cussed and then looked under the sofa.

"Here it is," she said. She reached in and pulled out a wad of cash. She counted out three dollars and handed it to me. "That should be enough."

I turned around and saw Jilly standing there in cut off blue jeans shorts and a blue tank top with Minnie Mouse on it.

"Oh, my. You look so beautiful," Dallas said with a wink at Jilly.

"Thanks," Jilly said. "You, um, look really good yourself."

"Oh, stripping does help to keep my body in shape. You'd make a helluva stripper with those titties of yours," Dallas said.

"I never thought about it before," Jilly said, turning a little red with embarrassment.

"Hey, it's Friday night. We have an amateur contest at the club. Thousand dollars to the winner. You should enter."

"Maybe I will," Jilly said with a smile directed at me.

I was grinning and trying hard not to laugh at what might have been the single most hilarious conversation I had ever heard. I walked out of the trailer, still grinning from ear-to-ear, when I heard Roan call out.

"Hang on, man. I'll ride with you," he said.

I just nodded, climbed into the Camaro and fired up the engine. We backed out and turned down the road which lead back to Frankford Ave. We turned right and began the drive to McDonald's.

"So, you and Jilly," Roan asked.

"Fuck if I know."

"We heard you guys ... didn't mean to ... but, well, anyway. I was wondering what was up with you two."

"I honestly don't know."

"What do you want?"

"To have a good time this week. Get home safely and try and get an interview with Bobby Cox when I get back."

"That's not what I meant, bro," Roan said with a laugh. "I mean, what do you want with you and Jilly."

"I know, man. I just don't know how to answer that question. She is ... too easy."

"Fuck, that's a helluva thing to say."

"No, I don't mean it like that. I mean, am I just settling for something that is safe. Or is there someone out there that I am supposed to be with."

"Yeah, okay."

"No, I mean it man. I just wonder if there is someone out there that I don't have so much fucking history with."

"You're a strange dude, Chaz. I ever tell you that? I mean that girl would crawl across broken glass to kiss your ass and your talking about 'someone with no history.' What the fuck does that even mean?"

"I don't know."

"You're a full-tilt emotional retard sometimes."

"Thanks, bro."

"No, I mean it man. You worry about some crazy shit like maybe there is someone out there? There's someone right in front of your fucking face and you're gonna chase that girl into some dumbass lawyer or accountant or whatever and she'll marry that dumb motherfucker because your retarded ass is all like, 'history and shit.'" Roan lit a cigarette and blew smoke out the window. "I think Sage or Jack hit you too hard as a kid."

"Maybe so."

"Fuck, I know so."

We went through the drive-in, placed our order and headed home.

Arriving back at the trailer, Jilly and Dallas were sitting on the sofa, drinking beer and laughing. Dallas had put some clothes on. A leather miniskirt and a lacy top with lots of cleavage showing.

"Hey, let's get out the fancy China," Rich said with a laugh. Dallas laughed as well.

Rich, Roan and I sat at the kitchen table, while the girls ate on the sofa and kept on talking.

"No, the funniest one was this little fellow. His name was Richard. But everyone called him Gumdrop," Dallas said, telling her stripping stories to Jilly. "He tipped me $300 one night. And he asked if he could have my panties. I thought, fuck it, why not, so I gave the fucker my panties.

"He came back the next week. Same thing. Three hundred dollar tip and request for my panties. So, I did it again. I ended up, basically, selling him ten pairs of panties over the next few weeks or whatever. So, one night, he comes in and says the same thing. I told him, I am out of clean panties.

"Now, his face drops all sad or something and he's like, they don't have to be clean."

Jilly looked disgusted, "Are you fucking kidding me?"

"Nope," Dallas said. "I sold him three different pairs of period panties and that mother fucker was happier than a pig in shit."

"What happened to Gumdrop," I asked.

"He was hit by a train," Dallas said matter-of-factly.

"I wasn't driving," Rich tossed in quickly.

We all fell over laughing. It was going to be an interesting night indeed.

CHAPTER 5

The Toy Box was a simple white building with 'castle molding' along the top of the building to give it a more dignified appearance. Perhaps, richer. The music inside was loud and the rotation was filled with every hair band the 1980s had produced. There were no shortage of blondes, a handful of brunettes and raven-haired buxom girls and one red-head with small breasts and large, erect nipples.

The nine o'clock crowd was a mixture of lonely hearts, wanna-be's, college boys with hard ons and wet dreams of fucking a stripper at night's end, and a small collection of possessive boyfriends strategically placed around the bar.

Rich was anything but possessive of Dallas. In fact, quite the opposite. He seemed genuinely thrilled with each and every dollar that went into Dallas' G-string or garter belt. Pointing it out in fact whenever Dallas received a large tip.

There were maybe five women in the bar, who didn't work there in some capacity and only three of them seemed pleased to be there.

Jilly was one of the three, who seemed to be quite thrilled to be in a common American strip club. She ordered Tequila Sunrises and downed two shots of Tequila separately.

"Liquid courage?" I shouted to her above the din.

"Yep," she said.

"Are you gonna get up there?"

"Hell yes. It's a thousand fucking dollars and a room full of strangers. Fuck it."

"You said that earlier as well."

She took a big swig from her Sunrise and kissed me on the mouth.

"I'm gonna win," she said as she winked at me.

It was 10 o'clock when the call went out for all amateurs to report to the DJ booth. The DJ was a forty-something guy with a bad suit and a mousey haircut. He had a 1970s porn mustache above his lip. He was the most cliche thing in the whole place.

Jilly bounced up.

"Here goes nothing," she said.

The DJ, Howard, walked to the main stage and quieted the crowd.

"Alright, alright, it's time for the Toy Box's Friday night amateur contest," Howard said. "Can I get a hell yeah, guys?"

The crowd responded with vigor as "hell yeahs," rose from all corners of the club.

"Let's meet our amateurs!" Howard yelled back at the testosterone-driven crowd. "First up is Brenda."

Brenda was obviously a college girl on Spring Break. Three guys roared approval for Brenda from the table she had been sitting at. Brenda was maybe five foot, five inches tall and looked to weigh about 150 pounds. But she had an enthusiastic smile, an attitude and a large bust line beneath an Ohio State t-shirt.

"Next up is contestant number two, Francis!"

The roar for Francis was a little larger. She seemed to have 10 or so friends in the club, and was also an obvious college student. Her t-shirt read, West Virginia University. Francis was much taller than Brenda, maybe five foot, eleven inches tall and very thin with bleached hair and blue jean mini skirt beneath her college tee.

"Next up, a real Georgia peach, Jillian!"

I was actually surprised at the size of the roar that went up for Jilly, since only myself, Roan, Rich and Dallas actually knew her and the four of us yelled as loud as we could. It was obvious Jilly had made some fans already. She waved at the crowd, her long hair bouncing about her breasts and shoulders. She was still wearing her Daisy Duke cut offs and her Minnie Mouse tank top. I was also surprised she had chosen the name, Jillian for the DJ to announce.

"And finally, Ramona!"

If Ramona was an amateur then I am a dentist, I yelled at Roan, who let out a laugh an a nod to the affirmative. The raven-haired beauty appeared to be about 35 years old and was certainly no stranger to strip clubs. She was almost exactly as tall as Jilly, who stood five-nine and had a much larger chest than Jilly, who had ample breasts herself. While Jilly was naturally endowed, Ramona's were obviously store-bought implants. For reasons I couldn't explain to myself, I suddenly wanted Jilly to win.

"Let's get it started!" yelled Howard into his microphone.

Brenda danced to Ratt's 'Round And Round' and stripped down to her bikini cut, pale pink panties. She had an enormous chest, maybe 42 DDs, and a pudgy belly, but she was as enthusiastic as a cheerleader. She got a nice round of applause when she was finished.

Francis danced to Metallica's 'Enter Sandman,' which Roan found to be quite pleasing. He even gave a wolf whistle when she was finished. She had also stripped down to her panties, also bikini cut, but dark red. She had small breasts and tiny pink nipples capping her small brownish areola. She got a louder round of applause than Brenda had received and clearly was the front runner.

It was now Jilly's turn.

Jilly had chosen The Rolling Stones' 'Honky Tonk Women' to dance to, it was one of our favorite songs, and I knew the moment it came out of the speakers she had selected the song for me. She took her time and hit the mark on the beat. She was actually very sexy as she first peeled off her tank to reveal her black bra. Moments later, she turned her back to the cheering crowd and removed her bra, dropping it at her feet. That received an even louder cheer from the crowd. She did have lovely 36C breasts with beautiful pink-brownish nipples, which stood taut and hard on her chest.

She continued her dance and slowly and provocatively she peeled down her Daisy Dukes to reveal her black thong panties. The roar of the crowd was deafening. But she wasn't done.

She twirled and spun, twisted and shook. She slowly worked her thumbs into her thong and slide the panties to the floor. I thought the place was going to erupt as she revealed her vagina for the world to see. But she wasn't done.

She bent over, exposing all, and waved through her legs at the crowd. They were in bliss.

The song ended and the roar was obvious. A new front runner had emerged.

Ramona had her work cut out for her. But she was an old pro. She worked the pole. She worked the crowd. She peeled through her clothes with ease as Motley Cure's 'Dr. Feelgood' poured from the speakers. When she was done, an equally loud roar, certainly equal to the one Jilly had received, went up from the crowd.

It was anybody's game.

Howard reemerged from the DJ booth, microphone in hand, to call the girls back onto the stage. One of the dancers, Ebony or Ivory or some obvious stage name joined him with $1,000 in hundred dollar bills in one hand and a dozen roses in the other.

"Okay, it's our moment of truth and time to crown a winner in the annual Friday night amateur dance contest," Howard began.

The crowd gave cheer.

"All those that think Brenda is the winner, let me hear you!" Howard said as he held his hand above Brenda's head. Brenda tried to wrangle more cheers from the crowd by flashing her tits, but it wasn't gonna work. Fourth place awaited.

"All those that think Francis is the winner, let me hear from you!"

Francis stood in front of the crowd and smiled, but she actually received less volume than when she had finished taking her clothes off.

"Okay, let's keep it moving. All those that like Jillian, let's make some noise!"

It was quite thunderous. Maybe some 200 people were inside the building, but it sounded like a thousand. Jilly walked out, a foot from Howard's hand raised above her head and gave a flirtatious wink to the crowd, and the volume increased.

"Well, it is up to Ramona now," Howard exclaimed. "All those for Ramona, give a yell!"

It was obvious that Jilly was the winner. Maybe there was simply no energy left in the crowd after cheering so loudly for Jilly, but whatever the reason, Jilly was going to walk off the stage the winner.

"I think we all know who gets the bed of roses and one thousand fresh dollars ... put your hands together for Jillian!"

Once more the crowd was screaming, whistling, clapping and hooting for Jilly, who graciously accepted her flowers, and smiled as she was handed her thousand dollars.

As she made her way back to our table, several men stopped her and added to her cash prize by handing her ten or twenty dollar bills.

"Told ya I was gonna win," she said to me with a grin, followed by a long, deep kiss as she tossed her arms around my neck and pulled me close.

A beast of a man appeared at the head of the table.

"Y'all are friends of Dallas, right?" he asked.

All heads nodded in affirmative.

"Okay, drinks are on the house. You did great up there Jillian," the large man said before disappearing back into the crowd.

"Who was that?" I shouted across the table to Rich.

"They call him, Mongo or something. He's the bouncer. One bad motherfucker right there," Rich yelled back.

The drinks flowed. Jilly had collected some twelve hundred dollars once the tips stopped coming to the table, and I was quite shocked that so many seeming losers would have so much disposable cash. Maybe they were morons. But I was floored at the amount of money she had received just from taking her clothes off.

I stuck to Budweiser beer in bottles and turned down repeated offers for shots. Someone was going to have to drive. Roan was hammered on a mixture of beer, shots and mixed drinks and he was beginning to look like a man that was going to be praying to a toilet soon. Jilly was high, but I couldn't tell how much was booze and how much was ego. Guys kept coming around the table looking to strike up conversation. Each time, she was polite, but at some point should would turn and give me a kiss or a hug to let them know she wasn't interested.

All but three seemed to get the message.

They were from Ole Miss and they were all about 22 years old. The leader of the trio was a freckle-faced kid with reddish-brown hair and a Panama City Beach airbrushed muscle shirt. At least he had some actual muscle.

The music was loud, but I overheard one line and that was enough.

"Hey, how about I give you a hundred dollars and you suck my dick," he asked of Jilly.

I moved her out of the way and punched him in the mouth. His mouth exploded in a sea of crimson. I landed the second blow right to the bridge of his nose, before he could get his hands up. His nose was shattered. And he fell to the floor. I leapt onto his chest and I felt tiny punches raining down on the back of my head from one of his friends. I ignored those and began to pummel the freckle faced kid in the face over and over.

I felt lifted and moved suddenly. I was carried out the door in a swirl of yells, curses and cheers. And then there was fresh air on my face.

"Fuck, you trying to kill him?" Mongo asked of me as I spun around to see who had removed me from the club.

"Fuck him. He asked Jilly to suck his dick," I told him.

Jilly arrived outside. If she was proud of her win, she seemed prouder still that I beaten the shit out of some college kid. She walked up and threw her arms around me.

"Are you okay," she asked loudly, but leaned in and whispered before I could respond. "I'm gonna fuck your brains out tonight."

Mongo assured us that there'd be no cops, but that we should probably leave just the same. The owner, Carl something, gave Dallas the rest of the night off and handed his business card to Jilly.

"You know you ever want to make some real money, give me a call," he said.

The five of us climbed into the Camaro with Roan and Rich in the back and Jilly sitting on Dallas' lap in the passenger seat and we headed to Rich's mom's house.

The ride over was mostly uneventful, but I noticed that Dallas' hand was high up on Jilly's thigh and she was whispering into her ear. Jilly laughed at something Dallas had said and the two girls began French kissing.

No one noticed but me.

Rich's mom Tammy was in the front yard with a fire going when we arrived. About eight other people were milling about the fire and it seemed that more were in the house.

"Roan!" she yelled as she noticed her nephew slide out of the car.

Roan walked roughly ten feet and threw up all over the sandy yard.

"Well, it's good to see you too, honey," she said with a laugh.

Introductions were made all around and I honestly don't know or recall who I shook hands with or man-hugged. Several were folks that I knew vaguely from previous trips to the PCB, and several seemed to have more of a memory for me than I held of them.

Finally, with Roan settled in a chair and Tammy taking care of him, Jilly and I escaped to the fire pit in the back yard, that held a smaller fire and no one else around.

"You didn't have to do that, ya know," she said.

"Do what?"

"Beat the shit out of that kid. I can handle myself just fine, thank you."

"Oh, I don't doubt that. You danced like a pro."

There was a sudden and pronounced silence.

"Wait," I said, my mind seizing on a previously unthinkable possibility. "You've done that before. Haven't you?"

Jilly sighed.

"My sophomore year of college. Dad was sick and mom was struggling to make ends meet. I took a job at the Gold Club for six months and our problems went away."

"Jesus, you never told me that."

"I know, dumbass. I'm telling you now."

"Why did you never say anything? How come you never called me up and said a goddamn word about any of this? You never even let me know there was a problem."

"What could you have done? Seriously. What were you gonna do that I couldn't do myself."

"I don't know, but something. I might have been able to do something."

"And to what end, Chaz? For what reason? To save me from having to work as a stripper for six months? Please. I was a big girl and the money was damn good. I put enough away that my junior year was paid for and daddy got his settlement from the paper plant the next year."

"I still wish I had known," I said. I pulled my crushed pack of cigarettes from my front pocket and tossed six broken ones into the fire before finding one I could light. I lit up and smoked as I stared into the flames.

54

"Do you love me," Jilly asked. "And before you answer that, I mean do you deeply love me? Am I 'the one?'"

I stared into the flames.

"Jilly, I have loved you for twenty years."

"That's sweet, but that's not the answer."

"Are you asking me are we going to get married. Is that what you want to know? Right now, this instant?"

Jilly sighed, and looked into the fire.

"No. That is not what I am asking."

There was a long silence that followed and I knew that any chance of me getting my brains fucked out was slipping away the longer I sat silent. But this went deeper than a night of great sex.

"Jilly, I want right now. I want this night. I want these moments. I don't have any deeper answers for you. You ask if I love you deeply, and the answer is yes. A thousand times, yes.

"But, do either one of us know who we really are away from the other one? And I don't mean the things we've done that we never mentioned. I still can't believe you were a stripper," and I made sure to smile at her when I said that so that she would know it wasn't being said as judgment or scorn for her tough decision all those years ago, "And I must admit, you make one sexy as hell stripper."

"This girl has some moves," she said with a laugh and two snaps of her thumbs.

"I want us both to be happy. I really do. I mean that above all else and I don't want to ever cause you anymore unhappiness."

"Look, okay, understand this," she started. "I need to be seriously laid. I mean seriously. So shut the fuck up and let's go find a place to fuck."

Tammy's property backed up to the North Bay, and after pulling a blanket from the trunk, Jilly and I found a secluded, but sandy spot along the water. Time seemed to slip away quickly as we found each other once more. At some point it dawned on us to return to the party — "We'll finish this later," Jilly promised. So we dressed, rolled up the blanket and returned to the gathering in Tammy's yard.

"Well, there you two are," Dallas said with a knowing look.

"Goodness. Jilly and Chaz. Y'all look so growed up," Tammy remarked. Tammy was now 51 and she had gotten pregnant with Rich, her only child, at 21. Her first marriage lasted roughly a year to Rich's father before he took off one night for a job in Texas and never returned. Six months abandoned, Tammy met a man named John White, who was maybe 10 to 12 years older than her. They married and moved to Panama City where he had a job waiting with Arizona Chemical. He ended up getting himself arrested on various charges and was killed one night when he fell asleep behind the wheel out on the Interstate. Police found several grams of cocaine in the car.

Tammy was a thin woman, with wispy gray hair and a crooked mouth. She'd always been attracted to the party life and how she made money was anybody's guess. She shared the home with Tom Duncan, her current boyfriend and live-in lover.

Dallas reached out and took Jilly's hand and the two girls headed into the house. I grabbed a beer out of a cooler in the front yard and sat down with Rich, Roan, Tammy, a small black man nicknamed, Dojee, a friend of Tammy's, Pamela, and two bikers, Rodney and Peter.

It was a motley crew to say the least.

CHAPTER 6

The conversation around the fire was deeply entertaining, even if it lacked in overrated things like actual facts.

"Man, I'm telling you," the biker named Peter said to Dojee, "That comet was sent here. That is no random thing, brother."

"I know, man, I know. The government is up to some serious deep space shit," Dojee said in complete agreement. He then took a big hit off the two-foot tall bong that the two were sharing.

"I mean, Clinton, man, he signs that law or bill or whatever outlawing human cloning. Seriously? They have to outlaw that? Like that is a thing or something," Peter exclaimed quite freaked out about the potential development. "They know something they aren't telling. I was in Phoenix last month and I saw them lights. Rodney and I were rolling to Bakersfield to see a guy about this job and boom! There they were. Just above our head."

Rodney nodded and added, "It was fucked up, man. Ain't never seen no fucking aliens before, bro."

"Preach, bro," Peter said.

"That's fucked up, man," Dojee said.

"Which comet? The Hale-Bopp," I asked.

"Man, I don't know it's name, but that shit definitely brought those aliens with it," Rodney stated as he too took a hit off the bong.

"You know, the thing is the government likes to keep us in the dark on shit like this," Tammy said. "The A-bomb? We had no clue until they dropped it. I'm telling you I was talking to someone the other day. I think it was Janice or ... Dojee, what is that nice little queer boy who comes round here every now and again?"

"Mickey?" Dojee replied.

"Yes, it was Mickey. He was telling me about this computer virus thing called Y2K that is gonna shut everything down," Tammy said. "I bet that is the aliens' plan. They probably gave us all that computer stuff and buried something inside of it to shut us down."

"Fuck!" Peter exclaimed. "I never thought of that."

"Like the Trojan horse," I suggested with an amused smile on my face. Although I was trying not to sound like a smart ass. This wasn't the time or place to correct such misguided thoughts and beliefs.

"What's a Trojan horse," Dojee asked.

"Damn, man, the Trojan horse. Like Noah and shit built that mother fucker to surprise the Greeks or the Romans or somebody and shit," Peter said, his grasp of history truly astounding.

"Yes, that one," I said, now more deeply amused than before.

"So, like, what's the purpose of a Trojan horse," Rodney asked, looking slightly befuddled. I assumed he thought it was a real horse.

"Man, the idea is that you hide shit in that bitch," Peter explained to him. "I bet that is what those fuckers did. This is why I ain't buying no fucking computer. Them aliens are probably all up in them mother fuckers."

Roan, who still looked a little pale, however, had heard enough.

"I think this is some of the dumbest shit I have ever heard," Roan said, his face painted in part-frustration, part-discomfort.

"Ah, you're just a non-believer, man. And it's cool, bro," Peter said dismissively, as if he'd been called out before and knew there was no convincing the 'non-believers.'

Rich, though, wasn't so unconvinced.

"Man, Roan, don't be that way. There is a lot of shit the government does that we don't know about," Rich began. "Like AIDS man. The world is like what, a few thousand years old and shit, and no AIDS. Then, one day AIDS? Naw, that is some deep dark shit."

I reached into the cooler and pulled another beer. This was getting far more interesting.

"Dude, c'mon, the government cannot just do shit like that," Roan said.

The group of Peter, Rodney, Dojee, Rich and Tammy laughed softly. A knowing laugh like, 'you just don't understand how deep down the worm hole this goes.'

Roan stood quickly, too quickly, and grabbed the armrest of the lawn chair for support. He swayed just a little and I am sure it felt like the Earth was spinning underneath him.

"I gotta piss," he announced to the small gathering in the front yard.

I decided to follow him. It seemed like the thing to do since he looked so unstable and I didn't want him smashing his head into a toilet or anything.

The crowd inside the house was much larger than I expected. There were only about a half dozen cars in the front yard and yet there were close to 15 people milling about the inside of the house. Jilly and Dallas were in here somewhere, but were nowhere to be seen.

Tom Duncan sat in his recliner and gave a wave as Roan and I entered the house. I'd met Tom about three years earlier on a previous trip to Panama, and he and Tammy had been together for the better part of a decade or so.

Roan made a right and headed for the bathroom, but I lingered as Tom seemed to want to speak to me.

"Chaz, how you been son," he asked.

"Doing well, sir," I responded.

"You still working for that big paper in Atlanta?"

"Yes, sir. Been there almost five years. It'll be five years in October," I said.

"What do you think about the Braves and that new stadium? Have you seen it yet," he asked. Most of the southeast, if not all, was Braves' territory, and I knew Tom was a big fan.

"Yes, sir. I was out there in February to take another tour," I told him. He looked positively amazed. "They have a pretty good team this year, so we'll see how they do."

"Oh, as long as they have Maddux, Glavine and Smoltz, they'll be alright. They just need to hit to support those guys," Tom declared.

"I think they'll have some offense this year," I opined.

"Be good to see them beat those fucking Yankees for the World Series," he said.

"That would be nice."

I heard a glass fall in the dining room and turned my head to see six people gathered around the long table playing quarters with red plastic cups. One of them bent over and retrieved their now empty glass, cursed, stood up and headed to the kitchen for a refill.

"There's some Purple Jesus in the kitchen that Tammy made if you like," Tom suggested.

"Thanks, but I gotta drive. Just sticking with beer tonight," I replied.

I turned and walked down the hallway toward the bathroom to check on Roan. I opened the door and saw Roan sleeping on the floor next to the toilet. I wasn't going to wake him. I thought an hour of sleep or so might do him some good.

I turned to the first bedroom, opposite of the bathroom and slowly opened the door. There was a single lamp on, but two people, clearly visible, were busy fucking, so I quietly closed the door and headed to the next bedroom; also on the left hand side of the hallway. I heard sounds, but decided to slowly open the door anyway.

The overhead light was left on and Jilly was laying on her back on the bed, with Dallas laying face down on top of her and slightly to Jilly's right. Dallas had two fingers working in and out of Jilly furiously. The crotch of Jilly's cutoffs pushed to one side. Dallas' mouth kissed and licked Jilly's neck.

I closed the door quietly and walked back down the hall.

"Hey, Tom. Where did you say that Purple Jesus was?"

Tom motioned me toward the kitchen and tossed out, "check the fridge."

I went into the kitchen, opened the refrigerator door to find a huge jug of Purple Jesus on the shelf. The fridge was loaded with a wide range of alcohol, but seemingly very little food. I pulled the jug and searched the cabinets for a cup or glass. I found a large plastic cup with the Florida Gators emblem on it. Screw it, I thought, it is clean. I poured the cup half full and took a swig. It was very sweet, but had a familiar warm burn as it went down my throat. Grain alcohol or some kind of moonshine, I guessed.

"Is that stuff any good," a woman now stood in the kitchen with me. She was 30-something and wearing a Def Leppard t-shirt over a pair of tight, ripped jeans and cuffed black boots.

"It's strong, but a little sweet," I responded.

"Hmm, I like sweet things. Pour me a glass, cowboy," she asked or stated. It was hard to tell. I'd never been called a cowboy before.

"Sure."

"What's your name." she asked.

"Chaz."

"Chaz. See, I knew you were a cowboy," she said with a smile.

"I never thought about it before and what's your name?"

"Samantha."

Yes, that fit. She looked every bit of a Samantha.

"I got a new tattoo. Wanna see it?"

"Yeah, sure."

She lifted her shirt, exposing her tiny breasts; above her right breast was a hummingbird hovering in front of a rose.

"Nice tat," I said.

"Yes, Glenn did the work for me. He's a pro."

"Sorry, I don't know Glenn. I'm from Georgia. Just down here visiting with friends," I offered.

"Georgia? I never liked Georgia. I got arrested in Macon once. Some shoplifting bullshit. The fucking cunt in the Macy's said I took some jewelry."

"Did you take it?"

She smiled. Then let out a little chuckle.

"Yeah, I guess I did."

I never knew that shoplifting was something someone could be unsure about it.

I pulled another plastic cup from the cabinets and poured her a half glass of punch, which she promptly chugged down. She held the cup aloft in front of me, and I poured her another cup. She took a sip this time and put the cup on the counter.

"So, you here with anybody?"

"Yes, kind of," I said. What else could I say?

"Hm, too bad. You look like a lot of fun." She winked, picked up her cup and turned back into the dining room.

I followed her in, not because I was following her, but because there was no other exit from the kitchen. There was a sliding glass door at the end of the dining room, so I pulled it open and looked back into the dining room, which now held about nine people. Samantha sat down in some guy's lap and tossed her tongue into his mouth. I just stepped back into the late night or early morning air of Florida, depending on how one slices time in the wee hours of a morning.

Rich was now in the backyard with Tammy and two guys that I hadn't seen or meet.

A deep silence fell over the yard and it seemed my presence here was unwanted. Especially by the two newcomers. I tipped my glass in their direction and walked along the walkway that lead back to the front yard.

I headed back to the small fire in the front yard and immediately noticed Rodney sitting with a .9mm in his right hand. I looked over at Peter and he too held a pistol, although I couldn't tell what kind. Some kind of revolver.

"Is everything okay," I asked.

"Sure thing. Right as rain in Spain," Peter said.

"Tammy and Rich are having a little meeting with some tenants that they rent to," Rodney began with a plausible lie. "They brought a couple of dudes that are sitting in the van over there," he waved his hand toward the street and my eyes followed to a white work van with two guys sitting in the front seat; it was impossible to know if there was anyone in the back. "So, we're just making sure they don't give Tammy any bullshit over this month's rent."

"Rental property is a tough gig," I said.

"Don't be a smart ass, college boy," Rodney said, with a look of, 'I'm smarter than you give me credit for,' on his face.

"I meant no offense, just making a joke is all," I said.

"No problem. You're a friend of Tammy's and that's good enough for me," Rodney said. "But, you still don't need to put your nose in another dog's ass, either."

"Good point."

Suddenly, I thought that perhaps I'd be better off back in the house sitting with Tom. If some bullets started flying over 'rent' money, I really didn't want to get caught in the crossfire. I went back into the house and headed first to the kitchen. I'd seen beer in the fridge and the hunch punch was just too sweet for my taste buds. I was actually surprised to find Jilly and Dallas standing in the kitchen, drinking beers and laughing about something.

"Hey, babe," Jilly said with a smile.

"Did you have fun," I asked. I don't know why, but suddenly I was pissed off, jealous and feeling betrayed. It was a strange mix of emotions.

Jilly either ignored the meaning behind the question, or simply mistook it to mean something else.

"Yes, it's been a good night," she said. "I mean, hell, a thousand dollars is pretty sweet. We should find a fancy place to eat this week and blow a hundred dollars on a meal."

"Yeah, I guess we should."

I walked past them both, opened the fridge and pulled out a cold Budweiser in a long neck bottle. Beer options were limited to Bud, Bud Light and Miller Genuine Draft.

"You okay," Jilly asked, looking into my face.

"I'm gonna let you two lovebirds talk this one out. You seen that son of a bitch of mine, Chaz," Dallas asked.

"Yes, he's in the backyard with his mom and two guys talking about rent money."

"Rent money? I wonder what in the hell that's all about. Well, I'll go find his sorry ass. That mother fucker probably got himself into some shit over something," and with that, she spun and exited the kitchen.

"What's wrong? Did I piss you off," Jilly asked.

"I saw you. I saw you two in the bedroom."

"That? You're pissed off about that," Jilly asked, with a bewildered look on her face.

"Hell, I don't know, Jilly. Am I supposed to be? Am I allowed to be? Do I need to be? I mean you tell me ... because I really don't know if we're two single people fucking, or a couple that just goes along with whatever feels right in the moment," I rubbed my face and stared out of the kitchen window. I was feeling like a dick. But I wasn't gonna back down.

"Look, that was just ... one of those things," Jilly said. "It just happened."

"And if that had been me and Dallas in there, would 'just happened' work for you? Would you think, okay, cool?"

"No, I guess not. You have a point. I am sorry. I was drunk, high and I did something ... stupid," Jilly leaned against the kitchen counter and crossed her arms beneath her breasts. "I dunno, I guess I thought you'd think it was hot or something. I have no idea what I was thinking."

"How was I gonna think it was hot? Were you planning on telling me about it later? I mean, unless I walk in there, how exactly do I find out about it?"

"Yes, I was gonna tell you. Dallas actually wanted the three of us to party later and I thought you'd be turned on by that. I fucked up," Jilly looked sincere.

I really didn't know what to feel, or even if I did feel anything. I was mad because I thought I was supposed to be mad. I thought I was supposed to be furious. But I wasn't anything. I was indifferent and that made me madder. Somehow.

Jilly sighed and looked defeated; like whatever thunder she had been building up had been swept away from her, stolen without a chance to sound. She pushed her hair behind her left ear and then picked up her beer and took a sip.

"Where's Roan," she asked.

"Passed out in the bathroom, next to the toilet," I said, and then I started laughing. "He's all curled up in there and I didn't have the heart to move him. Everyone's been pissing in the yard for like an hour now."

Jilly laughed with me and I walked across the kitchen and hugged her tight.

"I'm sorry," she offered. "It was a silly thing to do. I just ... it played out different in my mind."

"I didn't know you had a thing for girls," I said.

"Oh, I don't. I mean, well, it's different and can be fun."

"Not your first time, eh?"

"Oh, no. Ex-stripper, remember? Many of the girls at the club were gay or bi and we'd play around sometimes after work. It happens," she explained. "Besides, college is that time. No, I just, well, I saw Dallas naked this afternoon and I thought, she actually has a hot body. Do you know she's only 25?"

I was very surprised to learn that. She seemed much closer to 35 in a lot of ways. She was one of those people that was tough to pin down an age when you looked at them.

"Hm, I didn't know how old she was ... I thought she was older than us," I said.

"Yes, I think I did as well. She's been on her own basically since she was 15. She started stripping at 16 when she lied about her age to get a job at a club in Mobile or somewhere. I forgot where she told me she worked before moving to Panama City about three years ago."

"Where is she from," I asked.

"I think she said Baton Rouge, originally," Jilly answered.

"Let's get Roan and see if Dallas and Rich are ready to head back to the house," I said.

"Um, we might have to explain to Dallas ..."

"Hey, whatever happens, happens. Fuck it," I said.

"That's right, baby," she said with a squeeze. "Fuck it."

CHAPTER 7

We gathered up Rich and Dallas from the back yard first and then went to wake Roan from his slumber in the hallway bathroom. The two trailer park lovers waited for Jilly and I as we walked down the hall.

Only Roan wasn't there.

I looked at Jilly as if to say, 'I have no freaking clue where he could be.'

Jilly opened the bedroom opposite, but no Roan. I walked down the hall and opened the second bedroom door, but no Roan. There were only two choices left on the hallway, one was the laundry room, which was clearly empty as the door stood wide open and any glance in could prove. The second was the master bedroom and I was a little reluctant to go opening Tammy and Tom's bedroom door. I pushed aside my worries and tossed the door ajar.

Samantha was on her knees in front of Roan, who had his hands on either side of her head.

"Yeah. That's it baby. So nice," I heard Roan say; words I would never clean from my mind. I pulled the door shut and turned quickly to Jilly, who was behind me.

"He's busy," I said.

"No fucking way? I hope this one is legal," she said.

"Yes, I think she is very legal and somewhere in here is a guy that may or may not be her boyfriend," I said, letting the weight of that possibility fall on Jilly.

"Fuck. What do we do," she asked.

"I guess we stand here and act like we are talking. If anyone comes down the hall looking for a girl named Samantha, we tell whoever it is that she is outside," I said.

"You think pretty quick on your feet, white boy," Jilly said.

"I've seen this rodeo before, sweetheart," I said, in a terrible John Wayne impression.

"What the fuck? Now, you're a cowboy?"

"Hey, Samantha seemed to think so."

"What?"

"I'll tell you later. It'll crack you up."

We stood in the hallway for maybe a minute; staring at each other and smiling, occasionally. There was no awkward silence with Jilly, there was no awkwardness at all. We'd seen it all. The best and the worst. The most beautiful parts of who we each were and the ugliest parts of who we could be. The great comfort of knowledge. A knowledge gained from moments. The shared intimacy and the shared memories. She just was. As I just was.

I thought back to Spring Break 1991, just six years earlier, when a then 22 year old Jilly shocked me by entering a wet t-shirt contest. Now, in the light of her stripping admission it seemed much less shocking. But Jilly had been a serious child. A book worm. A reader. She was studious and controlled as a pre-teen. Driven and still polite as a teen. She never rebelled. Ever. Until, I guess she did. She stood there, amidst some 1,500 screaming college boys and girls and let them pour that pitcher of ice cold water down a paper-thin white tank top. Her nipples screamed through the fabric as they stiffened instantaneously against the Florida heat.

She was still rebelling. She was still trying to play some game of catch up for being the good girl. The nice girl. The smart girl. The polite girl. The honest girl.

She'd enjoyed shocking me by dancing at the Toy Box, and again when I'd caught her with Dallas. She wasn't upset that she'd been caught. I could see that now. She wanted herself exposed. She wanted her choices to be public; to not hide from anyone, least of all me who she really was.

The door opened and Samantha walked into the hallway, wiping her mouth.

"Well, hey there cowboy," she said. "Is it your turn?"

Before I could even begin to think of a response to that loaded question, Roan stepped into the hallway as well.

"Oh, hey guys," he said. "Everything okay?"

"Everything is grand, Roan. We were waiting on you so we could leave," Jilly responded looking a little ill with Samantha.

"Oh, cool. Yeah, well, I guess it is late," he said. "Hey, I got your number Samantha, I'll call you when we get checked into the hotel tomorrow afternoon."

"Sounds like a plan, sweetie," she said. She kissed Roan on the cheek and walked back to the living room.

We said a serious of short goodbyes, and whatever drama had briefly unfolded between Tammy and the two mysterious men in the backyard went unspoken.

We piled into the Camaro in exactly the same positions as we'd arrived with me behind the wheel, Rich and Roan in the back seat, and Jilly seated in Dallas' lap in the passenger seat. I pulled the

Rolling Stones cassette, Exile on Main Street, from my box of tapes and slid it into the player in the dash.

Tumbling Dice never sounded so good.

We drove straight back to the trailer park and dragged our tired, drunk, stoned bodies from the car and went inside. Roan piled himself onto the sofa, dragging an old comforter over his body, and gave a weak, 'good night,' to the rest of us. Jilly and I fell into the queen-sized bed in the guest room, while Rich and Dallas went to their shared room at the end of the trailer.

Sleep came over all of us quickly; at least judging by the silence, everyone went looking for the sandman. If I dreamed, I have no recollection of it. Sunshine poured over my face to waken me from my drunken slumber. I was actually in much better shape than the rest of our party.

I could hear Roan in the hallway bathroom, throwing up once again. Dallas had taken his spot on the sofa and was nursing a cup of black coffee.

"I made fresh coffee. Cups are above the sink to the right there," she said with little emotion one way or another.

"Thank you," I offered. I reached up and pulled a cup down. I poured a little milk into the cup, making sure to smell the milk for freshness first, and added two teaspoons of sugar, stirred the mixture, and took a sip.

"It's good," I said.

"My uncle taught me how to make coffee. I think I was eight or nine," Dallas remarked.

"Well, it is good," I said. I didn't know how much of this woman's life I really wanted to know about. Wasn't sure what questions I should ask; all of them seemed like a potential minefield.

There was minimal furniture in the trailer. The living room held the old sofa and a dark plume or purple cushioned chair. There was no TV, no coffee table, no end tables, no bookcases, and, no surprise, no books. I sat in the chair.

I laid the coffee cup carefully at my feet and opened my pack of cigarettes, lit one and lifted my cup off the floor.

"Do you have an ashtray," I asked.

"Yeah," Dallas said. She reached back over the sofa to a window shelf that was built into the frame of the trailer, grabbed a glass ashtray and handed it to me.

"Is it okay if I smoke in here? I should have asked first," I said.

"Oh, yeah, we do," she said. "So, you and Jilly?"

"Yeah, I think so," I said. "Hard to say."

"Y'all look like you've been together for a while, or something. She said you've known her most of her life," Dallas said.

"Yes, since elementary school," I offered. "We grew up in the same town, just a block apart."

"She's a real beauty," Dallas said. "She has that natural beauty. Most woman have to work at it, I bet she falls out of bed beautiful. I look like shit when I wake up."

It was hard to argue that statement, but to be fair, she had been drinking and smoking very heavily last night. Her hair was a mess, and as she finished her sentence, she ran her fingers through her hair and tried to shake it out. She had washed off her makeup at some point before bed last night and her face was actually much younger without all the makeup she had worn when I first met her.

"Yes, she is a beautiful woman," I agreed.

"Now, a woman like that ... well, she's gonna take some work. You have to earn that," she said staring at me like I was a convicted criminal or something. Her face softened, suddenly. "But I am sure you know that already."

And once again, she seemed older. It was really impossible to believe this was a young woman of 25. The sweet-twang to her voice seemed to disappear, still Southern, but not as Southern. I wasn't sure what response, if any, I was supposed to make, and then she continued.

"See, she's real smart to. And a guy like you, you'd be okay with a smart woman or a beautiful woman. I ain't to sure you can handle both in one package," she said without any trace of being vicious. She simply stated it as fact. "I know you got balls. That part is not in dispute. I seen you drop that bitch for disrespecting your woman — and you dropped his ass on a dime. No hesitation. No doubt. You just tossed up them dukes and went to town.

"And I know you got brains. She said you work for a newspaper or something like that and I imagine that takes some kind of skills. But the hearts of men are small little things. You guys spend your whole lives thinking with your brain or your balls and the heart shrivels. It's not y'alls fault, mind you. It's a way you were built kind of thing. Easy to own, easy to break a man's heart. And see, you're just smart, or dumb enough to know that and you're real good at making sure your heart doesn't get broke. I just wonder if you can handle all that she is. Can you make that leap of faith?"

I took a drag on my cigarette, took a sip from my coffee and took another drag on my cigarette. I'd never been so insulted, complimented and sized up before. I didn't know who this pint-sized stripper was and yet, she knew me better than my own mother.

Rich emerged from the bedroom and walked to the coffee pot.

"Just think about it, ace," Dallas said to me, before addressing Rich. "Fresh coffee, baby."

"Yeah, I can see that, I ain't fucking stupid ya know," Rich said with a snarl.

Rich fell into a chair at the kitchen table, lit a cigarette and blew smoke across the living room. He scratched his leg and then his bare chest.

"Damn, I feel like dog shit," he declared.

I stood up and stretched.

"I'm gonna check the weather," I said.

I opened the front door and walked outside, making sure to close the door tight behind me. I walked to one of the lawn chairs that had a small wooden table beside it, with an ashtray on top. I dropped my cigarettes and my lighter onto the table, and plopped into the chair, unceremoniously.

Across the street, a small dog, a pup of some kind, was sniffing after a large, gray cat. The cat seemed mostly oblivious to the pup. The pup saw me, and bolted underneath the trailer. I hadn't made any sudden movements, so I was little humored by his sudden disappearance. The cat sauntered across the street, stopped short of me, gave me a kind of once over and decided I posed no threat. He then rubbed against my legs and began purring. Something in the wind caught the cat's attention, and he too took off back across the road and under the trailer.

I sat for a minute smoking, the bright sun already above my head. It had to be 10 or 11 in the morning, and the sky was a clean, brilliant blue. Not a cloud to be seen in any direction.

Three dogs, large dogs, suddenly went trotting by. Two had collars, but the third, the leader of the pack, had none. They slowed as they passed by me, but kept moving and I was thankful for that since none of the three had a pleasant look.

The trailer door swung open and Roan appeared in the frame. He shielded his eyes from the bright sun and then walked toward me and the additional lawn furniture. He found himself a seat opposite me and placed his own cup of coffee on the ground.

"You okay," I asked. "You were on the sofa last night? Where did you end up?"

"Fuck," he chuckled. "I don't know what the fuck happened. I don't remember ever throwing up that much. I wonder if it was something I ate or something. Naw, ya know, I got up to puke and I guess I turned into Rich and Dallas' room. I woke up on the floor. Hell if I can remember."

"I know you started looking kind of green when we were at the Toy Box," I said.

"Man, I owe you an apology," he said.

"For what?"

"I like pussied out on you last night," he said, standing and taking a cigarette from my pack, lighting it and sitting back down.

"What? How so?"

"I just like was so fucked up or something. I shoved the one guy, the one that was hitting you on the back of the head, but that was about it," he said.

"Roan, don't worry about it," I said. "That was on me."

"So, I was drunk. What the fuck happened? Why'd you pound that dude?"

"He told Jilly he'd give her a hundred dollars for a blow job. So, I just knocked the shit out of him," I said. "I don't know. Just one of those things."

I blew out my poor attempts at smoke rings, which I'd never learned how to do properly. Roan laughed at my weak attempts and blew out a perfect ring of his own.

Asshole.

"So, how about them bikers last night. What the fuck were they even talking about," Roan asked laughing softly.

"That was some crazy shit," I said. "Did you hear the one say Noah built the Trojan horse?"

We both started laughing harder.

"I loved the guy, 'I ain't buying no computer.' Like, what the hell?" Roan said, laughing to the point of tears. He began to choke hard and I thought he might vomit again, but it was just a coughing fit brought on by the laughter.

"I'll never understand people like those guys," Roan said. "Freaking crazies, man."

"I guess so," I said.

"Naw, those guys are fucked up and you know it. Too many joints or something," Roan said. He turned his head to his right and began making a small kind of chirping sound. The gray cat came out from underneath Rich's trailer and leapt into Roan's lap and began purring loudly. "Do you believe in aliens?"

"Have you ever heard of Arthur C. Clarke," I asked him.

"I don't know ... sounds familiar. Who is he?"

"He's a writer. 2001: A Space Odyssey?"

"Oh, yeah, yeah. I saw that movie. What about him?"

"He said something that, well, it's one of those things that kind of sticks with you, because it has so much truth. It's one of those kind of indisputable kind of things."

"Okay, what did he say?"

"He said, there are two possibilities. Either we are alone in the universe, or we are not. And that both are equally terrifying."

Roan sucked on his cigarette.

"I bet that bitch could've built a Trojan horse," Roan said. We both were gripped by a fit of laughter.

Jilly stepped outside, her hair wet from what I assumed was a recent shower. She was wearing a red bikini top and a different pair of blue jean shorts over the matching red bikini bottoms.

"What's so funny," she asked.

"Trojan horses," I said between peels of laughter. Roan laughed that much harder.

"I obviously missed something," Jilly said.

I tried to catch my breathe and compose myself so that I could give her some kind of answer, but Roan's laugh had always been infectious. Once he started, it was hard not to laugh along with him until he stopped. Jilly sat down, a tall glass of Orange juice in her hand, and waited for the the two of us to settle down.

"Boys," she said, with a certain exasperation. "We have to get going. We need to get packed up, get some food and get down to the hotel. Check in is three and it is already eleven."

"Yes, mom," Roan said, with a chuckle.

We both knew she was right and we were both very hungry. We got up and gathered our belongings and got directions to a Waffle House from Rich. I packed up the Camaro as Rich and Roan worked out details on when and where we were to meet next. Spinnaker's was the most obvious meeting point and they settled on Tuesday night; if Rich could get away for a few hours: "I don't know. I got to get to work Monday for sure." I overheard snippets of Jilly and Dallas' conversation and it seemed obvious that Dallas was coming down to PCB with or without Rich.

The Camaro packed, final instructions and discussions concluded, we went through a round of hugs and then packed ourselves into the car. Jilly waved at Dallas as we rode off.

"Man, I need some fucking hash browns," Roan said.

CHAPTER 8

Originally, the plan, or so I thought, was for Rich to share a room with Roan, and I was still unclear as to why Rich had changed his mind. As I understood it, it had something to do with Rich not being in good standing with his employer and having taken too many "off days." I guess that wasn't that surprising. Rich seemed very different from the guy I'd known these last 13 years or so. Darker, meaner and on edge. I don't know if that was from some singular issue or a compound set of them. Who knows what really twists in someone else's gut. The struggles or demons they may carry. And, certainly, seeing a guy for maybe five to six days out of a whole year, once a year for 13 some odd years, didn't make me the best judge of what was going on with him. It wasn't like we exchanged Christmas cards, or birthday cards, or even occasional phone calls. It was one visit every Spring and we usually spent the week high or stoned or both. Sometimes all at the same time.

After breakfast we jumped on the Panama City Beach Parkway, crossed the Hathaway Bridge and then took the split onto Front Beach Road. We arrived at the hotel a little before 1:30 and we certainly could not have asked for a more picture perfect day. The Florida Board of Tourism would have been thrilled.

We'd rented four rooms on the fifth floor, on the side nearest the swimming pool. I still preferred swimming in a pool to the ocean. But I doubted that I'd do much actual swimming this week. The pool was usually choked off by dozens of people, if not more, and the crowds around the pool area could make it difficult to navigate.

That these were my thoughts spoke to how different I was at 28.

I tried to remind myself that I was here for a good time and to just go with the flow.

Sarah, Kaelyn and both their boyfriends, Reggie and Patrick, respectively, had been at the hotel since Friday afternoon and once we got settled, we went and knocked on the door to Sarah's room.

"Oh, my god!" the girls squealed and hugged and jumped around. It'd been a year since Jilly and Kaelyn, who now lived in Houston, had seen each other. Sarah lived in Buckhead, and she and Jilly would have lunch every now and again.

Once, our Spring Break trip had featured as many as seventy-five to a hundred seniors from Alexander Central. The first year after graduation, when it was decided that we'd all meet in PCB again we dropped to roughly thirty. The year after that about twenty friends made the trip. In each year that followed the numbers continued to fall.

Now, there were five 'Fighting Eagles,' standing in Room 534 at the Day's Inn in Panama City Beach.

And two poor guys along for the ride.

At least, as it turned out, I knew one of them.

Reggie Duncan had played football, basketball and baseball for Morgan County High. At six-foot-four, 220 pounds, he was a monster in high school sports. He was arguably one of the finest athletes that county had ever seen and no fewer than ten Division I colleges were following him in the hopes of landing his unique skill set. Just about a month after announcing that he was going to stay at home and go play football for the University of Georgia, he landed awkwardly on a jump shot and tore three different ligaments in his right knee. Surgery knocked him out for a year and by the time his body had healed, his grades had fallen and his ride at college was gone.

To his credit, Reggie didn't give into the temptation to just give up. Instead, he went to work for a guy who was a big fan of both the Bulldogs and Morgan County sports. A guy that liked Reggie. He taught him the paint business and now, at 29, Reggie had four crews working underneath him on industrial, commercial and residential paint jobs.

He looked to be in as good as shape as ever. His handshake was firm and his muscles toned.

"Hey, you're one of them Wilson boys, ain't ya," He asked, his brown eyes smiling in memory.

"Yes, my older brother was Sage Wilson," I replied.

"Damn, I remember him. He was a senior when I was a freshman I think," Reggie said. "They all said nobody hit harder than him."

"Yep, I got the scars to prove it," I laughed.

Interracial dating was still a new concept in the South and one that I had no issue with, one way or another. I could sense that Roan was a little startled at first, but I couldn't be sure that was because of the nature of the relationship between Reggie and Sarah, or that it was Reggie Duncan. *The* Reggie Duncan standing in front of him.

In our junior year, the year Reggie was a senior, big number 34 ran right over Roan, giving him a concussion. Roan lost two weeks of football.

Once the initial surprise wore off, Roan was excited to get to see Reggie once more.

"I'd like to say I remember that night — the night I played against Reggie Duncan — but I don't," Roan said.

Whereas Reggie stood tall and broad with his light chocolate skin, Patrick Holder was the exact opposite. Kaelyn's boyfriend was a musician in Austin and the two were in the middle of some kind of long distance relationship. Patrick was five-foot-six and maybe 150 pounds with bright red hair on one side of his head, the other side shaved. His eyebrows, nose and lower lip were pierced, along with what I counted to be sixteen holes combined in his two ears. He had a myriad of tattoos working their way up his arms and into his Red Hot Chili Peppers t-shirt. He was so pale that I worried his skin was going to match his hair in no time in the Florida sun.

Kaelyn was working for an oil company in Houston, owned a condo and drove a BMW. Patrick lived with two guys in a two bedroom apartment in Austin, drove a Volvo and worked delivering pizzas when his band, Blasted Eye, wasn't performing. It was a relationship that was either going to end in spectacular fashion, or last for the next 60 years. Love is a funny thing.

The three girls huddled up and made plans for our Saturday evening and night, while the guys and I stood on the balcony overlooking the Gulf of Mexico. It was determined that we'd hit the beach for a little while, come back up, everyone could get cleaned up, and then we'd find a nice outdoor patio and have an early supper before hitting the Strip.

The temperature was a warm 75 degrees by the time we hit the beach and there was a steady breeze that kept things on the cool-side. But the sun was big in the clear sky and Jilly, Kaelyn and Sarah were quickly laid out in bikinis. Like the other guys, I was wearing just long swim trunks and we had found some beach chairs to form a semi-circle to one side of the girls as they stretched out on beach blankets.

Roan and Patrick took off to buy beers for the party.

"So, what's your brother Sage up to these days," Reggie asked.

"Hmm, well, he's had a tough go of things," I said. "I guess you knew about that mess with the Whisnant brothers?"

"No, I don't know. I mean I don't recall ever hearing anything about that," Reggie said. "But I may have been off at college, or something. And, I never knew them anyway."

"Well, some shit went down and he got jail time and probation," I began. "Well, he had, I dunno, I guess a month of probation left and he caught a DUI near Lawrenceville. They revoked his probation and his first wife left. While in jail, I guess two guys made a run at him or something and he fucked both of them up pretty bad. The one guy almost died, which would have been a murder charge, most likely. It was bad time for him.

"He got remarried about two, almost three years ago, to a woman from Cartersville. She seems okay. I think they're talking about having kids."

"Man, I can understand. I'm divorced myself. We made it a year. I was too young, bro, just too young," Reggie said shaking his head. "Hey, now you had another brother, right?"

"Two other brothers," I replied.

"That's right," he said. "See, no offense, I always get you and Arlo mixed up. Y'all look so much alike."

"Well, he does have a good inch on me," I laughed. "But we do favor."

"Now, is Jack your oldest brother?"

"Yes, that's him," I replied.

"Damn, I was talking to him ... well, I painted his house," he said.

"The one in Winder," I asked.

"Yep, that's the one," he said. "It was a room or two as I recall, not the whole house. This would've been ... well, I think a year ago in March."

"That's right," I exclaimed. "I remember that now. He told me about that last summer. My mom's birthday is in July and we always get together for her birthday. It's kind of funny, we are like never together for Christmas and all of that. But her birthday was always easy to plan around."

"That's cool, man. Enjoy her. My mom died three years ago and it was hard, man. Real hard."

His eyes looked out to the ocean and I could tell by his face that the pain of missing his mother was very much alive in his heart, very tangible. Three years or not.

"I am sorry to hear that, Reggie," I said.

"You know she warned me not to marry Nesha," he said. "And I cussed her. Told her what a bitch she was being.

"She reached up and smacked me in the ear. Hard. Here I was a grown-ass man and my mommy is smacking me upside my damn head."

He shook his head and continued.

"I should have listened," he said. "But more than that. I never should have said it. When she was dying, she had the breast cancer, and she is laying there, and she looks me in the eye and says, 'I told

84

you so,' and she started laughing her ass off. Now, I'm crying my fucking eyes out, just balling, you know, my mom is dying and shit. And she is laughing and rubbing my head and she says, 'baby, nobody ever loves you like your momma.'"

Roan and Patrick returned with the beer and three girls. Shannon something, Michelle something and Emily something; all from the University of Kentucky. They smelled of frat houses and eagerness.

Jilly, Kaelyn and Sarah were friendly, but stand-offish. Roan had struck Panama City gold. And his wolfish smile was not doing him any favors.

The three female newcomers quickly surmised there was really only one single guy sitting here, and now it became a contest of who wanted Roan the most. After a beer my money was on Shannon. By the second beer, Michelle something and Emily something created an artful reason to walk down the beach on the hunt for a lost third cousin or some such, said their goodbyes, had a quick private conference with Shannon something, and headed due east.

Shannon something and Roan were quickly making up excuses of their own. I think Roan said something about a CD he'd left in his room, and they made their goodbyes and headed for the hotel. I thought of Roger back at the gas station in Alabama. I guess the devil walks in the daylight as well.

"Hey, Chaz," Jilly hollered at me.

"Yes?"

"Come here and put some lotion on my back," she commanded. I smiled. This was going to be a Roan conversation.

I crawled over the warm sand to her blanket, squirted a large load of lotion in my hand and moved my hands towards her back.

"Hold up," she said as she twisted her arms behind her back, undid the clasp of her bikini top, tucked the two tail-parts under either side of her torso, and I applied the lotion to her back once she was settled.

"I hope he got ID," she started.

"I seriously doubt he asked," I said. "But it appeared they had bought their own beer."

"How do you know?"

"I could see him by the beer cart, chatting with the girls while I was talking with Reggie. They'd already bought their beer."

"Hm. I hope for his sake she's 21," she said. "He gets arrested this weekend, Chaz, and that is all yours."

"Why's he all mine," I asked bewildered.

"He's your friend," she said.

"Wait. Hold on. I'm a little confused here," I said. "You've know Roan as long as I've known Roan and you never acted in all these years like he was 'my friend.' I was under the impression that he is 'our friend.'

"And didn't you call him and tell him the dates and he had to get his ass off of work so that he could come?"

"I did that for you, dumbass."

"What, like a late Christmas gift or something," I said. "I'm a little confused."

"I don't know what is so fucking confusing," Jilly said, a harshness to her voice that she rarely displayed. "He's been an asshole his whole life. And he drags you down. You don't see it, but you're different around him."

"C'mon, seriously? An asshole his whole life?"

"Yes, Chaz, his whole life. He clung to you high school, 'cause he was scared shitless of your brothers. He clung to you because you walked him through Algebra and English and Biology. And, oh, what happened when you went off to college? He fell on his face. That's what happened," she said.

"We went to the same college," I said, amazed at all that was suddenly pouring out.

"No, Chaz. We all went to the same college, but he had different classes. How many times our freshman year, not counting the drinking sessions at the Georgia Bar or the 40 Watt or wherever, did you actually see Roan?

"I saw him once on a Tuesday. Now he had classes on Tuesday and his ass was hanging out on the hill, chatting up girls. He never applied himself to anything, but getting laid," she said, her voice rising just a little.

"Okay, calm down a little," I said, with a touch of softness. I didn't know what if anything Kaelyn and Sarah could hear and I didn't want them getting involved in our small beach drama.

"I'm perfectly calm," she said. "I guess the point is Chaz ... I don't know what the point is. Fuck it."

I sat back and listened to the water landing on the beach.

"I"m going to swim," I announced to everyone and no one. I walked thirty feet or so and then sped into a full run before diving headfirst into a wave. The water was brisk, and the chill of it nearly took my breathe. It was still just the first week of April and the temperatures while mild still hadn't produced the warmer waters the Gulf is so famous for. I don't know how long I swam, or what thoughts I might have had. I just needed the motion; the time alone.

I wasn't angry or upset with Jilly. I just thought she was wrong. And I didn't know why I thought she was wrong about Roan. Roan just was. He was always going to be that one friend. That one friend that could make you a little angry, or a little happy, or laugh, or want to punch him. But you knew he was as he was always going to be. He could tell you little about anything involving history, arts, current events, or even who might be the Supreme Court Chief Justice; and he knew far less about anything involving literature, or philosophy, or theology — in fact, I don't know that Roan had even been in a church in two decades; he held no religious beliefs that I knew of and yet, he couldn't be described as an atheist. That would have taken some effort on his part to find atheism. No, he just was. He could be wrong-headed, foolish, cock-sure and downright arrogant. But then so could I. And maybe that was why I knew Jilly had to be wrong about Roan. Because some of the worst parts of Roan could be found in me and if Jilly was right about Roan, then she was very wrong about me. If Roan was 'an asshole his whole life,' what did that make me? She had to be wrong.

I emerged from the water far more frustrated than when I had gone in. I walked to my towel, collected my belongings.

"I'm going to get a shower," I said.

"No problem, man," Reggie said.

"I guess it is getting late," agreed Kaelyn.

Jilly just laid on the beach. Her sunglasses hiding whatever her eyes might have betrayed about her thoughts.

I tossed my stuff down beside the bed once I'd returned to our room and pulled out the clothes I'd planned on wearing out. Jeans, light blue button up shirt and my boots. I got into the shower and washed off the sea, sand and funk of a foul mood.

By the time I got out of the shower, Jilly was sitting on the edge of the bed. She got up and went straight into the bathroom without a word.

I straightened up my side of the room, hung my beach towel and shook out my hair. I needed a haircut. I liked to let my hair grow long in the winter and kept it shorter in the spring and summer. Jilly liked me with longer hair.

I sat on the balcony, smoking and waiting to see which Jilly emerged from the shower.

She finally came out of the bathroom, walked naked to her bed and began pulling out various sets of clothes and underwear. She finally pulled on a pair of lacy yellow panties and came out onto the balcony and sat down. She pulled a cigarette from the pack and lit it.

"I think you may be right," I finally said, unable to take her silence any longer.

"You're a dumbass," she said, exhaling. "And I love you."

CHAPTER 9

It had been a brutally hot summer in Georgia, 1979. The air was heavy with a thick humidity and each day of August had seen temperatures rise above 95 degrees. Jilly's 10th birthday party was planned for a Saturday afternoon and while 20 or so adults smoked cigarettes and drank a wide range of mixed drinks in the Branham's living room, complete with air conditioning, some thirty-five kids, ranging from 7 to 12 years old ran around on the red clay, through the thin Georgia pines and against the heat of the day.

Hide and Seek was still the most popular game of the day, and the one game that nearly every kid present at the party easily agreed to play. A group of boys, including my brother Arlo, who had been invited to the party, had tried to get up a game of baseball in the backyard. The girls, who outnumbered the boys twenty-one to fourteen, vetoed the baseball game. The girls wanted to play Red Rover, but the boys vigorously fought against that idea and, eventually, Hide and Seek became the choice.

Jilly grabbed my hand, "C'mon, I know the best spot. They'll never find us."

She pulled me along as we raced deeper into her backyard. We jumped a small creek, and she lead me to a thin trail that cut through a deeper cluster of trees. At the end of the cluster, a small clear area appeared and standing on the left side of the clearing was a large fir tree of some kind with branches that touched the ground in every direction.

Around the backside of the tree there was the smallest of gaps. Jilly dropped to her knees and climbed in through the gap. "C'mon," she hollered back at me. I fell to all fours and crept in to find the trunk of the tree. We were surrounded in a seemingly-magical canopy of fir branches. From the outside, no one could see in or see us.

"I love coming here," she said. "In fact, you're the first person I think I've ever shown this too."

"Great hiding spot," I said.

A single dandelion was growing out of a small patch of grass next to the trunk of the tree. I scooped the flower from the ground and held it in front of her face.

"Here," I said. "Blow this and make a birthday wish."

She closed her eyes tight, lost in thought for a moment, and then gave a big blow as the hundreds of tiny Dandelion puffs flew off into the branches of the fir tree.

"What'cha wish for?" I asked.

"That's a secret," she said, and then she kissed my cheek, and giggled.

We sat for a time and talked about the upcoming school year, "I hear we have Mrs. Mason for 5th grade," Jilly said.

"Yeah, my brother Jack had her, but Sage and Arlo each had Ms. Pennington. Jack said Mrs. Mason is nice," I said.

"That's what my momma said. She said I'd like Mrs. Mason. She does a lot of art projects and stuff," Jilly said.

"I'm no good at drawing," I said.

"I can teach you to draw. It's easy."

We talked about Star Wars and which television show was better or had been better: Buck Rogers in the 25th Century, Battlestar Galactica or Space 1999. We argued about whether or not Wonder Woman could beat up Superman; and we discussed what parts we'd improve if we had been the Six Million Dollar Man or Woman.

"I'd definitely want bionic legs so that I could run faster," I said.

"I'd want some bionic hands so I could punch people really hard," Jilly said.

After a while, it became obvious that we were the winners, and we could hear kids shouting our names for us to come out.

We took our time, but ambled back to her house.

"There you are," Mrs. Branham said. "Oh, Jilly, just look at your knees. You're a mess, child."

"She looks fine, Martha," said Mr. Branham. "Ready for some cake, kids?"

A loud cheer went up from 35 hot, tired, hungry kids.

Mr. Branham had borrowed an outdoor table from my dad and probably another from another neighbor. Three tables were then shoved against each other and 35 kids crowded around them with Jilly at the head of one side.

A large cake was brought out that read, "Happy 10th, Jillian Michelle."

Jilly listened as fifty-five people joined in singing Happy Birthday, blew out her candles and cut the first piece of cake.

After the cake, it was time for presents and I had, or my parents had, bought Jilly two new Star Wars figures — Princess Leia and R2-D2. I knew she liked both from the movie and didn't have any Star Wars figures that I was aware of. Plus, my mom had picked up some kind of a birthday card and I had scribbled, "*Hppy Birthday, Jilly. Your freind, Chaz.*"

My spelling would improve through 5th grade, thanks to Mrs. Mason.

Jilly seemed thrilled with the card and both of the Star Wars figures and I was the only kid she hugged after opening her present. Well, except for her best girlfriend at the time, Madison.

Following all the presents and the massive clean up, Jilly's dad rolled out a small stage he'd built for her. It even had locking wheels and these deep red curtains. Across the top, he'd painted, "The Great Jilly Bean."

"Hello, Ladies and Gentleman, boys and girls of all ages," yelled her little brother, Toby. "Prepare to be amazed by the one and only, Great Jilly Bean!"

Fifty-five sets of hands came together in applause and a few of the dads whistled loudly for the now 10-year old magician.

"Thank you, thank you very much," said Jilly, stepping from between the two red curtains carrying a cane. She tapped the cane on the floor twice and a bouquet of flowers blossomed from the top.

Several kids and a handful of adults oohed and aahed at the slight of hand.

Jilly worked her way through several tricks from disappearing quarters to a bunny trick that didn't go as planned. Her best trick was a cool card trick where she pulled an Eight of Clubs from her dad's front pocket. Even he was very impressed with that one.

The party broke up just before supper time so that moms could get their kids home for supper and baths and any late night chores they may need to complete. Due to it being summertime, and a Saturday afternoon, there had been quite a bit of fathers in attendance as well.

We piled in to my Dad's Chevy and he and mom made small talk for a while in the front seat, while Arlo and I discussed Phil Niekro's knuckleball pitch. It was a short ride home, but I overheard one bit of my parents conversation and I wondered what they were talking about.

"Roger must be a saint to take that woman back," my mom said.

"Yes, that Martha is quite the, um, handful, I'd imagine," my father replied.

"Well, I think he should have packed her bags up and marched her over to Tobias's house and said, 'best wishes,'" my mom said.

"Oh, don't say that Elizabeth," my dad said.

"You children sit back," my mother yelled at us, and I leaned back as my dad turned up the radio a little. Mom leaned in and whispered something into his ear, but I never knew what she said. I did know that Tobias was Roan's father. And Roan had not been invited to Jilly's birthday party. I didn't know why.

A now 28-year old Jilly stood in front of the mirror, brushing her hair and finishing her make up in preparation for our night on the town. She wore a yellow summer dress over a pair of black heels and had pulled out a black sweater to carry with her in case the night air became chilly.

"So, what do you think about Reggie and Sarah," Jilly asked as she worked on her eye liner.

"I dunno. He's a great guy. If they're happy, so be it."

"Her mother won't have them over for supper," Jilly said.

"Really?"

"Yep, her mom just won't accept it," Jilly said.

"Oh, she'll come around," I said.

"I don't think so. I really don't," she replied. "Hey, did your parents ever go to those key parties that the parents used to have in the 70s?"

"A what party?"

"A key party."

"What the hell is a key party," I asked completely naive.

"You've never heard of a key party," she said turning to look at me with complete exasperation on her face; shocked that I didn't know the term.

"I have no idea what you're talking about. None."

"Wow, I'm a little surprised," she said turning back to the mirror for one last once over.

"You look stunning," I said.

"Thank you," Jilly said with a smile. She sat down in the chair opposite me, at the small table in our room, pulled a cigarette and lit it.

"So, you gonna tell me what a key party is," I asked.

"Well, my mom and I were having this conversation about sex when I was home for the holidays," Jilly started.

"That's a strange thing to talk about with your mom," I said.

"You're not a girl," Jilly said. "I talk to my mom about everything."

That was a scary thought. I now wondered exactly how much her mother already knew about me.

"And she was wondering if I was getting laid and who I was sleeping with. ... relax, there's only been one other guy beside you this last year," she said.

"That is remarkably comforting," I said with a smile.

"Whatever stud. Anyway, she told me about something she and dad did during the 1970s. They used to go to these key parties," Jilly said. "Now, like you, I didn't know what they were either. I'd never heard of them. So, what happens is a bunch of couples come over to a house. They have a party. But all the husbands would toss their keys into a bowl or something. Now, at the end of the night, the women picked out the set of keys and whoever they picked out was who they went home with."

"Wait, hold on," I said. "You mean to tell me these women were going to have sex with some other woman's husband. At random."

"Yep."

"Fuck. So, why do people say the 1970s sucked," I asked rhetorically.

"Very funny," she said.

"And, wait, your mom and dad did this," I asked.

"Yep," Jilly said grinning. "Very shocking. My dad doesn't know that I know."

"Holy shit," I said.

"And that is why I know Sarah's mom will never accept Reggie," she said grinning even more.

"What does a key party have to do with Reggie, and Sarah's mom," I asked.

"Because at one of these parties, Sarah's mom drew the keys of this black couple that had come to the party. She refused to go with him. Mom told me all about it. She made quite the scene and my mom was embarrassed for the guy."

"What did your mom do," I asked.

"She took the keys and went home with the guy," Jilly said.

"No shit?"

"No shit."

"How many times do you think your parents did this?"

"I have no idea. She never told me that. It sounded like at least five times or more," Jilly said. "It was quite the shock."

"I bet so."

"So, I wonder now if your parents ever went as well."

I sat back, still trying to picture it all and now the imagine of my mom and dad having sex tried to scratch itself into my brain.

"Jesus, I just can't even," I said. "I don't even want to think about them having sex. Let alone with other people. That makes my skin crawl."

We meet everyone in the lobby; Sarah and Reggie, Kaelyn and Patrick, and Roan, who was alone. Shannon Something had headed back to her hotel.

"Have fun," I asked of Roan privately as Jilly made small talk with Kaelyn and Sarah on the walk to the restaurant.

"Yeah, nice girl," Roan said.

I just laughed.

We found a nice seafood place, with an outdoor patio, and got a large table that could seat us all. For the first time, I felt bad for Roan. A seventh wheel on a six person car. He looked alone as he sat. The girls talked about jobs, bosses, raises, responsibilities, and living alone or with a roommate. Sarah and Jilly each had roommates, while Kaelyn had her own place. The two bedroom condo in Houston. The guys, we talked sports, from baseball to football to basketball. We touched on politics, but moved quickly over that always touchy subject.

It was decided that everyone would pick up their own check, but when Reggie said to put Sarah's on his bill, I made the same offer for Jilly. Roan looked at me with surprise. And Jilly refused.

"I'll just pay my own," she said graciously.

Kaelyn added Patrick's to her check, without much discussion.

I ordered crab legs, while Jilly ordered a shrimp plate.

The table ordered a large plate of oysters and everyone dove into those when they arrived.

I was seated between Sarah and Jilly and they kept leaning over me to talk. Eventually I got up and switched with Jilly so that I could be next to Roan and the girls were all closer together. I felt bad for Reggie. He had Kaelyn on one side and Sarah and Jilly on the other.

"How's the job going," I asked of Roan.

"Oh, I guess okay," Roan said.

"Cool."

"Yeah, I mean it's all right. Eleven-fifty an hour isn't too bad, plus I get overtime," Roan remarked. "When I get back, we got two guys going on vacation, so I should be able to pick up about 50 hours a week, over the next two, maybe three weeks. It'll be a nice paycheck."

"Damn, I should go to work with you," I said.

"Yeah, right. You do okay at the paper."

"Not as well as all that," I said. "Newspapers are cheap."

"Great perks, though, I mean hell, you've met Greg Maddux," Roan said.

"He makes a lot more than I do," I said.

"You have a shitty curve ball."

"True."

Roan leaned up a little, lowered his voice.

"You and Jilly?"

"Good. No issues."

"Good. That's a good thing, man. You'll see," he said.

After dinner we hit a variety of different places, up and down the Strip. The drinks flowed, but everyone seemed to drink moderately. In several of the bars, it felt like we had stepped into time machines to 1987 or 1990 or 1992; the music was the same, by and large. The faces, different, but not very different. There was less denim, overall, than a decade ago. We stumbled back to the hotel at nearly two in the morning and said our good nights in the hallway.

Back in our room, I pulled my shirt over my head and went back onto the balcony to smoke. Jilly disappeared into the bathroom. When she emerged she was wearing a black teddy and nothing else.

"I think I made a promise to you the other night that I never really kept," she said, coyly.

"You did?" I only half-asked with a smile on my face.

"Yes, it involved your brains, I do believe," she said as she wrapped her arms around me, her breasts pressed into my chest.

Her lips found mine and the familiar gave way to a newfound passion. As she embraced me, I slid my hands down her back, cupping her ass, squeezing it; our tongues danced and the night moved in twilight grays, moonlit shades and the whispers of a world temporarily forgotten by us both.

Sunday morning brought a nearly empty beach. And six of us rose to take advantage of the quiet and as close to solitude as one can get on a Florida beach once spring arrives. Roan was nowhere to be seen, but I assumed he'd show up as soon as he woke.

Instead of sitting guys and girls, each couple paired off to enjoy some personal time on the beach.

I laid beside Jilly as she worked on her tan in a blue and gold stripped bikini, the bottoms of which had a tiny golden heart on the front.

"That was a lot of fun last night," I said.

"Yes, I was pretty awesome. You weren't bad," she said, trying to keep a smile from cracking across her face.

"Thanks, I do what I can," I said.

"Yeah, you know, a little more practice and you should be good," she said.

"Yes, well, I haven't had any practice, well, since, wow, since June when you came over for my birthday," I said.

"Oh, shut up."

"No seriously."

"Bullshit."

"I'm not bullshitting you."

She rolled over and sat up.

"You mean to tell me the last time you got laid was last fucking June. On your goddamn birthday." She looked astounded and a bit hurt.

"That's what I'm telling you."

"Are you a monk or something? What the fuck."

"No, just no one of interest, I guess. I mean, I started, well, I thought I started to see this woman, Lisa. She works at CNN. But she went back to her boyfriend," I explained.

"And nobody else?"

"No, just no one came along," I said.

"Wow."

"So, what about your little fling. Who was he," I asked trying not to sound jealous, but curious.

"Ah, Mark. He works accounts receivable at a place in Alpharetta," she began. "We met through Andrea. She hooked us up I guess in August."

"And?"

"Oh, I don't know. Nice enough guy. Nothing special in bed. Just no spark. I gave him the boot before Christmas. Didn't want him to feel obligated to get me anything," she said.

"That was nice of you," I said, just a touch sarcastically.

We spent the day on the beach and Roan never emerged. I knocked on his door once we went back up stairs, but there was no answer.

We did lunch, supper and had some drinks and before long each of the couples once more said their goodnights and departed to their rooms. It felt less like a Spring Break and more like a married couples retreat.

I couldn't blame Roan for disappearing into the throng of the real Spring Break, which went on all night long.

CHAPTER 10

Monday morning found the six of us, still no Roan, out by the pool for breakfast. Patrick and Reggie had graciously run out to Waffle House and brought us back a nice little morning spread of greasy eggs and bacon.

We all took turns in the pool, or all in at the same time, goofing off, swimming or just splashing about. Jilly and I got out of the water and sat in the chairs, while Patrick, who never got into the water, sat under an umbrella reading a book. *The Clockwork Orange*, I believe.

"The pool is awesome," said Jilly.

"Yes, it's pretty great," I said.

"I'm gonna get a drink. You need anything?"

"See if they have a beer, will ya," I replied.

"Sure."

She kissed me on the cheek and walked off. I watched her as she went, her bikini bottom swaying back and forth.

"She's hot," I heard a voice say.

I turned to my left to find a 12, maybe 13, year old boy sitting there in the chair next to mine. He also watched Jilly walk off. I chuckled.

"You think so, uh," I said with a little laugh.

"There are so many babes at this place," he said.

I laughed loudly at that remark.

"Yes, I guess there are," I said in a non-committal kind of way.

"Is that your girlfriend," he asked.

"I guess you could say that," I said.

"You're lucky."

"You think so?"

"Yeah, she's drop dead sexy."

I looked at the kid again. He had brownish hair, wet from swimming, but obviously straight, and a splash of freckles all over his nose and cheeks. He was thin, very thin, but not sickly thin, and his swimming trunks had Superman's emblem all over them.

"So, you got a girlfriend," I asked.

"Yeah, I guess," he said.

"What's her name?"

"Melissa."

"What grade are you and Melissa in?"

"Seventh."

"Where do you go to school?"

"Lancaster Middle. It's in Knoxville."

"Your parents here?"

"Yeah, my dad brought us down. It's cool and all, but it's noisy at night."

"Yes, it can be noisy."

"My parents won't let me go out at night. I still have to be in bed by eleven."

"Eleven? Man, when I was your age, I had to be in bed by nine."

"Seriously? Nine o'clock? Geez, my kid brother gets to stay up til ten and he's like seven. Your parents must've been assholes."

Again, I had to laugh.

"Those were just the rules. I had three brothers, so my parents had to keep us in line."

"Did you get spankings?"

"Yes, a lot of them. You?"

"No, my parents don't do that. They say it destroys self-esteem."

"Uh, that's ... different."

"So, you and your girlfriend ... y'all been all the way, yet?"

"All the way? Um, yeah, I believe we have gone all the way."

"I got to second base with Melissa, but she won't let me do anything else. I may break up with her when I get home. I dunno yet."

"How old did you say you were again?"

"I turned 13 in February."

"Well, there's no rush."

"Tommy, he's my friend, and he and his girlfriend, Pam, they went all the way."

"Did they? At 13?"

"Yeah. He talks about it all the time."

"That's not a cool thing to do."

"You don't think so."

"Nope. Only an asshole would do that. Is your friend an asshole?"

"No. Tommy's cool. He listens to rap," he said and reached for his Coke to take a drink.

"What kind of music do you like?"

"I like gangster rap. Public Enemy. NWA. The hardcore shit."

"Your parents let you listen to that?"

"Yeah, my parents are cool with it."

I picked up my cigarettes, lit one and looked over at the 13 year old, white, suburban hipster.

"Hey, can I bum a smoke off of you," he asked.

"No."

Jilly returned and sat my beer on the table, she had gotten a Bloody Mary.

"Who's the kid," she asked.

"I don't know, but he thinks you're drop dead sexy."

"Smart kid."

I chuckled and took a sip of my beer.

"Hey, kid, what's your name?"

"Brian."

"Well, Brian, this is Jilly. Jilly, Brian."

"Hi, Brian. How are you?"

"I'm great. You got great boobs."

"Brian," I said. "If you want to keep your self-esteem intact, you may want to avoid saying things like that to women."

"Oh, I'm sorry," he offered. "You're just really pretty is all."

Jilly pushed her sunglasses up her nose and tried to think of what to say next.

"Thank you, Brian," she said. She picked up her Bloody Mary and laughed softly to herself as she stirred her drink.

"You play sports, Brian," I asked.

"Yeah, I play soccer."

"Cool."

"Did you play sports in school."

"Yes, I played baseball and football."

"He won the state championship in baseball," Jilly suddenly added.

"Man, that's cool," Brian said.

"Well, I didn't win it. The team won it."

"Brian, he's being modest. He hit .535 his senior year with 17 home runs and 52 RBIs."

I looked at Jilly astounded that she could recall that.

"Wow!" Brian exclaimed. "Did you play baseball in the pros?"

"No, not even close. Just high school," I said.

"He had an offer, but he turned it down to go to college," Jilly said with a certain amount of pride. "Why did you turn that down?"

"I wanted to be close to you," I said, returning her smile. She knew that wasn't true, not entirely false, but she didn't push back.

"You should have taken the money," Brian said.

"You think?" I responded.

"Yeah. I mean who knows, you might have been famous."

"There is more to life than being famous."

"Not much more," Brian said, looking out across the pool like a young man who wished deeply that he was famous. If for no other reason than to be able to have his pick of any woman in the pool. He looked like a kid destined for a desk somewhere, in some nasty little office with a refrigerator where everybody has their name on what they brought to work for lunch. A kid who would one day drink copious amounts of coffee, smoke too many cigarettes, and drink a ton of beer ... a kid just like me.

"Well, maybe you're right," I said.

I stood up tossed my towel back into my chair, surveyed the pool and when I found an opening, took off and dove head first into the deep end. I pushed myself to the bottom of the pool, touched the slightly slimy concrete and looked around at all the bodies moving this way and that in the cool, clear water. It's a funny feeling to be a failure in the eyes of a 13 year old kid. Or maybe I was misreading his face; but he seemed to have an expression, one I'd seen before — on my dad's face when I told him I was turning down the offer — as I had left him at his table with his testosterone-filled fantasies, and hopes for sex with a bikini-clad college girl. I imagined him back at middle school in a few days, lying about how he'd scored with some 15 year old girl to his buddies in the bathroom between classes.

I recalled the phone call that June day in 1987, some guy with the Kansas City Royals. I couldn't even hear his name from my parents yelling with my brothers in excited voices. In the end, it was five thousand dollars and plane fare to some town in Oklahoma. Or go to college. I was good enough, I guess to have played at some small school, and several of those were interested. But when I got my SAT scores back and knew I could follow Jilly to the university, well there was no other decision to be made.

My dad was disappointed. I knew it the moment I told him. And if he did try to hide that disappointment then he certainly choose the wrong facial mask. It was in the eyes. I think he wanted to say his son played professional ball. Even if it was in some east of bum fuck Egypt kind of town. It was the thought, the dream. They'd had dreams for Jack. Which fizzled. Dreams for Sage. Which went up in smoke. And dreams for Arlo. Which never were going to materialize.

I think my dad felt he was 0-for-4 on sons.

I'd found an old photo book once in one of his chests up in the attic. In it were old newspaper clippings from the Athens paper. He'd been quite the athlete in his day. He left high school and joined the Army. He married my mom when he got back six years later and they settled into married life, and had kids. I guess he hoped one of them would do what he'd been unable to do.

My senior year, I hit safely in 33 straight games. The team went 29-4 and won the title. But my dad bragged to all his friends that I wasn't held hitless by any team we played that season. You could see his pride in that.

Even though our football team had gone 6-5 and I was just average; he took his pride from my baseball season.

I had other thoughts, other ambitions. Even if I didn't know what they were.

I launched myself back to the top of the water, took in a deep breathe and swam back to the side.

I climbed out and saw Brian's chair empty.

"Where'd the kid go," I asked Jilly.

"I dunno."

I sat down and began to sip on my beer. I watched the frolic. I watched the dance. I watched the kids being kids, as I had once been. The conversations all filled with hopes that they'd lead to sex. It was in the face of every guy. It was on the face of every girl. Harder to see, but there. You could see their minds, as they tried to decide if he was gonna be a lucky one. Was this their stranger in paradise? Or just some nice guy buying them a drink and talking about life in whatever college town they had come from. There were the cool guys. The nerd guys. The frat guys. The sports guys. The metal guys. The biker guys. Guys with raging cocks. Each and every one on the prowl. The hunt.

The women played their part. The bikinis. The shaved legs. The sunglasses. The not-interested look on their faces. The but-I'm-not-*not*-interested look there as well. They were enjoying the hunt. The prowl. They loved the eyes and the once-overs. They loved being chatted up; if it was the right guy. Their kind of guy. If not, then the game was quickly over for that poor guy.

The prowl went on like this year after year. Hunting season for humans; each and every spring.

"What?" I said. Jilly had been talking. I'd heard none of it.

"Jesus, were you even listening to me?"

"No, sorry. I was lost in thought."

She looked over the crowd of men and women and back at me.

"No, it wasn't a girl," I said. "I was just thinking about baseball."

"Really?" she said.

"Yes. I haven't thought about that stuff in a long time," I said.

"You wondering if you made the right choice?"

"I dunno, maybe, maybe not."

"Do you remember that article you wrote about that woman with the three kids that was evicted from her apartment?" she asked.

"Yeah, that was about two years ago. Why?"

"You're good at what you do, Chaz. You are. You have a gift. You make people feel something for other people," she said, paused to light a cigarette and continued. "You should be proud of that, is all. I think you sell yourself short. You don't see the impact you can have.

"That woman got a new, nicer place to live because of your article. You made a difference in four lives. How many ever get to do that. Famous or not."

Sarah and Reggie joined us at the table, followed moments later by Kaelyn, who paused briefly to kiss Patrick on the top of his half-shaven head.

"What a great day," Kaelyn said.

"I am loving this pool," Reggie said with a laugh, as three college girls in string bikinis walked by.

"You're just liking the scenery," said Sarah with a smile.

"Yes, the scenery is nice," Reggie said. "But I got myself a sexy little thing right here,"

He scooped up her hands and kissed them.

"Where's Roan," Kaelyn asked.

"I haven't seen him," I said.

"I hope he's okay," Kaelyn said.

"I'm sure he's fine," I responded. "He's probably hooked up with that Samantha girl, or whoever."

"How about we go out and get some lunch?" Jilly asked. "Maybe we'll just bump into him out on the strip."

We packed up our belongings and headed for our rooms. I wasn't sure what our odds of finding Roan on the strip were, but I couldn't imagine they were very high.

After lunch it was decided to split up, guys and girls. The girls wanted to do some shopping and were going to walk west, while the guys were going to head back east towards the hotel and check out some of the various haunts along the way.

"If I find him, I'll tell him to call the hotel and leave a message for you at the front desk," Jilly said. "This way when you get back to the hotel, you'll at least have some answer from us."

"Are you gonna walk back," I asked.

"Sure, we'll be fine," she said.

"Just stay in the crowds and don't get separated from the girls," I said. Spring break could bring out the worst in human behavior. Something that never crossed my mind half a decade earlier.

"I'll be fine," she said, leaning up to kiss me on the cheek.

We walked into six different clubs, two bars and one pool hall. We checked out six different swim and surf shops and two tattoo parlors. About the third club, we started drinking. A beer here, a shot there.

Patrick was quite the detective. He stopped waitresses and bartenders, tattoo artists and shop girls. He gave each a brief physical description and probed with follow up questions.

There was no Roan. And I wasn't the least bit surprised. And I wasn't even alarmed.

I was certain that Roan was in a hotel hot tub or pool or bed with some strange. He was not going to be a tag along. He was going to live it up on this trip to Panama City Beach. And if someone was worried about him then so be it.

We decided to loop around behind the strip and walk along the back roads for a bit. We had nothing else to do and the drinks were beginning to hit home. Reggie spotted a small bar named, McGoverns and it was decided we'd try there.

We found three barstools, empty, and grabbed them while we could. The bar, like so many other places was filled to near capacity. If not over. We ordered beers and Patrick began his interrogation of the bartender, a tall woman, who was maybe 30.

The questioning proved fruitless, but the beer was cold, so we ordered another round. I felt someone saddle up alongside me and then a hand on my shoulder. I turned to see who it was.

"I thought that was you," said a female voice.

I looked at the face, the hair and suddenly it came back to me. Lexie. The waitress from Alabama.

"Hey! Hello there. It's Lexie, right," I had to talk a little loud over the din of the bar, even at mid-afternoon.

"That's it. Your name was Chaz, wasn't it," she asked.

"Yes. What are you doing here?"

"Oh, my plans changed. I came down this morning with a friend of mine, Brenda," she turned and pointed to Brenda, who sat at a table against the wall. She had purple hair, tattoos and a decidedly masculine look about her. "She's harmless," Lexie offered for no reason whatsoever.

"Oh, good to know," I said with a smile. Lexie turned toward the bar and tried to flag down the bartender.

"She has a crush on me," Lexie said. "And I'm not really into girls, and not into Brenda. But she is good to me when I need something."

"That's nice."

"So, you gonna buy a girl a drink or what?"

I raised my hand and tried to flag down the bartender as well. She flew past me with a 'I'll be right back,' on the way by.

"They are very busy," I said.

She looked deeply at me, like she was trying to read something off of my face.

"Yes, it would seem they are."

The bartender, however, was good to her word and suddenly appeared in front of us.

112

"What do you want," I asked of Lexie.

"Bud Light," she said.

"And give me another Bud."

The bartender was gone and back in a flash. She dropped our beers, collected the money and was gone again.

"So, tell me about yourself," Lexie asked.

I was standing in dangerous waters now. It was as if I was on an icy lake, all alone, thousands of miles from any help. And I could hear a crack beneath my feet. Caution. Go slowly. Answer carefully.

She lit a cigarette and turned to face me in full, awaiting my answer. The crowd surged slightly and she was pushed into me just a little. I felt the hardness of her nipple beneath the fabric of her t-shirt as it brushed against my arm.

I was in big trouble. The ice was cracking faster.

CHAPTER 11

"I still think their best album was *Goo*. I know everyone says *Daydream Nation*, and I get that. I do. But I think *Goo* was just fuller somehow; more well rounded," I yelled into Lexie's ear as the music of McGovern's was at full throttle.

"I'm not arguing that," Lexie said. "But *Daydream Nation* was more natural, I thought. Less of a commercial version of the band."

"I don't think *Goo* was commercial. You think *Goo* was commercial?" I shouted at the pixie-headed musical expert from Alabama, who just happened to wait tables.

"God, yes," Lexie yelled back. "It was their *And Justice For All* album. The sellout album."

"Really? I don't see that. I think for a sell out record it would have been way more accessible. I mean including 'Mote,' and 'Titanium Expose.' I don't see those as commercial songs."

"But they were. They were a cleaned up version of what Sonic Youth had done before," she said. "Okay, what's your favorite Replacements album?"

"That's easy, *Let It Be*."

"See? Again, you like the cleaned up version of that band," she laughed, but not at me. Just at the direction of the conversation.

"Honestly? You think *Let It Be* was a commercial record?"

"Of course it was. They were suddenly caring about being famous. About the big time. Prince had put Minnesota on the map by '84 and The Replacements released *Let It Be*? C'mon, that had alt-radio written all over it. They were the REM of the north at that point."

"I'm not sure I can see that exactly," I said.

Reggie and Patrick had departed about four hours earlier, or so I assumed. I remember them tugging at me, but at that point I was deeply engaged in conversation about The Cure with Lexie and told them to go on without me. I told them I'd be along soon.

"Do you listen to Sugar?" I yelled at Lexie. The music was loud. The beer was cold. And I was young. I was alive.

"Yes, of course. I fucking love Sugar," she said.

Her own friend Brenda had left with a girl about an hour earlier.

"Okay. Favorite song," I asked.

"Hmm. I'd say, 'Helpless.' And yours?"

"I liked, 'A Good Idea.'"

"Oh, that was dark. I liked that one as well. Look, are we gonna talk all night or do you want to fuck?"

And there it was.

The wind blew strong on the day we won the state championship. It was the first of June and the 4A Championship was at the baseball stadium at Georgia Tech in Atlanta.

We'd won the first game 3-2 on Friday night and trailed 4-1 in the sixth inning of Game 2 on Saturday afternoon.

115

My coach, Coach Bruce Ellington, was a pudgy little man. He'd played catcher in the Detroit Tigers farm system in the 1960s and ended up at Alexander Central after a friend suggested the position to him. He was in his 24th year of coaching when I was a senior.

There were two on base, a man at third and first, when my at-bat arrived in the sixth. One out.

I took the first pitch for a strike and Coach Ellington called time.

"What the fuck are you doing son," he asked in a whisper that only I could hear. "This is a first pitch, fastball guy and you stand there."

"Sorry, coach."

"Fuck, son."

"Sorry, coach."

"Okay, he's gonna go off speed and off the plate. Take this one for ball one. But be ready because he is coming back with the heat on pitch three. And you better fucking swing."

The pitcher, from a school in Rome, was a tall, lanky righty. He tossed the change well off the plate for pitch two. Ball one.

I stepped out, took a breathe and stepped back in.

I could see the seams of the ball out of his hand. It clung there. Framed. I hit all of it. The ball cleared the left field fence and we were tied up, 4-4.

I could hear Coach Ellington in my mind.

"Fuck, son. She just grooved a fastball over the plate and your just fucking standing there with your dick in your hand. Get up there and swing."

And there it was.

"Yeah, let's get out of here," I said.

"I got a place. It's not far," she offered.

"That sounds good."

We walked roughly four blocks to a one story house that sat in the curve of a road. A single palm tree stood tall over the house. The lights were on all over the house and a party appeared to be raging on the inside.

"C'mon," she said, taking my hand and dragging me inside.

The place was filled with twenty-somethings, all wearing the latest in alternative rock gear. Combat boots and ripped jeans. The 1970s punk movement had returned and were selling clothes to the disaffected masses.

Brenda sat French kissing her new girl on the sofa.

Lexie pulled me to a bedroom in the back of the house, opened the door and appeared to check to see if it was safe to enter before pulling me through the doorway.

"You want a beer," she asked.

"Yeah, that'd be great, actually."

"Okay, hang tight," she said, disappearing back into the hallway.

I took in my surroundings. The bed was framed with a boxed wooden headboard. The headboard was filled with a variety of items, including a tattered copy of The Hobbit, three old candles, an angel made from plaster, and an old Sex Pistols sticker stuck against the wood. The walls were filled with a range of posters — from Van Halen to Led Zeppelin, from The Misfits to Metallica — and framed pictures of all variety. A framed print of Salvador Dali's Swans Reflecting Elephants hung above the bed. There was a beat up dresser opposite the bed and a mirror hung above the dresser. The bed had a striped print comforter pulled neatly across the top and four pillows lay near the headboard.

"I grabbed a Budweiser. You drink those, right?"

"Yes, that'll be fine."

Lexie handed me my beer, took a swig of her own and leaned back against the dresser.

"Are you sure you want to be here," she asked with a thin smile on her lips.

I didn't feel nervous, or guilty for being there. But I wasn't sure why I was there either.

"No, I'm good," I said, trying to flash a confident, sexy smile.

"Good?" she said with a wicked curl to her lips. "How about we see if we can make you better."

She sat her beer on the dresser and pulled her tee over her head, letting it fall to the floor. Her breasts were on the small side, but perky and firm. Her pinkish-brown nipples stood erect on her chest against bottle cap-sized areola. She walked towards me and grabbed my hair, gave a playful, yet firm, tug and tossed my head backwards to drive her tongue, forcefully, into my mouth.

Our mouths were tight and hard, each against the other. Her tongue slowly, but strongly, circling around mine. Her hands lightly followed my arms down to my waist, where she gripped the bottom of my shirt and pulled it swiftly over my head; our tongues returning to their delicate dance.

She had straddled my legs, her ripped jeans tight against the flesh of her legs and beyond, and our chests pressed into each other. Her nipples brushing against me like two small finger tips, tracing some butterfly flight pattern over my chest. The touch enflamed me further. My member pressed, hard, against my own blue jeans; trapped, pinned, against the soft cotton of an old pair of Levis.

It was an exquisite pain. The pressure building as I awaited her move to release me; as I am sure she awaited my move to release her from the pressure building inside of her own jeans.

There was a flow.

A natural balance.

A touch, a moment; form and shape in a cascade of colors. Her dirty blonde hair in my face. Her blue, deep blue, almost purplish eyes, flashing into mine. Her slightly tanned flesh; the myriad of pinks, ranging from pale to rosy. I wanted to breathe in this painting of life. And oh, those glorious smells. The soft lavender hints lifting off her naked shoulders and throat. The smallest touch of jasmine from her hair. The raw cinnamon flavor in her mouth. I wanted more. I needed more. To drink her in. And to drink and drink again. This was a drunkenness that lead to a different set of prayers. A drunkenness that produced a different kind of spinning room. A drunkenness that needed no program, no support group, no interventions and no hangovers. A delightfully, delicious drunkenness that made me only want to drink more.

She reached between our bodies and worked the button at the top of my jeans. She unfastened that link in what seemed to be a cloth prison, encasing me. Give me release, my body screamed. Her hands returned to my chest, my arms, my neck, my throat, my face — everywhere her hands — but where I desired them, needed them, the most.

My own hands found the small of her back, her Venus' dimples just above her waist line were well defined. Her flesh so soft. She was firm and fit, but not overly thin. I was loathe for girls that seemed walking skeletons. Her shoulders, collarbones, and throat were graceful, yet strong. She was stunningly feminine without seeming girlish; tight, and naturally toned, without seeming masculine or tomboyish. At 25, she was a complete woman.

I cupped her left breast in my right hand and lifted her nipple to my mouth. I flicked it with pressure in my tongue; hard, yet not too hard. A soft moan escaped her throat. I flicked it again, harder now. Her moan rolled on her tongue. I traced the circle of her areola, then licked her nipple harder still. My mouth took it in now. I felt her head fly back, her face staring up at the ceiling as she whispered, "Fuck, yes."

Those two words, those two little words — "Fuck, yes," — sounded to my ears like all the tumblers in a lock falling into place. I lifted Lexie up, felt her knees pinch against my sides, and turned to face the bed with her in my arms, clinging to my torso. I lightly tossed her onto the bed, and I reached for the button and zipper of her jeans. Her hands beat me there. She worked the fasteners, and pushed her jeans down. I grabbed the cuffs at each leg and gave a large tug that pulled them all the way off. I tossed the jeans in a backward motion, toward the dresser; not really caring where they landed.

As she had been naked beneath her t-shirt, she was also naked beneath her jeans. The sight of her now naked on the bed. There was a reason there were so many thousands of naked women captured in art; so many thousands of naked painted ladies on canvases across the world, hanging in so many galleries. The form was perfect. God. Angel. Beast. Happenstance. Devil. Darwin. Some strange brew of stardust and time. Whatever the push that gave creation to such beauty, deserved my worship and prayers.

Lexie had the tiniest triangular patch of pubic hair, trimmed close to the skin; a light brownish color to the hair. To the right of the patch, was a black heart tattoo, while a small black star was tattooed on the opposite side. Jilly kept her bikini line very smooth, but had a thicker patch of pubic hair on her mound. By comparison, Lexie was nearly completely shaven. Her well defined hip bones stood out against her tight tummy and a larger, more natural triangle appeared to the eye as I looked down on her — a triangle that seemed to run across her belly button and then seemingly angled in from each hip bone to the point where her pink vagina waited.

I lifted her left leg slowly and gently kissed her ankle. I playfully kissed her small toes and then returned my mouth to her ankle and calf. Using both hands, I lightly kneaded at the muscles in her leg. Allowing myself the pleasure of feeling her skin as my kisses brushed down on her. I made my way to her thigh and then skipped across her womanhood and began kissing and caressing her right leg in a similar manner.

Then I fell on her. Diving into all that she was as a woman. Her fingers took my hair, holding me. Her legs wrapped around my back. Time and moment merge. Image and flash of image. A snapshot with eyelashes, eyelids acting as physical shutter. The visceral meeting surreal and real. Time and moment again; the flesh filled with an ancient, powerful desire.

I heard a call of my name. Hair pulled tighter on my scalp.

I lifted my own hips just high enough, and held them high just long enough, to peel my own jeans from my body. And then I made the climb. My mouth found her flesh again and again. The bits and pieces of who she was. The physical marks of womanhood; I found them all. Flickers. Touches.

And the night unfolded.

A dream of the youth that was fleeing my body hour by hour, day by day, year by year; a pace that seemed to quicken. That dream now captured in a night. Held. And held again. The force and the gentle of who we are when flowing in the intimate. The muscles, the skin, the emotion of our sex and the newness of she to me and I to her made for something unlike any other moment of physical love that I had previously experienced. The days of gawky, lanky, unsteady, unsure, self-conscious, self-doubt, embarrassed, quick, rushed for time, and most certainly uncertain love making where released and past.

This new man now stood in my skin. And I didn't know him.

Gasps, cries and moans of pleasure will fill the ears, but leave memory and float away over time. The knowledge that they were once there, once sounded, never leaves. The images will cloud and fade like old photographs, but the soft image is better than none at all. The touch of skin, so familiar, is easily recalled, even if the touch is removed by decades. The creation of a new memory, with a new lover, can either remain alive and front of one's recall; or be wiped clean and forgotten. I knew I might sooner forget my name than this night with Lexie. This night. I knew I would smell her, see her, feel her, touch her and taste her forever. That was the hope. The dream. Maybe it would prove foolish and false. But in the heat, the sweat of it all, I thought I'd never forget.

Time slips away and the night seemed to speed along as we intertwined, clung and realigned our bodies, one to the other.

Several times her moans became more guttural and she would clasp harder on my shoulders, her nails digging into my flesh. Each time she issued a series of new cries, new gasps; all with a new tone, urgency and frequency. The spasms of muscle and tissue deep inside her.

Finally, I emptied myself into her.

There was music coming from another part of the house. She curled up against my chest. I struggled to find and light a cigarette with my left hand, as my right was pinned beneath her. Once lit, I blew smoke into a grayish room, toward a grayish ceiling.

"Do you need anything," she said sleepily, her voice now strange in my ears. Different than I had recalled.

"No, not at all," I said. "I need to get up and head back."

She curled tighter to me.

"Will she mind," she asked.

"Who?"

"Your girlfriend. The girl from the diner."

"Yes. I don't know what I will say to her."

"Lie. If she throws you out, come find me. We can go anywhere you want. I have nowhere else to be and no one else that I am with," she said.

I half-chuckled, "What about your job? Your family?"

"I quit. And I have little of any family."

The reality. Harsh and sudden. I didn't even know her last name.

There was a song on the air, pushing through the walls and I smiled. 'Cross The Breeze' by Sonic Youth from the *Daydream Nation* album was playing in some part of the house.

I closed my eyes and drifted off.

The sun hit my face and a blood-curdling scream gave voice in my soul, head. I flung myself up and forward towards the dresser. This had to be a bad mistake. Had to be some foul dream. Whatever lie I might have been able to pass off four or five hours earlier was going to sound much thinner to Jilly's ears now. A lie that would only lead to more questions and a deep well of doubt.

I dressed quickly, turned and realized as I gazed down at a sleeping Lexie how little I actually regretted. I was going to regret lying. That I didn't want to do. Truth, then? What would that get me.

Where did that road lead. To my surprise, Lexie opened her mouth and spoke.

"Don't tell her the truth," she said. "She will live with a lie, even a terrible lie, if she loves you. The truth will not be so easy for her to handle."

"You don't know Jilly," I said, but not aggressively or even defensively.

"Do what you need to do," Lexie said.

I turned toward the bedroom door.

"Wait," she said.

I turned back around and she stood naked now. She was beautiful. She walked to me and leaned up on her toes and kissed my mouth softly.

"I'll be here, if you wish," she said. "Go," she added, pointing towards the door.

I walked out of the house and down the block. I made the turn at the corner when the fear set in.

"Fuck," I yelled into the morning sky. I assumed it was somewhere between 8 and 9 a.m., but I wasn't certain.

My feet began to speed up and suddenly I found myself running like I hadn't run in 10 years. I felt the smoking in my lungs then. The burn. I fought through it. My feet pounding the pavement. I must run faster, I thought. Fear. Regret of something. Regret of something. I wasn't sure what.

The moments that I had been with Lexie seemed like a blink in time; or even a strobe light-like series of blinks. Now, as I raced through the streets of Panama City Beach, wondering what to say to Jilly, the time seemed stretched somehow. My feet I feared would never get me to the hotel.

Twice, I stopped in raw panic that perhaps I had made a wrong turn — certainly, I should have been back at the hotel by now — and both times I could hear the ocean to my right and I knew I was running East, and in the correct direction. Finally I saw the sign for the hotel.

I stopped outside the lobby and tried to catch my breathe. I stood for a moment thinking, I am already late, a few extra minutes will make no difference now. I took advantage of my sudden calm to sit on a bench and light a cigarette. I needed to think of a plausible lie in case the truth would not come from my lips. The truth. The lie. The swing went back and forth.

I stamped out my cigarette, found the elevator and made the walk down the hall to room 532. I could hear noises coming from Roan's room, so he must have finally returned.

I slide my key gently into the lock and pushed the door open.

Jilly sat in a pair of blue jean shorts, a pale gray sweater and her hair pulled into a ponytail.

She sat with her legs drawn up to her chest and she faced the open glass door to the deck.

She turned toward me, with tears in her eyes.

I have fucked this up so bad I thought. My mouth quivered as I tried to decide between lie and truth.

Jilly spoke first.

"Roan is dead."

CHAPTER 12

Roan's face was bloated, bruised, cold and dead. Lifeless, he lay on a metal rolling table, a single sheet draped over his body. A name tag of some kind was attached to his toe. A single large gash was obvious, running up from his forehead and into his scalp, and the back of his head appeared matted with blood, dirt and God only knows what else. The room was cold. Life was colder.

Jilly stood near me and held my hand. I hated myself for that. That she would hold my hand and comfort me at this time. I wanted to scream my truth at her, to lay bare all the wrong I had done. But words found no voice in my throat or mouth. I was in shock. A profound shock as if all the world was in on some great cosmic joke. Instant karma was going to get me and did. I was waiting for a punchline I knew would never be delivered. I waited for Roan to rise and begin to laugh after pulling off the meanest practical joke ever delivered. He lay still. Death never laughs.

A man in a white coat sat scribbling notes at a nearby desk. He had a neatly trimmed goatee, white from age, and green and brown horned rimmed glasses. He was as solemn and professional as the room. His name badge identified him as Earl Carter. Earl looked up from his desk, offered a thin smile and returned his gaze to his paperwork.

We'd already confirmed the identity of Roan Phillip Bishop, 28, of Decatur, Georgia. It sounded odd hearing the detective say it in such a formal fashion. He was just Roan.

Earl rose, clear plastic bag in hand, and approached us.

"These are the items we found with your friend. They've been processed and cleared. It is my understanding that his father is on the way down, but I can release these items to you both, if you wish," Earl said in a steady voice.

"Yes, I thank you," I mustered up.

Looking into the bag, it appeared a t-shirt, jeans, socks, Roan's wallet and a lighter were all he had with him at the time of his death.

"When, um, when did he die? Do you have a time of death," I asked.

"I'll let you speak to the detective about that. I believe he had some questions," Earl said.

We were shown into a small room with a table and four chairs. Three bare walls and a fourth that featured the door to the room. Time was lost to us in that room. Fifteen minutes or five hours; it was impossible to tell. We sat. We waited.

Jilly rose at one point, opened the door and walked down the hall. I could just hear her asking for directions to the ladies room. I stared at the ceiling. When she returned, she again reached out and held my hand.

"I'm sorry," was all I could find.

"Not now. Please," she said.

There was a patch of light brown on one of the ceiling tiles. It looked as if the building had a leak. The shape of the patch looked like a Volkswagen Bug and I had no idea why it caught and held my attention. But the patch seemed out of place. A flaw in an otherwise flawless and clean environment. Perhaps this room was used so infrequently that no one had noticed. I wished to be a kid again. To lay in the back of the car on some trip, some vacation and stare up at the clouds from the backseat and see the shapes the clouds produced. I wanted to play the blink game and close my eyes so just a sliver of image could creep in. I wanted Roan to be alive. To be my buddy again. To be my friend again. I had so much I never said. Things I thought I should have said. I wanted someone to come and replace the fucking tile.

Finally, Detective Aaron Ledbetter arrived. He came into the room carrying a folder under his arm. He was well-toned, fit, and even the cut of his suit seemed to suggest a man who worked out often. He appeared to be in his late thirties, but he could have easily been a decade older.

He shook our hands and offered his condolences for our loss. The introductions were no sooner out of the way when a second man entered the room. A tall, lanky black man who introduced himself as Detective Wilton Tilly. Tilly appeared to be nearing sixty and had the look of an extremely studious man.

Tilly sat, casually, in the chair next to Ledbetter and lit a cigarette. He had small patches of gray around each ear, but the rest of his hair was at least two shades darker than his skin tone. He looked kind. It was in the eyes. It was a trait that seemed out of place to his profession. He was patient, and that was a trait that probably served him well. He had time. He was in no rush.

Ledbetter seemed in someways similar to Tilly. He wore a wedding band and I was betting he had children, at least two. He had a close crop haircut, light brownish hair and a scar on his chin.

"The first thing we need to establish is eliminating suspects," Ledbetter began, his voice fatherly, almost patronizing. "Now we do this in several ways, of course, but I think first we'd like to eliminate anyone in your party. From there, well, the investigation will be able to move quicker if that possibility is eliminated."

Jilly and I nodded our heads.

"When is the last time either of you saw Mr. Bishop?" Tilly said, speaking in a deep, yet gentle voice, with a strong Bayou accent, perhaps Louisiana or Mississippi in origin.

I spoke first.

"Saturday night, or early Sunday morning."

"It was 2 .m., on Sunday morning," Jilly said clearly. "We'd gone for dinner, the seven of us, and then out to several different clubs. We all returned to the hotel and then went off to our rooms."

"Was anyone with Roan when he went to his room," Tilly asked. Ledbetter was making notes, but I felt sure the room was probably being recorded.

"No," Jilly said. I shook my head in agreement with her.

"Was there any trouble at the restaurant, or any of the clubs? Any problems with anyone in the street," Tilly asked.

"No and no," Jilly said. "No run-ins of any kind. It was a fun, peaceful evening."

"Any reason you can think of for Roan to leave his room and the hotel that night?"

"Well, yes, of course," Jilly said. "Roan was the only single friend in our group, at the time, and he probably went looking for girls, or to just continue partying."

"That's something he would have done," Tilly asked.

"Yes," Jilly said.

"Mr. Wilson, now it is my understanding you are Mr. Bishop's closest friend," Tilly stated.

"Yes, sir."

"Know him well, then?"

"Probably better ten years ago than now, but I feel like I knew him pretty well," I replied.

"I assume you agree with Ms. Branham that Mr. Bishop probably left the hotel to continue his good time, or to look for female companionship, correct?"

"Yes, sir."

"Now, in speaking with the staff at the hotel, one staffer, luckily, recalls your friend leaving around 3 a.m. This staffer recalled him because your friend stopped and asked him for directions to a place called, 'The Grunge,'" Tilly adjusted in his chair, took a long drag on his cigarette and continued. "No such place exists that we can find in Panama City or Panama City Beach. We, of course, have underground clubs that pop up from time-to-time, and we will certainly make every effort to learn what we can, if indeed this is an underground or illegal club.

"But I must ask, have either of you been to such a place, or heard of such a place. And let me say, because I know that while on vacation, people will often do things they may not do in their personal lives at home. Certain inhibitions, or certain taboos one may hold ... well, even morals, can be challenged in such a place and during these kinds of trips. It is Spring Break and I have been a cop for 32 of them. So, please, do us a favor in helping your friend. Do not be embarrassed to tell us something, even the smallest piece can help solve a case like this."

"I have never heard of any such place, Detective Tilly," I said.

"Nor I," Jilly said. "And if we had, I assure you that I would tell you. I have no idea how he even would have heard of such a place. What kind of club is it, or do you know?"

"No, idea," Tilly said. "Again, we can't find that one exists, but our investigation is only just beginning."

"Where was Roan found," I asked.

"West Beach Drive. It's here in Panama City. There's a sand road, kind of a dirt area with a patch of trees," Tilly said. "He was discovered laying in the shallow waters, along a rocky beach area by a man out for a jog. We were able to clear the jogger as a suspect quickly, if that helps."

"How long do you think he'd been dead?"

"We are still looking into that. I don't have any answer on that or his toxicology at this time," Tilly said, as he looked reassuringly into my face. He wanted me to believe that this case was going to be worked. And then it dawned on me. Tourist. Murdered. White male. Of course. This murder came at the height of Spring Break with thousands of young college and high school students descending on the community. Millions of dollars would pass hands. A murdered tourist was not good for business. It explained their patience, their kindness. They wanted us to feel comfortable that this had high priority. And perhaps it did.

"Is it fair to say there isn't a primary suspect at this time," I asked.

"Yes, that is fair to say," Tilly said. "What do you do for a living son?"

"I'm a journalist, a reporter," I said.

"Cover news, eh?"

"Sports," I said.

"Very nice," Tilly said. "And you Miss, what do you do?"

"I'm a project manager, basically," Jilly said. "Employed by the Georgia Department of Transportation."

"And you both live in Atlanta, correct?" Tilly said.

"Yes, sir," we replied simultaneously.

"Do you cover the Braves, son," Tilly asked.

"Mostly high schools and some college," I explained. "But I do get to pitch in and help out in covering all the professional teams as they need me."

"Very nice," Tilly said again.

"Detective, how was Roan killed," Jilly asked.

"I am not at liberty to disclose that at this time. For one, I don't have the medical examiner's report, yet," Tilly said. "There is a lot that makes very little sense. It is a rare crime here. And, to be honest, most of our murders are usually related to some form of domestic violence. It is rare for us to have a tourist murdered while here."

"And is it your thought that this place, this 'Grunge,' may have played a role," I asked.

"That is not something I am prepared to answer, one way or another," Tilly said. "He may have never found the place. He might have been mugged on the way there."

"Was he mugged," I asked.

"Well, I don't know that yet."

"Was anything missing from his wallet?"

"I don't know that, son," Tilly responded. "I do know there is $419 in his wallet. In cash. So, I am guessing, no, that he was not mugged. But, suppose the mugger ran off. Got scared. Something spooked him, or her, and this person wasn't able to finish the act and take the money. We don't know yet. We do have officers out on West Beach asking questions."

"And I hate to ask this," Ledbetter spoke up. "And I don't ask to upset either one of you. Did either one of you kill Mr. Bishop?"

"No."

"No."

"Do either one of you know who might have killed Mr. Bishop?"

"No."

"No, sir."

"And Detective Ledbetter is accurate, we are not trying to upset you further at this difficult time, but as I said, it helps us to eliminate suspects as quickly as possible and we both appreciate your honesty at this difficult time," Tilly's voice was reassuring, but his eyes held suspicions. Not accusations, but you could see he wasn't prepared to 'clear,' anyone just yet.

Both detectives shook our hands, again offered their condolences for our loss and showed us the way out.

We stood on the sidewalk in the middle of the day. A warm, beautiful Florida day. Our lives forever changed. Now altered by some as yet, unexplainable horror. I was sleepwalking. I had to be. This had to be some kind of mistake. There was no reality where this could have happened. My reality. We're supposed to be drunken fools, maybe one last time, but fools and the frolic of fools, the dance of fools. This was a week of stupid smiles, drunk smiles, and the smiles of 2 a.m. captured in fire light with laughter in our ears and topless girls. This was not the week my best friend was supposed to die. A guy I really no longer knew and didn't deserve the right to call 'best friend.' When was the last time Roan and I had hung out? The weekend before Christmas, maybe. Work. Always work. I did evenings and nights; he did break of dawns and days. It was a phone call. A promise for beers. A broken promise and a late phone call to say I was sorry, and how I'd been tied up at work on this assignment or another. My friends? My current, real friends. What the hell were those? I had people I worked beside. People I laughed with over some arrest or some crime or some sports event or some current event or some Saturday Night Live episode. But friends? No. I had none of those. I had Roan and I had wanted rid of Roan. I wasn't a kid and I didn't need a childhood pal. And I needed a childhood pal. In the pale grasp of adulthood I had a child's mind and a man's body and the damned confusion of a spirit built out of less than air. I had no soul. I was a walking, working zombie. And I was alive.

Jilly drove my car back to the hotel, I sat quietly beside her. She opened the door to our room and I floated to the deck. She poured me a drink and I sat, frozen and stunned, on a deck overlooking one of America's greatest weeklong street parties. I wanted to weep at my stupidity and the shallow stupidity of a generation. No challenges. No wars. No great economic calamity. I'd faced nothing in my life more traumatic than not finding a desired gift under a plastic Christmas tree. Everything else had been the angst-ridden drama of youth.

My friend was dead. My friend was dead. My friend was dead. I stared at the sea.

I sat for some amount of time. I found myself needing to be closer to the water. I pulled off my boots and my socks and my shirt and tossed them to the floor. I lit a cigarette.

"I'm going for a walk," I said to the room. Jilly may have responded.

I found myself on the sand, with only my tattered jeans.

I walked into the water, deeper still, and then I wept.

134

My friend was dead.

CHAPTER 13

My momma tried to get us involved in church at an early age, much like her parents had done. She got little if any help from my father, who had given up on anything church-related while in the military. "If foxholes are the only place God ever shows up, then he isn't much of a God," my dad said once. My father's logic and worldview were always shaped by that which he could touch and see. Mystical stories, fantasies, or fairy tales of any kind he found silly, at best, and insulting to a world that could use some tangible positive change, at worst.

My momma was another story all together. And I think the differences between the two actually helped their marriage. My momma was always trying to get my father "saved," or to at least help in the ongoing hunt for a missing Jesus. My father was always just slapping her butt and saying, "maybe next week, hun."

My brothers dipped out of church one after the other, with Jack being the first to stop going when he turned 13 and my dad needed his help with changing a lawnmower belt one Sunday. After that, Jack never went back. Sage was next, arguing weeks later with my momma that if Jack didn't have to go, then why did he. My father, in his way, agreed with Sage and made him sweep the carport and rake leaves, while momma dragged me and Arlo to church. It was another three years later, when Arlo turned 11, that he was able to stop attending as well.

That left momma and I to get up on Sundays and make the ride to Alexander Methodist Church. I was nine then and still enjoyed getting momma all to myself and the fact that she made pancakes for me every Sunday, since I was a "good boy, who goes to church with his momma." It would be another year before the bribe of Sunday morning pancakes lost its appeal.

Alexander Methodist was like so many other seemingly millions of churches in the South. All brick, stained glass windows, large white doors at the front and a huge golden cross sitting high atop the church; often painted against a blue sky, that cross was the highest point in Alexander for many years. In the early 90s, as Georgia transitioned from a 'southern' state to a bizarre mix of modern, international and, in pockets and individual communities, cosmopolitan place, a hotel chain built a 17 story hotel next to the Interstate. In roughly thirty years, Georgia went from KKK cross burnings atop Stone Mountain to the home of openly gay singer Elton John.

That transition was hard on the members of Alexander Methodist. They had held onto a Georgia of simple black and white for at least a hundred years. At least three generations had passed through the doors of that church with little cultural change at all. Suddenly, there were Russians and Koreans and Hispanics and Indians and people from places ending in "-stan," living across the whole metro Atlanta area. The Olympics would come and go in 1996.

Atlanta boasted one of the world's busiest international airports, and geographically, one of the largest. A city of hustle, bustle and two hour traffic jams.

But in 1979, long before the changes would arrive in north Georgia, as I turned 10, I too joined my brothers and father in 'non-membership' status.

"But momma, they don't have to go," I recall saying, as I waved a hand in the general direction of my three brothers.

"Honey, just come with me today and see if the message doesn't speak to your heart," my momma said.

"But momma, the game is on today," I said, referring to a football game I wanted to watch. My momma was smarter than that, however.

"Oh, Chaz, please. That game doesn't start until 1," she reasoned. "We'll be back right in time for kick off."

Suddenly, something unexplainable happened.

"I'll go with you," Sage, then 15, said. He pushed back from the kitchen table, carried his empty plate to the sink, rinsed, and placed it into the dishwasher. He walked toward his bedroom without further word.

"See? Your brother is going," momma said. "Jesus is working in his heart this day."

"Fine," I said and stormed off in the direction of my room to get dressed.

The car ride was uneventful, and the message, delivered by Pastor William Bennett, was something about doing for others, about sacrificing for others. I guessed that Sage had sacrificed for me, so I thought that was something. The car ride home was equally uneventful and Sage hadn't said maybe more than three or four words to me. Even during the 'greetings,' portion of church as I had turned to shake hands with neighbors, and folks I'd spent my whole life with, and offered "Peace be with you's," and other similar greetings, Sage hadn't shaken my hand. He just shoved my head and grinned.

Later, sitting at home, I walked into his room.

"Hey, why'd you go to church with us," I asked.

"Hell, I dunno. You're my brother, so I thought I'd kind of stick up for you a little," Sage said. "But, I ain't going next week. That place is boring."

"Well, thanks for going."

"Yeah, well, whatever."

Sage's version of Christian charity was a little murky.

I sat now staring at Sage as he sat opposite me at Welldon & Family Funeral Home, serving the people of the Gulf Coast since 1954. At least that's what the sign out front said.

Sage had left Atlanta after getting a phone call from my momma, who I had called Tuesday evening to give the news of Roan's murder. Now, on Wednesday morning, here he was. He was the darkest of the four of us, his hair a darker brown and his eyes almost black, having a deep brown tone. He looked more like my dad. The other boys, Jack, Arlo and myself, took after momma. Fair hair and bluish eyes. Yet, Sage was probably the least-favored child of the four. Brooding, moody, sullen and crass; his arms covered in poorly done, greenish tattoos displaying girls, crosses, motorcycles and guns, his huge frame was intimidating to many. And unlike some men of large size, who have a kind of 'teddy bear' soft side or jovial personality, Sage looked like a man always on the edge of violence. He was the one person you wanted on your side. And why he was here now, having driven through the night to get here, was a total mystery to me. As so much about Sage was.

The receiving room at Welldon's held fourteen people altogether — myself and Jilly, Kaelyn and Patrick, Sarah and Reggie, Rich and Dallas, Roan's aunt, Tammy, Sage, Mr. Gilbert Welldon, the funeral home director, Mrs. Maple Welldon, Gilbert's wife and receptionist for the business, and Roan's parents, Tobias and Denise.

I don't know when the last time Tobias and Denise had seen each other was, but they appeared friendly toward each other and made no display of any personal hard feelings toward the other. They'd split up in the 80s, and were officially divorced about a month before we'd graduated high school. Roan lived with his dad the last month of high school, at his old home, while Denise had moved to Cummings, Georgia and, as I understood it, rented a small house there.

They'd flown down together from Atlanta to Jacksonville, picked up a hopper to Panama City and rented a car, together. Now, they worked together to get the funeral arrangements for their only child in place. I wondered how they were handling all of this, so calmly, so matter-of-factly, but then I thought that they may be in shock as well. While I had called my momma, it was Jilly who had tracked down both Tobias and Denise, through her own parents, to give them the awful news that their son was dead. Murdered in Panama City.

The hotel had graciously given Roan's room to his parents since it'd been rented for the week anyway. Jilly and I had offered up our room, figuring we could bunk down with either Kaelyn and Patrick, or Sarah and Reggie. The offer was made so that Tobias and Denise wouldn't have to be uncomfortable sharing a room after so many years apart. Each room had two queen beds and both Tobias and Denise refused the offer saying they'd be fine.

I stood up and headed for the door to smoke a cigarette. I felt Sage rise to follow me.

"What did the police tell you," Sage asked, once we were outside, as he lit a cigarette of his own.

"Not much," I said. "They have the body, and I guess from what Mr. Bishop said, it won't be released until Friday at the earliest. They are doing an autopsy today."

"Did they say where he was? Or where he was going?"

"They mentioned a club called The Grunge. How they knew about that, but didn't know where it was located seemed a little weird," I said.

"How'd they know about that," Sage asked, taking a draw.

"They said someone who worked at the hotel told them they recalled Roan asking for directions to the place."

"And where was he found?"

"Somewhere off of West Beach Drive, they said."

"Huh."

"What?"

"Well, I'd be willing to bet that whoever Roan talked too gave him some kind of directions to the place."

"Why do you say that?"

"That seems like a pretty good distance from the hotel to where he was found, don't you think? It just seems like a good starting point is all."

"A good starting point for what? Look, what the fuck, Sage ... I mean, I am really glad you're here and all, but you're not exactly Magnum Fucking P.I., you know?"

"Yeah, no shit, fuck-bird. But do want to find out who murdered your friend or not?"

141

"Sage, man, look, I'm not sure what the fuck I want. Jesus. Are you serious with this? What are we gonna do, go kick down some doors? Fuck some people up? And what then? This isn't something you and I can just go off and do. This is a big fucking town — "

"It's not that fucking big."

" — and the the cops here will figure this out," I finished.

"Yeah. I'm sure they will."

We sat smoking for a minute in silence. A lone black dog was eating something in one corner of the parking lot. Something that looked to have been wrapped. Probably a discarded hamburger or something. The dog finished the meal and trotted toward Sage and I. He stopped short about ten or fifteen feet away and stood, sizing us up. He sniffed the air, seemingly checking for any free food we might have or might have tossed him. He barked once, turned and trotted away.

"You gonna help me with this or not?" Sage finally said.

"Yes, I'll help you."

"Good."

"So, what's the big plan then," I asked, with probably a large dose of sarcasm and doubt in my voice.

"Just gonna follow the example set by Dr. Martin Luther King, Jr.," he said, with a sudden flash of the boyish charm he held long ago.

"What the fuck are you talking about?"

"Damn, I thought you went to college and were a smart boy and all and you don't know Dr. King?" he said with a large dose of smart ass in his own voice.

"Yes, I know who Dr. King is. I am asking ... oh, fuck, I don't even know what I am asking."

"Men often hate each other because they fear each other," Sage began. "They fear each other because they don't know each other. They don't know each other because they can not communicate. They can not communicate because they are separated.

"Dr. Martin Luther King, Jr.," he said, drawing again on his cigarette. "I had some time in jail to do some reading, college boy. So, yeah, we're gonna go communicate with some folks, so they don't fear us. If they don't fear us, maybe, just maybe, we can learn who killed Roan. And then that person will get to fear us."

Jilly came outside and sat down on a bench next to the one Sage and I occupied. Sage rose, stomped out his cigarette.

"I'm going back in," he said.

Sage stood up and stretched his six-foot-six frame. He wore light, dusty brown cowboy boots, similar to my own, although his own feet were probably two sizes large than mine, and a dark pair of Levis with a collared, button up blue shirt. The sleeves were rolled up high, revealing a few of his tattoos. He slapped his hand on my shoulder and turned to go back into the funeral home.

I looked up and saw Jilly looking at me. A look of grief mixed with sympathy. I hated myself. Her blue eyes were soft and kind. She either didn't suspect my recent unfaithfulness, or had decided not to call it up. Maybe Lexie had been right. Maybe Jilly would forgive any lie, no matter how pale and weak, but the truth, if tossed into her face, would only make her angry. Angry for wanting to believe the lie. For buying into the lie.

"How are you holding up," she asked. There was a deep kindness to her voice. I didn't deserve her.

"I don't know."

"It just doesn't feel real, does it," she asked. "I just wish he'd have asked us to go."

"Go where?"

"That club. Grunge? Whatever it is. I wonder why he didn't want us to go, or even asked us to go?"

"I don't know. Roan could be ... I think he probably knew it was some single person kind of place, maybe. Maybe he didn't want to be seen as a third-wheel."

"I guess," Jilly said. "Do you have a cigarette?"

I pulled open my pack of Camels and tossed one to her, then gently tossed her my lighter. She lit up and tossed the lighter back to me.

"Sage got here very fast," she remarked.

"Yes, he must have flown down in that truck of his," I responded.

"What's he driving?" she said as she turned toward the parking lot to survey the various vehicles in the lot.

"That Ford 350 over there," I pointed out.

"Damn. That's a big ass truck."

"He's a big ass." I said.

Jilly laughed softly.

"He loves you," she said.

"Yeah, I guess he does."

"He's probably violating some parole or something even being here," she said.

"Yes," this time I laughed softly as I spoke. "He probably is."

We returned to the parlor the Welldon's had assigned to us. There was one other funeral party in another part of the building. A deceased elderly woman, I believed based on the crowd of family and friends who went to and from the other parlor. Upon entering our little room, which was remarkably well furnished, I noticed Sage speaking quietly with Rich. That could only mean trouble. Tobias was speaking with Mr. Welldon and the two seemed to be coming to some agreement about something or another. I sat next to Roan's mother and softly put my arm around her back.

"I'm sorry," I said.

"Oh, dear, you have no reason to be sorry," she said. "He was always happiest when he was with you and your brothers. He loved it at your house."

She looked off as if caught in a sudden memory and then spoke.

"Remember that one year it snowed, and I think Jack was driving then and he took all the boys off to Carter's hill to go sledding," she started.

"Yes, vaguely."

"He pitched such a fit as I tried to get him dressed. He kept thinking that y'all would leave without him. He loved just being around you. You were like a big brother to him, I think."

"He's a good friend," I said, realizing I'd spoken about him as if he were still here. Still among the living.

"You two were like a regular Tom and Jerry, always one, you get the other," she said with a smile. "I always felt bad for your mother having to feed so many boys, so often."

"Yes," I said with a chuckle. "Between us, I think there were always some eight to ten boys in and around the house at supper time."

"And Sage, are his problems, um, behind him," she asked with motherly concern in her voice. But also a touch of gossip.

"I don't know. He is a hard one to figure out sometimes," I said. I looked up at my brother and now he was engaged in conversation with Dallas and Tammy. Jilly stood with Kaelyn and Sarah. Poor Reggie and Patrick looked kind of lost and trapped at the same time. I am sure neither one of them had figured their vacation would turn out like this. At least Reggie knew about Roan, even if they'd never been friends, but Patrick was a total stranger to nearly everyone here, save Kaelyn and he looked totally out of his element. Mrs. Welldon more than once looked at the punk rock attired Patrick as if he were an alien from another world.

Sage was suddenly alongside me.

"Come smoke with me," he said, his eyes suggesting it wasn't a suggestion.

We made our way back outside.

"Take Jilly back to the hotel in a little while and then meet me at Rich's trailer. Dallas thinks she might know someone who knows about this club, Grunge."

"Sage, are you still on probation." I asked.

"Dude, if I'm not in jail, then I'm on probation. That's not your concern."

"Look, I'll hang out and whatever, but if you do find something, you, no, we have to go to the police."

Sage looked at me as if I was some kind of salesman, trying to sell him on a time share or an idea that was as foreign to him as Greek.

"Yeah," he said. "Exactly. That's exactly what we'll do."

This was a mistake.

"Sage," my voice seemed to trail off. I didn't know what to say to him.

"Kid, he was your friend," Sage said. "Now, I think I'd be pretty pissed off knowing someone beat the shit out of my friend, killed him and left him laying on a strip of sand. But that's me.

"I've known that little shit-heel friend of yours since I was 13 years old. And, you know, I liked that kid. He made me laugh. Now, somebody stomped out his life and I plan on making sure whoever did that finds out that I, for one, don't think that is something you just get away with. Join me, or don't. But I know what I'm going to do."

There was no turning back. If I agreed with Sage then I was opening a door in my life, one I might not be able to close ever again. I was four inches shorter than Sage, and he had more than 50 pounds on me. I moved in close against him, my eyes hard.

"We find something, we call the police. Understand?" I spoke with just the slightest threat in my voice. Sage merely blinked.

"We'll see."

CHAPTER 14

Roan had taken after his father, Tobias Bishop in a lot of ways. You could see some of the youthful stockiness in Tobias' build, the way his shoulders were cut. Tobias had the same thick black hair that Roan had sported. It was even parted the same, right to left. Tobias stood on the sidewalk in front of Welldon's now, smoking. It was nearing mid-afternoon and a decision had finally been made to seek out lunch, or an early dinner and then go back to the hotel. Denise Bishop wanted the young people, as she called us, to go swimming. "Y'all came down here for a vacation. A little swimming will do the mind and the heart some good," she had said. Tobias had agreed with her, even saying he might need to buy a swimsuit. They were each trying to use some levity to lessen, even in some small measure, what we were all feeling.

"Are you going out with your brother later? Over to Tammy or Rich's," Tobias asked.

"Um, yeah, I think so."

"Keep an eye on him, Chaz," Tobias said. "He's angry and people do foolish things when they're angry."

I shrugged my shoulders, searching for the right words.

"I don't know why he thinks this is his fight," I said.

"He's your brother. It's always his fight."

I looked closely at Tobias and suddenly my mind was filled with the story of key parties and swinging that Jilly had told me about. Maybe Roan had gotten his natural interest in the opposite sex honestly.

"Did you have brothers," I asked knowing very little about Tobias' upbringing. I think he'd been born in southern Georgia, near Valdosta, but I wasn't sure.

"Yes, I do. I have three brothers and four sisters. Grew up on a farm. Pigs, mostly. Hell of a thing growing up on a pig farm. Place always smells of shit."

He suddenly rolled up his left sleeve and held his arm out for me to see. A nasty scar cut up his forearm toward his left elbow.

"How'd that happen," I asked.

"Pigs, of course."

I nodded my understanding, although I truly didn't understand.

Tobias must have sensed my lack of knowledge concerning such and expanded his explanation.

"I was seven and I fell in with the pigs. My arm hit the trough and one snatched it up. Bit right to the bone, damn near snapping my arm," he explained. "My dad was nearby and shot the pig dead. I got lucky that all I got was a scar and a whippin.'"

"It was my brother, John who'd dared me to walk the fence in the first place. He got a whippin as well. Just one of many times we took a whippin together. So, I understand brothers. And yours, well, he thinks he has to do something for you. He probably has his reasons, but you need to be sure he doesn't get himself in more trouble."

"I'll do what I can," I said.

"Your dad didn't want Sage coming down here, but your momma called him," Tobias explained. "I think she wanted to send someone to look after you. I think she'd have been better off sending Jack. Jack has his head about him. Sage, well, he's one tough son of a bitch, there is no doubt about that. But his head, it's probably three eggs short of a full dozen."

I had to laugh at that.

I lead a mini-caravan back to the hotel. Tammy, Rich, Dallas and Sage headed back to Rich's trailer, while Jilly, Kaelyn, Sarah, Patrick, Reggie, the Bishops, and I went back to the Days Inn. We departed to our rooms, showered, changed and met in the lobby to walk down the strip towards a seafood supper. We went to the same restaurant as we had on our first Saturday night in Panama City Beach.

Our orders taken, the conversation turned toward stories of Roan, moments shared and recalled. There was more laugher than tears.

Sitting on the deck, I had one moment of panic. I thought through the crowd, which I could see passing by on the sidewalk, I caught a glimpse of Lexie. The haircut was similar, and even the body size, but the young lady was not Lexie.

Later, we joined that throng, the crush of bodies along the sidewalk. Cars, bumper-to-bumper, backed up on the Strip.

Evening had fallen by the time we made our way back to our rooms. Kaelyn, Sarah and Jilly were going to go swimming, but I had promised Sage I would meet him at Rich's trailer. And despite my reservations, I was going to keep my word.

"Are you sure about this," Jilly asked sensing my indecisiveness.

"Look, knowing Sage, we'll go to a couple of strip clubs, ask some questions and then call it a day," I said. "There won't be any trouble."

Jilly stood, her back to the water, wearing a sundress. It was a splash of light purple with darker purple swirls, swishing this way and that, on the fabric. Her hair lifted and danced in the constant breeze off the Gulf waters. She wore sandals on her feet and a single gold bracelet on one ankle. She lifted her cigarette to her lips, a dark red lipstick, and took a draw. She exhaled and looked down on me with grace in her blue eyes. A sudden breeze caught her hair and threw it playfully around her face. Oh, how beautiful you are, I thought. And I am the world's biggest fool.

I had chosen, once more, my favorite cowboy boots and my favorite pair of Levis and a simple white t-shirt for the trip to Rich's trailer. I gathered my belongings — keys, wallet, two packs of cigarettes and lighter from the dresser — and walked back onto the deck.

Jilly now faced the water and I wrapped my arms around her as the Wednesday night sounds of Panama City Beach reached our fifth story room. I kissed the back of her head.

"I love you, Jilly," I said. "Please know that. I love you."

"You're still a dumbass," she said, playfully.

"I'm beginning to think you are right."

"Just don't do anything fucking stupid," she said, spinning in my arms. "A little stupid, I can deal with. Fucking stupid is off limits, okay?"

"Okay," I said.

I made my way to the elevator and into the lobby. From there I walked to the parking lot to my car.

I saw the well dressed black woman walking at me with a guy in tow. He carried a camera.

"I'm sorry to bother you," she said. "I'm with WPCB and I was wondering if you'd answer a few questions for us."

"About what?"

"I understand you lost a friend. Murdered the other night in Panama City, is that correct?"

Suddenly there was a light on and I naturally shielded my eyes against the glare of the bright light.

"Um, no, I think you have the wrong guy," I said.

"Look, I have ..."

"Listen, I'm a reporter myself," I said.

"Really? Where?"

"Atlanta. And I understand you have a job to do, but I have somewhere I need to be," I said and walked past her.

"The death of your friend has a lot of people talking you know. There are stories floating around out there. Don't you want people to know the truth?"

"I don't know the truth."

The ride to Rich's trailer was the first time I'd been alone, totally alone, in days. The silence in the car was somehow refreshing. Just me and my thoughts. Thoughts in snippets; glimpses into memory. The past, present and an anger for the future now ahead. And for the first time, I was feeling angry. I was feeling vengeful. I wanted to hit somebody, to shove somebody, to kick somebody. I wanted to feel powerful. I wanted power over death. Power over loss. Power over grief. And pain. This fucking pain. My heart was choked in it now. Roan. He was a good dude. A happy dude. He made people laugh. He made people laugh with a joy of just being. He had a way with ladies and he had a way with other guys. He could make you feel comfortable. He put you at ease. He was always looking for a good time, a party, a girl, a beer, a smoke, a stiff drink, a shot, a toke, another girl, and another party. He was head strong at times, to be sure. He was stubborn and had a stubborn man's vision of rights and wrongs; and he could speak up at the wrong time and say the most dreadfully wrong things. But dead? No, he didn't deserve that. Perhaps my mother had sent the right brother after all. For Sage was many things; chief among them, the embodiment of all things mean and angry. I needed some mean and angry.

Sage's truck was parked in the street and I knew Rich's Nova on sight, but a third car was behind Sage's truck and I didn't think it belonged to Tammy. It was a Mustang. A 1972 or 74 by the look of it and in good shape.

I had to park behind a Chevy Chevette on the street, two doors down from Rich's trailer and walk back up to his place. I knocked on the door and slowly let myself in.

Sage sat on the sofa, with Dallas on the other end, smoking a joint and talking to the two people at the table, a man and a woman.

"Hey, sweetie," said Dallas. "How are you doing?"

"I'm fine, Dallas," I said and pulled up a chair at the table. "Where's Rich?"

"I dropped him off at his momma's place and brought his car back here."

I looked at Sage. He grinned at me. The son of a bitch had fucked Dallas.

"Let me introduce you sweetheart," Dallas started. "That's Christopher and Morgan. They're friends of mine. This is Chaz, y'all. Morgan, tell Chaz about Grunge."

Morgan was about 19 at the most. Very young with small breasts in a halter top and ripped up blue jean shorts. She had a tattoo of Mickey Mouse on her right arm and a large rose running down her left calf.

Christopher was about 35. He wore khaki shorts and an Iron Maiden t-shirt from some tour in the late 80s and Converse sneakers. He had his long hair pulled back into a ponytail, and I assumed he played in a band.

"Well, um, I don't know where to start," she said, looking back at Dallas for guidance and support.

"Honey, Chaz is family. Just tell him the whole damn story. He's not gonna judge you darling," Dallas said with a flash of a smile and a quick look in my direction that seemed to suggest I needed to reassure this girl.

"Morgan," I said. "My friend is dead. Please just tell me what you think I need to know."

Sage stood up, walked to the fridge, pulled two Budweisers, sat one in front of me and returned to the sofa with his own. I popped the cap off, took a swig and looked at Morgan. She took a deep breathe and began.

"I was 17 when I met Mr. Rivet. He was a photographer then, mostly nudes and fetish stuff. I did a few photo shoots with him and hoped that maybe I'd go to Hollywood or something. Anyway, last year, I was old enough to finally do porn and he had me take this role in a movie, 'Little Chicks, Big Dicks,' and it was you know, okay, it paid like five grand and so I did another one. Well, he got me into some strip clubs, doing the featured routines. That's where I met

Dallas, at the Toy Box one night," she slowed long enough to take a sip off her own beer and I took a big swig of mine. "So, he suggested that I branch out into these 'art house' gigs. He said I could make seven to ten thousand dollars doing those and I thought why not.

"So, the first one wasn't too bad. It only paid three thousand, and all I had to do was walk around naked while people talked and stuff. A couple of guys groped me and a couple of women, but that was it. So, I told him I wanted another gig and this one was eight thousand he said, but more intense. I was tied up to a pole in the backyard of this rich guy's house and people covered me in paint and then whipped me. It wasn't so bad. It hurt, but not awful. It was kind of sexy," she took another sip and I took another swig.

"The next gig was the same money, but I was put into a dog cage, naked and folks ... well, they pissed on me. About ten or twelve guys."

I'd heard enough.

"Morgan, I'm sorry, but what does this have to do with Grunge?"

"I'm getting to that," she said, slightly offended that I'd interrupted her. "Last summer, I got a call from Mr. Rivet about an underground club that needed some girls. Now, I'd done about twenty movies at this point, mostly anal, and he thought I'd be good for this gig. It paid ten thousand dollars for one night. I was driven to a warehouse in Panama City, bent over a table and tied there, naked. I was used all night long. Maybe a hundred people, maybe more. I don't really remember. I was using a lot of drugs back then."

"So, you know where this place is then," I asked.

"Well, no. I mean that's just it. They move around. It goes from house to warehouse to garage to airport hanger," she said. "It is never really in the same place twice and I don't even know who runs it. I told Dallas this already."

She took a deeper drink from her beer.

"It doesn't even stay in Panama City from what I understand. It moves along the Gulf and across parts of Florida. Christopher knows," she said pointing at her male friend.

Christopher was maybe five-foot-ten and appeared to weigh about two-hundred pounds, all of it soft. What he lacked in physical appearance, he made up for in pseudo-intellect and a smarmy personality.

"Yeah, bro, I drove some bitches back and forth to the different locations. Always picked up a cool grand for driving and keeping my mouth shut," he said. So much for the latter, I thought.

"Yeah, I mean, you know, it's like your basic fuck and cum club, but they run different house music. It's like shitty jazz one time and maybe some kind of European rap the next," he continued. "You never really know."

"Who was your contact person," Sage asked from the sofa.

"Oh, this guy named Dillon. He's super cool. He owns a music store. You know, selling guitars and drums and shit."

"You got a number for Dillon, or a location we can find him?"

"Nah, his number changed or something. But his business is called Rocker's Edge. I bet they're open. He usually works late and stuff."

I looked at Sage, who shrugged and said, "Sure, why not. Let's go and see Dillon."

CHAPTER 15

The Rocker's Edge sat in a mostly derelict shopping center. Only four businesses appeared to remain in any state of operation, with a Chinese takeout place on the far, western end of the strip mall to a nail salon, Painted Talons, and an appliance repair business simply called, Procter Repair. The music store that Dillon operated sat on the eastern end of the mall, three empty businesses sitting to its right and two empty places to its left before one could walk in the door at Procter's. The shop was lit up with a large amount of neon in the front windows, with what appeared to be old band flyers announcing local concerts taped all across the outside of the windows in a random, haphazard manner. The sign above the business was a cutout of an electric guitar with the words, Rocker's Edge painted in a fiery font.

We parked roughly fifty feet from the front door and tried to get a feel for the foot traffic flowing in and out of the business at almost 9:30 at night. The place seemed to be fairly busy and must have enjoyed a solid reputation among local musicians.

"Well, how about we go in and browse for a little bit," Sage suggested. "Just see if we pick up anything or hear anything."

"Sure," I said. I wasn't convinced this path was going to lead anywhere. A former drug-addicted, porn star having kinky sex was not exactly a startling revelation, and I wasn't convinced this Grunge place even had played a role in Roan's death. But it was a starting point and I was willing to humor Sage in his quest for justice.

We had driven Sage's Ford pickup to the music store and the enormous truck filled nearly four parking spaces. Sage had been sure to park away from the store and with the small amount of business in the lot, I doubt his unusual parking style offended anyone.

Sage's musical tastes ran to 1960s and 70s rock and ventured little from that genre. He had installed a CD player into the dash and we sat listening to The Doors' *Morrison Hotel* while we had eye-balled the music store. Roan had enjoyed The Doors as well. I recalled him lip syncing to Jim Morrison on countless occasions, and he even pulled off a passable imitation of the former California singer, with his hops, skips, jumps and snake-like slither. Once, in the midst of the pursuit of some girl, Roan had video-taped himself lip syncing to The Doors song, "Love Street." It was intended, I suppose, to come off sexy or filled with his deep emotion, fleeting as it was, for his love interest. Instead, it came off comical, and Roan spent months trying to live down the various imitations of himself imitating Mr. Mojo Risin.

"You ready," Sage asked.

"Yeah, let's go look at guitars," I said.

The interior of Rocker's Edge was surprisingly spacious. Guitars — electric, acoustic and bass, joined by banjos, mandolins, violins, cellos and harps — hung in racks along the walls and from the ceiling. Rows of keyboards and a wide range of PA equipment ran down the left hand side of the store, with an equally diverse collection of drum kits running down the right. There were low-lying shelves filled with guitar strings, guitar picks, drum sticks, sheet music and five stands filled with old records. Five apparent customers, not counting Sage and I, mingled among the items and it appeared two employees lingered behind a counter. Faces locked in apathy, neither seemed very interested in selling anything to anyone.

An older black man sat in a chair in the left corner of the store playing guitar through an amp, with the volume turned low. Even from my distance to him, it was obvious he was talented with the instrument, but what was not so obvious was whether he was a customer or an employee.

I wandered around listening to the sound system pumping out Soundgarden's "Black Hole Sun," while Sage walked to the counter in an effort to strike up a conversation with the two disinterested employees. The one was a woman, small with purple hair and a black leather vest over a ripped up Soul Asylum tee shirt, and a black and white striped mini skirt; while the other was a male, heavy-set with a distinct Elvis-style pompadour and thick black sideburns. He wore a trendy pin stripe Zoot suit that he must have paid handsomely for; it appeared to have been tailor-made. To his credit, Sage deftly struck up a conversation with the pair about the records that were for sale and began to explain how he'd heard that the store might have a copy of some rare Big Star vinyl he was looking for. The male salesperson of course claimed to know nothing of any such record, while the female seemed intrigued by the huge guy with the sweet southern accent asking about the power pop band.

"I don't know," she said. "Dillon will be back soon and he might know."

"Oh, man, that's right," Sage said, snapping his fingers once for effect. "I was told to ask for Dillon. So, I'm sorry that I jumped the gun there."

"It's no problem," she said sweetly. "So, you live around here?"

"No, I'm in from Georgia, visiting family, and one of my cousins suggested this place, is all," Sage responded.

I walked away as Sage continued to flirt and be flirted with by the glorified cashier. I walked past the record bin and flipped through several of the old records and came across a Leadbelly album. It was a 1954 10-inch Allegro Records recording called, "*Leadbelly's Sinful Songs,*" and it was priced at five dollars. I knew this one was leaving the store with me and put it under my arm as I continued flipping through the records. I eventually walked to the other side of the bin and the black man, who had been playing guitar looked up and flashed a smile. His teeth a beautiful pearly white, with one golden cap on his bottom row.

"How you doing this evening, young man," he asked with a rich, deep southern voice.

"Well, sir. And yourself."

"Hmm, well, I am here testing out this Gibson and trying to make a hard decision about a new guitar," he said.

"I heard you playing when I came in. You're very good."

"Thank you. Been playing since long before you were born," he said. "But I ain't had a guitar now ... oh, hmmm ... let's see I guess it was 1982? Maybe 83."

"Why's that?"

"Ah, my house got broke into and it had to be 82 or 83, I think now, and they took all three of my guitars," he sounded mournful.

160

"That's an awful thing to have something stolen from you," I said.

"Yes, yes it is. What record you got there?"

"Oh, Leadbelly."

"Leadbelly?" his eyes rose and his face seemed on the verge of full laughter, but he held it in and the mirth crossed only through his eyes. "What is a young, white boy like you doing listening to Leadbelly."

"Oh, a few years ago this band called Nirvana did one of his songs."

"Which one?"

"Where Did You Sleep Last Night," I responded. "And I have a couple of cassettes of Leadbelly back home. But I have never found a record until now. So, I am going to get it."

"Powerful music. Powerful music."

"Do you play any of his songs," I asked.

"Let me see that record a second," he said reaching out with his right hand. His hand was worn like old leather; it appeared hardened and his knuckles each looked as if stones had settled beneath his deep dark skin. He gave the record's track listing a once over.

"Oh, yes," he said softly. "I know several of these." He paused and looked back over the racks of guitars. "Hand me that Martin," he said.

I looked over the rack and then back over my shoulder, uncertain which of the acoustics he was asking to see.

"That one there," he said pointing at a pale rosewood guitar with a rich brown finish. I pulled the guitar down and gently handed it to him. He placed the Gibson in a stand up rack near his feet. It was then that I noticed for the first time his worn tennis shoes. An old pair of Nikes, that had clearly carried him for a long time.

He plucked at the guitar, checking the tuning and then he began. The music soared off the instrument and was soon joined by his deep, well-balanced baritone voice.

"John Hardy, he was a desp'rate little man, He carried two guns ev'ry day," he opened and soon everything in the store seemed to cease. Two people saddled alongside me, listening to the elderly black man with a voice born of bourbon, a voice comfortable in its age. "He shot a man on the West Virginia line, An' you ought seen John Hardy getting away. You ought to seen John Hardy getting away." His fingers danced up the fret board with ease, relaxed; his face filled with purpose and poise. His eyes shut tight as he wound out this plaintive tale of murder and woe. The song poured out of him with such ease, like a man simply walking down a street, with little effort. And save for his tightly shut eyes, there was nothing in his body that suggested he needed to concentrate at all. "I been to the East and I been to the West, I been this wide world around. I been to the river and I been baptized, And now I'm on my hanging ground."

A small round of applause went up for the singer as he finished and I turned around to Sage, who was smiling softly and clapping as well. From the corner of my eye I noticed another man standing in the doorway. I turned a little more to see a man of roughly fifty, with a long white beard and long white hair standing, motionless, against the frame of the door. He shook his head softly and then walked towards the gathering standing around the black singer.

"Edward, Edward," he said, shaking his head softly. "Are you ever gonna buy one of these guitars, or are you just here to give free concerts to my customers."

The black man chuckled softly.

"No, Mr. Dillon. One of these days I will buy one of these guitars as soon as I find the one that falls in love with me," he chuckled a little louder at that.

Dillon smiled down at him.

"Well, let me know when you find the one you want to sleep with for the rest of your life," he said and began to walk towards the counter.

I pulled sixty dollars from my pocket, folded it twice and slipped it to Edward.

"Thank you for playing that for me. It was beautiful," I said. "I needed to hear that tonight. Thank you."

"You a mighty heavy heart. Ain'tcha son?"

"I guess you could say that." I walked away before he could see how much money I had given him and have to fend off any argument about him accepting the money or not.

As I made my way to the counter I could hear Sage speaking with Dillon about his phony search for a rare Big Star album.

"Radio City, you said," I overheard Dillon ask of Sage.

"Yeah, it's the one with the red cover. A shot of a ceiling and a light bulb or something," Sage said continuing his little deception.

"Geez, I don't know," Dillon said. "And it was your cousin who thought I might have a copy?"

"Yeah, he was saying I needed to check out the Rocker's Edge and ... well, this is the place, right? I was just kind of hoping you had a copy," Sage said.

"Hm. I really don't think I do."

I walked to the counter and placed my record down. The Zoot suit rang me up, placed the record in a bag and handed it back to me.

"Do you know anyone that might have a copy?" Sage pressed on.

"Not off hand," Dillon said as he began to walk slowly toward the door that I assumed lead to an office of some type. Sage trailed him. Dillon stopped at the door and looked at Sage as if to suggest, sorry, but I can be of no further help.

"Oh, well. I was just hoping to get lucky is all. You know how it is," Sage said.

"Sure, no problem. I wish I could have been more of a help. Is there anything else you're looking for?"

"How about another record?"

"Which one?"

"Damn," Sage said scratching his heavily-stubbled chin. "I can't think of the name of the band, but they released an album called, The Grunge."

Dillon's skin turned as pale as his hair. He swallowed.

"I'm sorry? What's it called?"

"The Grunge," Sage said calmly, his eyes clear in the meaning.

"I don't think ..."

"It may just be an urban legend," Sage said suddenly. "You know, one of those things like Mikey choking to death on Pop Rocks or some guy's dick. Maybe, it wasn't an album at all."

The packages Dillon had carried into the store with him seemed to slump to his waist as his hands lowered and he looked trapped and uncertain of what to say next. Sage filled the silence for him.

"I bet that it's just some fancy, high rollers excuse for a good time," Sage said. "You know, make up a story about an imaginary recording to impress a lady and next thing you know, well, everyone is talking about it.

"I bet you could prove how right someone is about this whole thing. I guess the easiest thing to do would just be give me some directions on how to find that rare recording."

"Look, I can't …"

"Oh, sure you can," Sage said.

Dillon was a small man. No bigger than five-foot-eight at the most. He'd probably been a musician most of his life and his love of music had probably afforded him contacts with a large and diverse range of people in his lifetime. But I was certain he'd never seen anyone quite like Sage, who towered over the diminutive shop owner.

He spoke softly when he finally spoke.

"Step into my office, please."

Dillon straightened his packages in his arms, pulled keys from his belt, unlocked his door and lead the way into a back room. The three of us walked across the storage area to another door that Dillon simply opened. He placed the packages on his desk.

"I, um, keep the information you need in my safe," he said, nervously.

He turned toward the floor safe next to his desk and spun the dial on the front, pulled the lever and opened the safe.

"So," he said, rummaging through the safe. "How did you hear about The Grunge."

He was withdrawing his arm when suddenly Sage brought his boot down hard on Dillon's right arm. The crack was loud and Dillon's eyes flew wide and sound tried to escape from his mouth. Instead, he vomited right into his safe.

"Holy shit," I heard my own voice say aloud. My mind was blank. My body was numb. I felt as if I'd seen something wrong, something that could not possibly have just happened in front of me.

Sage lifted the small man with one hand and tossed him onto his desk and into the wall. He lowered himself to the safe and pulled out a .9mm handgun.

"Now, that's interesting," Sage said, showing the gun to me and then holding it, non-threateningly, in the direction of Dillon. "Were you expecting us to rob you or something? Or do you always shoot people that ask about The Grunge?"

"I wasn't gonna shoot you," Dillon said through clenched teeth and a pained expression on his face. "I was just gonna try and scare you away."

"Do I look like I scare easy," Sage asked with an amused look on his face.

"No. No, you don't."

"Then why try? Unless you're scared of something more than me, right?"

"You could say that."

"Yes, I guess I could. So, where were we ... The Grunge."

"Look, I don't know what you have heard, but you don't want to get involved in this. I am begging you to please just walk out of here. I won't say a word about my arm, or anything else. Just please leave."

His eyes travelled from Sage to me and back and forth again as he spoke. He wasn't trying to see if we'd cave in, he was desperate for us to cave in and leave.

"Listen," I said. "The other night my friend was killed. He was looking for The Grunge. I don't even know if he found the damn place, but I need your help."

"I am helping you," he said. "Please, just leave this alone."

"Dillon," Sage said. "It's too late for turnaround. You just tell us who we see and where we go next. Got it? That's it, man. That's the deal. You're still gonna keep your mouth shut, because you don't want your name dropped in the next conversation I have.

"And I can either drop your name, or the name of some made up bellhop at a local hotel. The choice is yours, man."

"Who is Mr. Rivet," I asked.

"Ha! A nobody. Just a two-bit pornography, who occasionally sends a girl up the pipeline," he said. "Did he tell you about The Grunge? Because his ass will be on the line."

"Dillon," Sage started. "Tell me about a 'somebody' then?"

CHAPTER 16

Men break. There is in fear a place where courage can be overcome. And in this truth, we all shutter. For if even the bravest can have pause, then what hope may we hold? If the measure of our heart cannot withstand, not overcome, and the waves or the hurricane of fear overtakes us and we drown in those moments, what weight did our life have? We stand and face that mirror, that proverbial abyss, and wonder, what could break me?

Dillon had his answer now. And he spilled out a tale of sex. A tale of debauchery. A tale of power and money and those who hold high in the palaces of men. A place of rare air. A timeless place, occupied by few, and passed from one generation to the next, always trying to find a more base existence, always trying to find a way to express a meanness built from the emptiness that fear can bring. Even to the powerful. For none is immortal. And in that, our fear of death, our fear of the vast emptiness that may follow, then all bets are off. No promise of golden halls and fertile, ethereal planes can overcome that fear.

Dillon knew little of the names, or the next location, but he had one honest lead. One honest moment of confession. For his soul was now cleansed.

The house Dillon directed us too was a single story ranch style home near Lake Martin. The house sat on a single lane dirt road and based on the appearance was no more than a decade old. To the left of the house sat a children's swing set and trampoline, and I was hoping that we were in the right place, or that there were no children inside the home.

Sage's threats against Dillon, to visit all manner of pain upon him if he was lying, may or may not have worked. There was really only one way to find out and that was to ring a door bell; which at eleven at night seemed like a bit of a dice roll. The various possibilities of what we may next discover were rolling around in my mind. Sitting in the cab of Sage's truck, my main concern was that this was a false lead and that we would find some nice little family scared by our late night visit for no reason. If that proved true, Dillon was in for a world of pain.

An older man opened the door, matching the description Dillon had given us perfectly. Dillon had not lied. Now, the question was had Dillon alerted this man with a phone call. Based on the man's demeanor, Dillon had not broken from that promise either.

"Yes, can I help you," he asked. His eyes were sizing us both up and this man of seventy showed no fear. He was too close to death to fear other men. His face was pocketed with brown spots and red spots, his eyes swollen and bluish. His arms looked like two rubber bands that had been stretched by decades of heavy-lifting, but whatever muscle might have once filled the skin was long gone. Replaced by a white cheese of fat and weakness. The eyes still held.

"We are looking for a man. A Mr. Wise," Sage asked.

"And what do you know of Mr. Wise? How have you heard this name," he asked back.

"May we come in and speak with you? I have lost a friend, murdered, and we mean you no harm. But I am looking for some answers," I spoke softly. I hoped that my act of meekness would not be misread as weakness. I wanted this man to be at ease and I didn't want a repeat of the violence visited upon Dillon. His decision hung in the air, but he finally tossed the door aside, gently, and in his right hand, once hidden behind the door, he held a double barrel shotgun.

"Jesus, does everybody in Florida meet strangers with guns," Sage asked, rhetorically.

"It's the times we live in, son. The times we live," the old man said in reply. "Come. Come on in."

The foyer opened out into the living area, which was spacious, and well-appointed. Two large leather sofas were placed opposite each other, separated by a large glass table sitting atop a solid piece of marble. To the left, when entering, stood a fireplace, while to the right a low wall divided the living room from the kitchen. Two sliding glass doors lead out from the living room to a partially visible patio area. The solid wall that separated the glass doors held an enormous abstract painting of a naked woman. I didn't know the painter.

"Have a seat," the old man said waving at the sofa to his left. He sat on the opposite sofa, with his back to the kitchen and ours to the fireplace. There was no fire burning, but the ash hadn't been swept in quite sometime. I had a feeling we were not alone with the old man.

"You boys, you want something to drink then," he asked.

"That'd be great," Sage said.

"Yes, sir," I added.

"What do you want? I have everything from brandy to wine," he said.

"We'll just take two beers, in bottles. Caps on if you don't mind," Sage said. He seemed paranoid. Which seemed pointless since the old man had a double barrel shotgun laying across his lap. Why poison us, if he could just shoot us? But then again, it was a nice living room.

"Milas! Milas," he yelled.

A young, light chocolate-skinned girl came out of a closet beside the fireplace. The sight of her was shocking. She wore a black leather collar around her neck, off of which two chains fell to similar cuffs around her wrists, and then fell further to two more cuffs around her ankles. With the exception of the apparatus, she was naked.

"Sir," she asked.

"Two beers, caps on. Go," he said, his voice hard, almost snarling.

She shuffled off toward the kitchen, the chains lightly clinking together, but they were long enough to afford the young woman a wide range of motion. In addition, she seemed to display no discomfort wearing them, nor did the chains and cuffs appear to be uncomfortable to her skin. She had a strange tattoo or brand of some kind on her right butt cheek, and the back of her legs showed welts and raised lines. She'd been whipped. Not too recently, but certainly within the last three days.

"So, how can I help you then," the old man asked, his voice gentler now.

"First, I assume you're Moffitt," Sage asked.

"Hm. Yes, and how you know that name is most curious to me," Moffitt said.

"A little bird sang for us," Sage said.

"Well, there are exactly three 'little birds' that know me by that name. The name, Moffitt. And one of them is getting your beer from the kitchen as we speak," Moffitt said. "I'm going to hope that you did not hurt Dillon too badly.

"He is a good man. A hard-working man. He lost his wife to cancer eight years ago. I bet you did not know that. But then, how could you, right?"

I felt a little sick in my stomach.

Milas returned, the chains clink announcing her presence in the room, and placed the two unopened beers, Coronas, in front of Sage and I.

"I thought slavery was against the law," I said.

"Slavery? Son, Milas is here for pleasure," Moffitt said. "Isn't that right, Milas?"

"Yes, sir." She had an accent but in the three or four words she'd spoken, I hadn't been able to place it, yet.

"So, I guess then she can leave whenever she wants?"

"I am sorry," Moffitt said. "But did I knock on your front door? Is this not my home, then? Have I brought this woman into your home to insult you? No. I think not.

"Now, you mentioned a murdered friend. Ask about him, or get the fuck out of my home."

I pulled my beer from the glass table and using my keys I popped the lid off the beer and took a large swig.

"Fair enough," I said. "My friend was killed early Sunday morning, and found face down near West Beach."

"I am sorry to hear that, but I am not understanding how this brings you to my door," Moffitt said.

Milas sat, on her knees, with her hands laid lightly into her lap. Her face and eyes looked down toward the plush rug that ran underneath both sofas and the coffee table, but didn't cover the entire room. The flooring was made from some kind of teak wood. Moffitt was stroking her head like a pet. I was feeling a little sicker in my stomach watching the display. Something was off about this pair.

"He had asked for directions to a club called, The Grunge," I said.

"Of course."

Moffitt's face twisted up into heavy thought. For the first time, I could tell he was weighing whether or not to shoot us. I doubted Sage and I would be the first people he'd ever shot. And my inquisitive nature was suddenly peaked by this off-beat man. He wore a faded white t-shirt over tan, knee length shorts and his feet were bare. The nails on his toes yellowed and cracked. His head was topped by a whiff of white hair, swept from left to right, but thin enough that it did nothing to cover the large hairless expanse of his head. He had an old, fading U.S. Navy tattoo on his right forearm; arms that crossed over the shot gun laying in his small lap. I wondered what kind of man needs a phony name. Especially a man of some seventy to seventy-five years of age.

"Can you tell us if the club, or whatever it is, was open on Saturday night," I asked quickly. I was hoping to give him as little a reason as possible to shoot us. I knew he must now be wondering exactly how we had obtained not only the name of the club, but his name as well. If he began to wonder about Dillon's health and well-being, he just might be more concerned for his own. My hope also extended to wanting a fast 'yes or no' for an answer and then perhaps we could move on. If I could convince Sage that we had followed the line as far as it would take us.

Moffitt sighed heavily and leaned back into the sofa.

"I am now 74 years old," he began. "I was born in 1923. I have a touch of colon cancer, or so my doctor tells me. I've had one heart attack. I was fifty-six at the time. It was a small attack, but I quit smoking and started eating healthier. You know, less meat more green shit. I've buried one wife. She died of cancer in '88. Ovarian. Awful, awful illness.

"I've had two brothers, both dead. I joined the Navy in 1940, before I turned 18, and I saw men blown into pieces on several islands and at sea, all over the Pacific. One of my brothers was killed at the Battle of the Bulge. The other died in Korea."

He scratched his chin and continued.

"I tell you this because I need you both to understand that as I look at the two of you, I can see the resemblance. One that I am sure many folks miss. It's obvious he is an older brother," waving his hand at Sage, but maintaining eye contact with me. "And whatever you did to Dillon to get my name, well, the same won't be done to me. One of you will catch a lot of lead and the other will have to either beat me to death, or maybe make a run for that truck of yours. Because if the survivor hesitates, well, he too is gonna catch lead as I reload this monster."

He tapped the shot gun in his lap softly.

"Now, I am sure I appear as an old man to your eyes; soft and slow. I can assure you that I will not miss."

"Sir ..." I started.

"Son, this conversation is over. I don't know how or why Dillon told you the name 'Moffitt,' or told you about 'Mr. Wise,' and I certainly hope for his sake that you left him laying dead somewhere. And that will be on your head. When his body is found, if he is dead, it will be your description that will go to the police in an anonymous phone call. I'd suggest you both go back to Alabama, or Georgia, or Tennessee, or wherever you two hillbillies call home ... if he's not dead, well, once his body is found," and he let the ramifications of that sink in before continuing. "That same phone call is gonna be made."

He wrapped his right hand around the long wooden stock of the gun, his finger softly tapping the trigger.

"I want you both to walk out of here. I'll give you the proverbial head start. Or this can happen here and I can tell the police how you forced your way into my home. It's your decision."

"Thank you for your time, sir," Sage said. He tipped his beer up, finishing off the remaining beverage in the bottle, and then in one fluid motion he hurled the emptied bottle across the room, smashing into Moffitt's head.

The impact created a large gash above Moffitt's right eye as his head was thrown back by the blow. His knees heaved up and suddenly a blast from the shot gun blew pieces of Milas' head all over the carpet, floor, table and me. She slumped over, instantly dead. I looked down at the bits of blood and brain matter on my arm and then back up in time to see Sage straddled on top of Moffitt, punching him three or four times quickly in the face.

Moffitt was unconscious and I wasn't sure if he was alive.

"We don't have much time," Sage said. "We need to get what we need and be out of here in about five to ten minutes, tops."

I was staring at Sage.

"Hey! Hey, kid!" I heard him yell at me. Everything seemed so far away. The light was dim. My head was heavy. I felt a wave of nauseousness wash over me, then pass. Darkness brushed. Suddenly, there was a splash of cold water in my face. Sage came into view.

"Pull it together," he said. "We don't have time for your pussy shit. Get up and walk around the sofa, that way, and go through Moffitt's dresser, closet, anything you can find. Do not get your finger prints on anything. And do not walk through the blood on the floor. Do you understand me?"

"Yes," I heard my voice reply.

Sage walked around the sofa, picked up the beer bottle he had hurled at Moffitt and sat it next to mine. "These leave here with us," he said.

I rose and walked to the bedrooms. I bypassed two guest rooms and a large guest bath in the hall on my walk to the master bedroom.

The room sat at the end of the hall, the door ajar, and I walked inside the enormous bedroom. The bed sat in the center of the room on a small one step rise. There was a large oak armoire to the left between two doors. I assumed one lead to the bath, while the other lead to a closet. The bed faced a wall-length expanse of windows, the windows all facing Lake Martin. The wall to my right displayed an odd collection of whips, chains and devices and items I'd never seen before. It looked like something out of a strange horror movie.

I pulled open the doors to the armoire and moved items around, gently, with the back of my hand. It was filled with a wide range of clothing items; socks, underwear, shirts and slacks. Nothing of any importance.

A scream came from the living room. Moffitt's voice. I didn't want to know what caused it and I stepped into the closet. There was a dresser along the far wall, and I had removed one t-shirt from the armoire to cover my hand. I used my covered hand to pull and close each drawer one at a time. The top right drawer held a small black

176

box with a golden symbol on the top. A symbol of some kind of bull, or oxen.

I covered the box with the t-shirt, lifted it out, and opened the lid. There was a myriad of items in the box, including military pins or medals, rings and one black book. The book contained fifty to sixty unusual, and seemingly made-up, names, with some kind of a code number next to each. Below each was what appeared to be some kind of oddly written addresses.

Entries like:

The Hopper. 9737-2.

Road. Wilson. 42. A.

Mr. Rabbit. 111665-1.

Back. Tabletop. 735.

I put the book into my back pocket, closed the lid and placed the box back into the dresser. I folded the t-shirt and laid it atop the dresser and walked back to the living room.

Sage was straddled atop Moffitt, the shot gun pointed up at Moffitt's chin. Sage held a pair of pliers in his right hand, crushing Moffitt's nose with his grip. Sage's left hand held both of Moffitt's wrists back behind his head. Moffitt's face was a mixture now of pale white, yellow and green. The right side of his face was awash in blood from the open gash above his right eye, and his face on that side was beginning to swell.

"I found something," I said.

"Did you hear that Moffitt," Sage asked. "My brother found something."

I walked the long way around, trying to avoid the blood, but mostly trying to avoid seeing Milas's naked, headless, lifeless body in the floor. I pulled the book from my back pocket and began reading the entries.

"Fuck you," Moffitt said, spitting blood. "Fuck you, both. Kill me."

Sage looked back at me.

"He's not gonna tell us anything more," Sage said.

"He's not told us anything at all," I said.

"Go look out at the patio," Sage said.

I turned and walked to one of the two sliding glass doors that opened onto the patio. I knew what was coming next. In the reflection, I could still see a fuzzy image of Sage and Moffitt. Sage reached his hand between his legs and there was a roar as the shot gun took Moffitt's head off and slung blood, bone and brains all over the ceiling, and the floor behind the sofa.

Sage stood, wiped his hands with the towel he held. He picked up both beer bottles, wiped down the glass table, partially, avoiding the splatter of Milas' blood upon the table so as not to smear it, and surveyed the room once.

"It's time to go," he said. "You got that book, right?"

"Yes, I have it," I said.

"Good," he said. "Look for a Mr. Wise and read the entry to me."

CHAPTER 17

The entry on Mr. Wise, like all the others, was written out in some kind of odd code:

Wise. 071749-2.

Harbour. Kings. 3016.

Sage stopped at a gas station, bought a Panama City map and then poured over the various street names. One leapt out at both of us. Kings Harbour. Back in Pretty Bayou. If the 3016 represented the physical address then the house was only about two miles from Rich's trailer, and maybe three miles from Tammy's house; both of which were in Pretty Bayou.

"It's worth a shot," Sage said.

"It's very late," I said. "It's close to one in the morning, in the middle of the week. Do you expect to find someone awake? Or are we now to the point of just kicking down doors and killing people?"

"Let's just see what we see. How about we do that?"

"Sage, we just killed a man," I felt a tear on my cheek, wiped it away and then ran my hand through my hair to cover up the fact that I was crying. I didn't want Sage to see that.

"Kid …"

"No, man. No. What the fuck are we doing? What are we doing?" I choked up. The weight of it was crushing. The blood. I was still finding specks of it on my arm, my shirt. I felt nauseous once again and doubled over. Nothing came up.

"Kid," Sage said softly.

My arm flew up at him; please stop, I thought. Please don't.

I tried to find words again. This buzz in my head was turning into a chorus of violent, black ringing; all screaming in unison, all screaming my guilt. What had we done? What had we done?

"Kid, the cops are going to arrive and find a naked girl in chains. A young naked girl," Sage said. "They're going to find a 74 year old man, with colon cancer, holding a shot gun. They're not gonna find any evidence of a forced entry. No real signs of struggle.

"I'm not trying to make you sick here, but Moffitt's head is gone. There is no evidence of getting punched. They're going to think, old guy can't get it up or something, gets depressed, kills the hooker — and that is what they are going to think she is — some kind of sex worker. And they are gonna think that he offed her and then himself. Case closed."

"And what will we think," I asked.

"I'm gonna think we offed an old, creepy bastard, who liked to own and rape young woman. I got no issue with it."

"We might have had something if Milas had lived," I said aloud. An incomplete thought, but all I had.

"Maybe. Maybe not," Sage said. "That wasn't how I wanted it to go down. I knew the shot gun was close to her head, but I didn't think ... well, I didn't want that girl to die. But I don't know what she would have told us, so, there it is."

Sage had parked his truck next to the air tank at the gas station and the place held some twenty gas pumps and a large convenience store. It was lit in greens and reds. A large sign, "Stop-N-Go," stood high over the parking lot. Even in the late hour, a dozen cars were scattered around the lot. Some stood pumping gas, some inside shopping for beer, or cigarettes, or late night snacks; a dope smoker's paradise of potato chips and candy bars just inside the doors. Three skateboarders worked the sidewalk nearest us. They popped their boards into the air; spinning, catching and rolling. Sixteen, maybe. Life moved around us. The ballet of the living.

A police cruiser pulled into the lot, parked and a young pudgy officer got out and went inside.

"Let's get going," Sage said.

"Hang on a second," I said. Something caught my eye. One of the teen skateboarders stood, his board standing on its back edge as he leaned against it. A myriad of stickers ran across the board, but one was prominent — "The Grunge."

I walked slowly towards the trio, casually. I didn't want them to bolt thinking they were going to get harassed by some older guy over skateboarding. I figured the cop may do that soon enough and I needed to hurry, but not be too rushed.

"Yo, kid," I tossed at the skateboarder with the sticker. "Great board."

"Yeah, thanks, bro," he said in his casual, 'whatever, man,' kind of way.

"Hey, that sticker? Is that the club, 'The Grunge,' or something else," I asked.

"I guess. I got it in a surf shop off Front," he said.

"Which one?"

"Ah, Perfect Wave, or Rollers."

"You ever been to that place?"

"Nah, man. I don't know anything about it. I just liked the sticker."

For a secret club, the word around Panama City Beach, and someone spreading it on a bumper sticker, seemed counter-productive; even foolish. But then again the sticker may have simply been the product of someone who'd heard the phrase and liked it enough to print it. Kids would certainly have a reason to gravitate to it. To embrace it. Grunge, while on the way out, still held a certain cool among the teens of the south, and I imagined most of America. It had been a bit of a sudden flash. Here and gone. A new age hippie movement for rebels without a cause.

"Thanks, kid."

I walked back to Sage's truck.

"What'd you say to the kid," Sage asked, as I climbed into the Ford.

"He had a sticker on his skateboard for Grunge, which I find really odd," I said.

"How so?"

"You're running some kind of secret, underground sex club, or something, right? I mean what else kind of place can this be? So, you have this underground sex club and you're printing bumper stickers to sell in surf shops? Or someone is printing them. But why? I mean what's the reason to advertise a club you want to keep secret? I've looked at this black book and there are probably sixty names in here ... and okay, why the dash and then number? The number is always a one, two, three or four. On everyone, and each and every entry. I thought the first series of numbers was a birthdate, or at least that makes the most sense, but why the dash? And why the different numbers? And yet, as weird as the numbers are, they probably aren't or weren't weird to Moffitt. I mean I have to assume this is his handwriting throughout the book. Why was he keeping it? What was he noting for himself? Blackmail? Did he want some kind of record in case they, whoever they are, came after him? And with him dead, does this book have any real power? The bumper sticker, though, I can't figure that out at all."

"What if the bumper sticker is a way to lure young kids in," Sage asked. "You saw Milas. What was she 21? 22 tops."

"I thought she was younger," I said. "The make up makes it hard to judge her age."

Sage fired up the engine and pulled out onto the road to begin the trip back to Petty Bayou.

"What if you're right, though? What if the bumper sticker is a way to lure kids, or teens, or whatever. But where would you lure them to? I mean if this place moves around, and is so hard to find ... it doesn't make a lot of sense," I said.

"Is Moffitt in the book?"

"Yeah, he is."

"Hm."

"I don't know why, though. Why keep a book with your own name in it?"

"Well, one, it may not have been his. Maybe he offed someone for the book and was keeping it safe — "

"Safe? Just burn it, if it's not yours," I interrupted.

" — and two, was there a number by his name?"

"Yes. A number one."

Rolling the window down, I pulled two cigarettes from my pocket, one for Sage and one for myself, and lit my own. White smoke soon filled the air and streamed out the windows, twisting and turning in the rushing air.

"Are you working," I asked.

"You don't want to know the answer to that one, kid," Sage said.

"Fuck, man, seriously? 'I don't want to know the answer.' What the fuck does that even mean?"

"It means you have a nice, clean candy ass job in a building downtown, right? I mean, you get a paycheck with all your little deductions marked down in neat little boxes, right? Well, my job pays cash, when it fucking pays off. And the less you know about, the better it is for you," Sage said. "Jesus, I thought you went to college? How can you be so fucking stupid? Fuck, do I have to draw you a goddamn picture? Or have you sketched it out in that, what, thirty-forty thousand dollar brain of yours?"

"Forget I asked," I said.

"Maybe this Mr. Wise will have some answers," Sage said.

"Let's try not to kill him first."

We needed an answer about Roan. I didn't know if any of this lead back to Roan. And that was churning in my mind more than anything. What if all of this, this wild goose chase, and one man with a broken arm and fearing for his life, and another dead, with a young girl, accidentally killed alongside him — she was innocent in all of this and still dead — lead back to nothing. Proved nothing. Solved nothing. Did nothing. I was a bystander to my brother's uncontrollable rage, a rage against a world he'd never found his place in. I was walking side-by-side with the same guy who'd punched his high school football coach. The same guy who'd driven some kid into a tree face first at a party one night and then pissed on his bleeding head. The same guy who'd put the Whisnant brothers into the hospital for beating me up as they tried to defend their sisters honor. An ass-kicking I still felt I deserved. The same guy who'd told my dad to fuck himself on countless occasions before storming from the house; always to come crawling back with tears and apologies. The same guy who'd put three different inmates into jailhouse infirmaries with a myriad of broken bones all for something as simple as a cigarette or a stare. This was the guy that was leading the charge. This was the guy now calling the shots, and I was once more a kid brother just along for the ride.

A ride across one of the classic Southern party cities; perhaps only Daytona Beach, Florida and Myrtle Beach, South Carolina rivaled Panama City. Whereas Charleston, South Carolina, Savannah, Georgia and the majestic New Orleans, Louisiana could provide great food, great music, classy parties and cultured entertainment, save of course the indulgence that was Mardi Gras, Panama City was more about blatant youthful drunkenness and sloppy sexual conquest. Very little class on display.

The rest of the drive, itself, with the night air off the ocean, was mostly silent after our initial questions and conversation about our intended destination. Sage navigated our way with ease. And that can be quite the feat. For there are very few Southern cities where the layout of roads makes any sense. There can be no discernible pattern in many of the millions of twisting Southern roadways; some of which can even turn ninety degrees in one direction or the other, even at a four way stop, and continue with the same name. One is either born with a good sense of direction or one will become accustomed to hearing things like, "turn at the third tree on your left," or "watch for where the fence stops and then go two miles and turn right."

Thankfully, Sage was one born with a natural sense of good direction. Even if he was unable to apply that to the course of his own life.

We crept slowly down Kings Harbour Road, reading mailbox and house numbers as we went until we found a 3016. It looked like something off a postcard. A magnificent structure. Grand, elegant, and obviously the product of great wealth.

"Give me the book," Sage said. "I think I have a plan."

Suddenly, I felt like a foot soldier following General Custer over a hill on the plains of the Dakotas.

The house, a Spanish Colonial that is popular across Florida, was truly enormous. I imagined it must have held eight to ten bedrooms, and probably as many baths, from just a precursory glance. An eight-foot tall fence, finished in white, like the house, with the matching reddish-brown tile caps across the top, began at the front of the home and circled around into the backyard. The property had to have been close to an acre and a half, perhaps two. There were two black wrought iron gates, which gave access to the backyard on either side of the home, and a walkway that broke off from the main circular drive that one could take in either direction to reach the gates. The driveway spilled into Kings Harbour at two points and I thought we were fortunate that the home owners had not had the gate built to cover the entire property; just the backyard was fence-lined.

Sage and I, after climbing from the truck, stood looking up and down the empty, darkened street. There were no signs of late night life in this privileged neighborhood. No spring breakers throwing up into the grass, or flashing their young tits at a crowd. Here, all was still and silent.

Tapping my arm, Sage said, "Come on, this way," and lead me towards the gate on the right-hand side of the house. He gave the gate a once-over, checking for alarms, and he gently lifted the unlocked handle to the gate and swung it open. The walkway continued through the well-manicured yard, winding this way and that until it opened out to a beautiful in-ground swimming pool. The pool was shaped like three inter-locking circles, with the center circle the largest in diameter. A long, twisting slide worked its way through a wall of stone, plants and waterfalls on the far side of the pool.

"Wow," Sage said softly. "That's nice."

We turned in unison to find a beast of a dog, softly and deeply growling. The Rottweiler was easily a hundred pounds, its dark eyes focused and trying to determine which target to go for first. It picked Sage.

The black dog, silently, leapt at Sage's left arm. Sage offered up his forearm and, in one smooth motion, allowed the dog to bite down, while twisting the animal to his chest and belly. Sage launched himself hard onto the cement with the dog pinned underneath him. Reaching quickly up with his right hand, he locked the animals neck and gave a violent twist. There was a tiny yelp that escaped the dog's mouth, then silence.

Sage stood up, four deep puncture wounds on his left forearm, and cussed under his breathe. Reaching into his back pocket, Sage pulled a bandana and wrapped it tightly around his arm to try and stop the bleeding.

"I think we're still okay," he said, once more looking closely at the house for any signs of alarm.

"The dog didn't make much noise. We're lucky it didn't bark," I whispered.

"Well, come on. Follow me," Sage responded quietly, while grimacing through the pain.

The vast majority of the back portion of the house, along the first floor, was covered in glass windows and doors; all facing the swimming pool. The second story was mostly darkened, with a tiny light appearing in one window, perhaps a lamp, while the third story was completely dark and featured the least amount of windows of the three story structure.

We crept along the patio area slowly, gingerly even, like two wounded men not wanting to alert the enemies, or prison guards in some war film. A living area portion of the house suddenly came into view and it appeared there had been recent activity in the home. It also quickly became obvious, we were in the right place.

A woman, with red hair, was naked and sleeping, or appeared to be sleeping, in a dog cage, complete with a water bowl. She was collared in the same way Milas had been collared, but there were no chains binding her neck to wrists to ankles; just the cuffs and collar.

A second naked woman, raven-headed, was strapped, spread eagle to some kind of 'X' shaped beams, with two clamps attached to her nipples; her nipples pulled by some kind of rope, attached to the clamps, toward the ceiling. She appeared to be awake and breathing heavily.

I took a step toward the lit room, toward the sliding door that opened into the room with the two naked women, when Sage gripped my shoulder, "Wait."

His eyes narrowed and he looked closely at the house; his eyes moving from window-to-window and back again.

"What," I whispered. "What do you see?"

"Nothing, I just want to be certain that there are no cameras, or motion sensors."

Sage stepped slowly to the sliding glass door and quietly pulled it open. We both cautiously stepped into the room. The raven-headed woman, attached to the X-shaped board, was laying on her back with her feet pointed towards the pool area and her head closest to the wall opposite the sliding doors. A large vibrator had been strapped to her left leg and was running at what seemed to be full speed. Her chest and tummy heaved up as she reached an orgasm, her voice softly moaning in pleasure. She had headphones placed over her ears and it was quickly obvious that unless she opened her eyes, she was not going to be aware of our presence.

Sage bent low to check on the girl in the cage and whispered that she was sound asleep.

He crept across the room and clamped his hand down tightly on the raven-headed girl's mouth. Her eyes flew open in shock and Sage raised one finger on his free hand to his lips to silently ask her for her silence. He nodded to me to turn off the vibrator, which I did. A little blue on-off switch on top of the device was easy enough to find. Sage removed her head phones and leaned down to her ear.

"We are not here to hurt you in any way," he said gently. "Nod if you understand."

She nodded in the affirmative.

"I am going to remove my hand, okay? And I do not want you to scream. Can you do that for me," Sage asked, again with a softness to his voice.

She nodded her understanding and Sage slowly removed his hand from her mouth.

The young woman took a deep breathe, but was true to her word and didn't scream. Her eyes darted back and forth as she tried to size up Sage and I, and I assume try to explain our sudden presence in her mind.

Sage, still whisper quiet and gentle as a lamb, asked her name.

"It was Kimberly," she said. "But Mr. Wise calls me Blackbird."

A tear rolled from her right eye down her cheek. She was terrified. And not of us.

"Kimberly, how long have you been here," Sage asked.

"I don't know. Two years now, I guess," she said.

"How old are you?"

"I'm twenty."

"Where is your family?"

The tears came flooding down, but she held her voice and for the most part her composure.

"California. San Diego. I was taken in Mexico. It was June of 95 and ..."

"Shush, shush, it's okay. It's gonna be okay," Sage said. He stroked the girl's hair gently. "What can you tell me about the girl in the cage? Do you know where the key to the lock is?"

"He. He would have it ... and he calls her Ginger," Kimberly said. "I don't know her real name. But I think she is seventeen or eighteen."

I turned toward "Ginger" and bent down for a closer look at the lock and the girl. She had fresh welts and bruises on her buttocks, back of her thighs and the back of her calves; just from what I could see in the position she slept in. There was a brand on her left butt cheek; a curious circle with a square inside of it followed by a triangle inside of the square. The skin around the brand wasn't red or swollen, and I assumed it had to have been done at least six months ago or more.

While I was turned toward "Ginger," Sage had removed the clamps from Kimberly's nipples, and released the hooks holding her neck, wrists and ankles to the board. She stood and wobbled briefly, but was quickly able to gain her balance.

"Thank you," she said softly. "I've been there for several hours. He likes ... he likes forcing me to cum for him."

"Yes, I do dear," said a voice from behind me.

Sage and I turned at the same time, while Kimberly turned white and passed out onto the floor.

"Oh, my," the strange man said. "I do believe I have frightened my sweet Blackbird."

His voice was syrupy, high in tone and deeply Southern. He stood no more than six feet tall and appeared to be at least fifty years of age. In his right hand he held a .357 Magnum.

"So, gentleman ... too what do I owe the pleasure of your sudden, and most illegal, visit into my home," he asked.

"I guess you're Mr. Wise," Sage stated, taking a step forward.

"Oh, no, no, no," the man said with just a touch of mirth in his voice. "That name should never come from your lips, darling."

CHAPTER 18

The week before Jilly, Roan and I took off for Panama City, Dexter King, the son of slain Civil Rights leader Dr. Martin Luther King, Jr., sat in a small room at the Lois DeBerry Special Needs Facility with James Earl Ray, the man convicted of killing his father in Memphis, Tennessee on April 4, 1968. At some point in their reported conversation, King looked across the table at Ray and said, "I just want to ask you for the record, did you kill my father?"

Ray, reportedly, replied, "No, I didn't."

King believed him. He left the room more convinced than ever that something, or someone, bigger than Ray, some force with more power, more pull, perhaps even more reason, must have killed his father. Maybe, he needed to believe that. Maybe, sitting in the room with Ray, an aging, scrawny white racist he came away with the belief that this tiny man could not have killed someone as great as his father. His father, who stands with the giants of peace, could not have been slain by this puny little man. Perhaps, the perception of Ray, looking weak, frail after nearly thirty years of jail time, and failing organs played its part in convincing the son that this man could not have acted alone. If he acted at all. It must be go deeper, must run higher up the food chain. There must be some dark, clandestine operation at work. Because surely to kill a great man you must need an equally great hate, an equally great passion to see him dead. It must take an equally great man, or men.

Not this puny man.

As Mr. Wise stood waving his .357 casually and asking questions about how we had discovered him and his home, the reverse hit my mind. The possibility that Roan wasn't killed in any deep, dark, sex slaving operation or by the operators of such a disgusting operation. What if out there, right now, as I stood staring down the barrel of a powerful handgun, a tiny little man with frail bones was smoking one of Roan's cigarettes or looking at some artifact he'd looted from the body right after killing Roan.

That thought was more frightening than Mr. Wise, whoever he really was. What if we were wrong? And in being so wrong, we had traveled a path that had only brought us to our own demise? Or worse. This man had money. Lots of it. Whatever else I didn't know about Mr. Wise, I knew that much. And men with money have friends with money. Money, the long infamous root of all evil, could make any story, stake any claim and the truth was always for sale in America.

Mr. Wise leaning casually against a wall spoke and I snapped from my thoughts.

"This is going to be a fun night for you two lovebirds," he said. "I called some, well, I hesitate to call them just friends. They are special friends. Talented men. And tonight, you two will get to sing with new voices. It's gonna be a wonderful performance."

Sage started laughing. And laughing.

"Oh, I have amused you, have I," Mr. Wise asked sarcastically.

"Old man, look I imagine having a tiny dick is an awful thing to have too live with, and I am sure that fucking up some bitches gets you all jazzed up and shit, but you got this playing out all wrong man," Sage said. I knew he was making his play.

In October, 1980, on a blustery Sunday afternoon, 20 young boys gathered in the backyard of Roland Tolbert, a roly poly, 14 year old, then freshman at Alexander Central High for a pickup game of tackle football. Roan and I were the only 11 year olds there. Sage, then 15, was picked as captain and quarterback of one team, while Larry Parker was selected as the other. Parker, as everyone called him, was 17 years old, a senior and the varsity quarterback for the Fighting Eagles. Parker picked me with his fifth overall pick. I was thrilled and I was shocked that he'd bypassed some nine to ten other guys, including Roan, who went last, but also to Parker's team, to take me. "Don't let me down kid," he'd said after selecting me.

Our team went up early 7-0, although we didn't kick extra points, when Parker rolling to his left found his number one pick, David Pointer, wide open in the corner of the end zone.

Sage answered with a seven play drive that ended when he executed a perfect pitch play to his number one pick, Alex Gilbert.

Pointer, like Parker, was 17, a senior and a wide receiver for Alexander Central. Gilbert was also 17, a senior and the team's starting running back.

The sun was setting behind us as the air grew chill and the score knotted up, 49-49, when I tried to 'not let Parker down.'

Sage's team had the ball and it had been decided they had one last play or the game would end in a tie. Everyone had to get home for supper or a scolding soon.

Sage broke the huddle and I rolled to my left. He was coming my way. I knew he was coming my way. I didn't know, and still don't know, how I knew. Maybe the eyes. Maybe it was a look he gave me; a kind of 'where is that kid brother of mine playing' look.

The ball was snapped, and some sixteen boys executed their blocks and assignments as Sage came to the hole. He faked the pitch to Gilbert and Parker drove hard at his buddy and star running back believing that he would get the ball. But Sage didn't pitch. And I stood between him and the end zone. Sage lowered his shoulder into my right shoulder and knocked me clear off my feet. I hit the ground and felt the air escape from my lungs. I recall the fire in my eyes as the tears burned. I rolled over, tasting blood in my mouth, to see Sage's backside as he sped the length of the field for the game-winning score. And I hated him.

But I learned.

Sage's right hand was slowly inching now around his waist band for the .9mm he had tucked there. In another part of the home, the front door was opening, and Mr. Wise turned his head to the sound.

The gun was in the air now and two, three, four bullets screamed across the expanse from Sage to his target; an impish fifty something with a sadomasochistic sexual appetite. Three found flesh.

Mr. Wise's .357 barked twice, almost simultaneously, in response to Sage's shots. One bullet crashed into the wall next to Sage's chest — the shots brought a blood curdling scream from Ginger, who woke to the gunfire and the shots brought two racing figures into the room. Mr. Wise's second shot also found flesh. Sage's right side was a brightening pool of crimson.

The .357 fell from Mr. Wise's hand and I made my play. The only play I had.

I dove onto the pistol and gripped the black handle. I saw two .9mms being raised at Sage, who had turned his pistol to the two new arrivals. Sage squeezing his trigger. I was squeezing the trigger on my newly acquired pistol. The two strangers squeezing theirs.

Silence.

Five men lay on the ground. Two naked women lay on the ground. Four men with blood-stained shirts. One man, I; alive.

Screams. Two girls found voice in the aftermath of madness and their song sang out.

"Quiet! Be quiet," I yelled at the two young girls. "Kimberly. Kimberly, I need you to get the key off of ... him." I pointed at Mr. Wise, but refused to use that name any longer.

Racing to Sage's side, he looked up and chuckled.

"Well, fuck," he said. "That didn't go down like I thought."

"How bad is it?"

"Bad."

He had two gunshots on his right side; the original one from "him" and a second one now on the hip from one of the two strangers. A third gunshot, also delivered by one of the two strangers, was just below his collarbone on his left hand side. Reaching for Sage's boot, where I knew he always kept a knife, I withdrew the blade and began cutting stripes from his shirt and mine, stuffing the fabric into two of the holes. The one on his hip looked to have grazed off the bone and the bullet didn't enter into his body. It actually looked to be the most painful of the three. The bone had to be fractured.

"Can you stand? Walk?"

"I don't know. Give me just a minute. Listen, we don't have too much time. We have to get the fuck out of here with these two girls," Sage said. "Grab the wallets and anything you can out of the pockets of everyone. Got it?"

"Yes."

I walked quickly to the three bodies on the floor. One was still breathing. Barely. But he was alive. Barely. An olive-skinned man, maybe thirty, with black hair swept back with some kind of styling gel. He'd be dead soon. Soon.

I went on my knees and checked "him," first. I pulled several items from the pocket on his housecoat, but found nothing else.

Looking up, two naked girls stood staring down at me.

"Kimberly, listen," I said. "You have to leave here with Sage and I ... I am Chaz, that's my brother, Sage over there." I moved to the dead stranger, leaving the barely alive one for last. "Please, you must find clothes, a jacket, anything you can find. Put it on. Do the keys you found take off those chains?"

"I don't know," she said. "Are they dead?"

"Yes. And if we don't move fast, we might just join them," I said. "Please move quickly. Wait! Is there anything in the house you can think we might need, as far as evidence, grab it. Okay?"

"Okay."

Kimberley guided "Ginger" off, past the three dead or dying men.

I stripped the two strangers of their wallets, two hotel room keys, car keys, one pack of Marlboros, one Bic lighter, a wad of loose cash, one pack of gum, and one condom. The one dead stranger was also roughly thirty with bleached hair and two earrings in his left ear. I grabbed a towel down off a kitchen counter as I raced through the house and wrapped everything I had found into it. I tied it off and returned to Sage.

"Can you stand up," I asked.

"Yes, I can. We have to fucking move. We are running out of time," Sage said.

It had all seemed so loud inside the room that we both assumed the whole world had to have heard the gun fire and placed six billion some odd calls to 911.

The girls returned to the room, their chains gone. Kimberly wore a pair of men's boxers with a sports coat over top. The girl called "Ginger" wore sweat pants and a Florida State t-shirt.

"I didn't find anything. I'm sorry," Kimberly said, on the verge of tears again.

"It's okay. Time to leave, alright?"

Hoisting Sage up, I let him lean onto me. His weight was difficult to balance for the first several steps and I feared I was going to spill over at any point.

"Fuck," he said. "Just let me limp to the goddamn truck."

The four of us went out the front door, and I was smart enough to open the front door of the house with my shirt over my hand. Maybe I left no fingerprints anywhere else. Too late now.

The air outside was heavy, but silent. We went racing across the grass to Sage's truck.

"Is everything okay," I heard a voice say. It was in front of me, across from "his" house.

"Yea, just drunk," I said trying to sound like a fun-loving idiot.

"I thought I heard gunfire," the man's voice said. He stepped into the light. Bald, sixty-something and rich.

"Oh, yeah, that fucker," I said pointing back to the house. "He was shooting his goddamn guns at the TV. He lost a bet on a baseball game or sumthin." Act drunk.

"Oh, well, you know that's against the law," he said.

"Sorry, dude," I said. Sage and the girls were into the truck on the passenger side. They never came into the good light, I thought. He'll never see the blood on Sage.

"Well, I am calling the police," he said. "No need for that bullshit around here."

"Ah, man," I said reaching into my pocket. I found two clean one hundred dollar bills. "Bro, no need for the law, man. Just some kids, man."

I handed him the money. He looked down at it and then back at me. Act drunk. Act high. Be stupid.

"Well, I hear anymore bullshit and I am calling the police. Some of us can't get drunk you know. We have to work."

"I understand, bro. I mean, ah, sir. Sorry, sir man," I giggled like an idiot at the mention of 'sir man.' Time to go.

I spun and climbed into the driver's seat. Sage handed me the keys.

"Where we gonna go," Sage asked.

"I know a place," I said.

I drove us back to Panama City Beach; back across the bridge. Have to get out of Pretty Bayou, I thought — "Ginger" was speaking. — I can't go back to Rich's or Tammy's. Have to get out of Pretty Bayou — "I've been there for seven months," she cried, softly. "Seven months. They fucking branded me." — What the fuck have we gotten ourselves into? — "Me as well," Kimberly added. — I can't go back to the Day's Inn. How do I get Sage through the lobby — "I mean they fucking branded me," the girl called Ginger said. — How did Roan get to West Beach, that night? — "What's your real name," Kimberly asked her softly. — What was he doing looking for The Grunge? And why? — "Sierra. My name is Sierra," she responded. — I can't go back to the Day's Inn. What do I tell Jilly? Or Kaelyn?

Or Sarah? Or their goddamn boyfriends? Or fuck. What do I tell Roan's parents? Can I tell them? I think your son was murdered by sex traffickers, but I have no evidence of that. Just some theory I am working on — "They pulled me off a street ... I was in Mexico City with my parents," Sierra started, but the tears overcame her. "They ... they raped me for days." She was choking back tears and grief and shame. — This can't be happening now. I just cheated on the one girl I think I love. My best friend is dead. I am on Spring fucking Break — "They beat me. He fucking beat me. I tried to make him happy. I did. I tried. I promised. I sucked his dick. And still he fucking beat me." — That leaves me with Lexie. It's the only person not connected. No dots — "I know, sweetie. It's all gonna be alright," Kimberly said stroking Sierra's hair. "Isn't it Chaz? It's all gonna be alright." — No, no, it's not gonna be alright — "It'll be fine, Sierra," I heard my voice lie into the air. — It's all we've got. A girl I fucked once. A girl who brought me coffee once. A girl I gave a really big tip to because I thought she was pretty. A house I've been to once. Who's fucking house is it? There may not be a bigger dumbass than me right now. I could hear Jilly saying the words. Jilly. I have to get back to Jilly — "Chaz is taking us somewhere safe," Kimberly said. Sierra was in full sob. Her words garbled and choked in her throat. Tears streaming down her face.

Safe.

I pulled the Ford into the only open space on the street in front of the house that Lexie had brought me to just two nights earlier. The house we had fucked in.

Safe.

I hope she is here.

200

CHAPTER 19

"What the fuck is this place," Sage said angrily. The pain etched and clear upon his face. He was pale. Very pale.

"It's someplace safe," I said.

He kept shuffling his feet and he was in no position to argue. The two girls stuck close by our sides; fearful of the entire world and all the lights, sound and motion that came with a Spring Break night. Twice, just walking up the sidewalk, Kimberly gripped my arm as some sound or movement spooked her.

The front door stood open, while a screen door was pulled shut, but there was motion and activity everywhere, including five or six stoners who laid in the yard looking up at the night sky, passing a large joint. I heard one say, "Fuck, I am tripping so hard. Look at those muthafuckers covered in blood."

Pulling open the screen I stepped inside and saw Lexie's mean-looking lesbian friend, Brenda sitting on a bar stool by the kitchen.

"Come on," I said turning back to Sage, Kimberly and Sierra.

In the light of a home, with the full blaze of warm bulbs in the overheads, and the carnage, bloodshed, drama and hysterics somewhere a bridge away, we looked like four blood-stained ghosts. The full grip of fear, the tingle of confusion, upon us. I looked down at myself, my body, in this light, and saw the brownish stains of blood and the stench of it in my nostrils. The metallic smell of it pouring still from Sage's weakened body. A man so strong, weakened by the three tiny pieces of lead. We stood in this light, full of merriment and frolic, the full rush of youth, and all eyes stopped and stared at the four creatures tossed into their midst like something from one of the slash-and-hack films from the previous decade. The camp counselors never survive, and the fucking teenagers always die first. Especially the bikini-clad, or the token minority. And here we stood four blood-stained ghosts, breaking the mood. The ultimate party foul, the ultimate buzzkill. The eyes telling the brains, something is not right here. And silence followed, save for music, loud music meant to drive the mood and enthusiasm of youth, as the brains processed and accepted the reality of four ghosts standing in their midst. I felt like apologizing. And I felt like telling them all to fuck off. In the end, I asked for Lexie.

Sage wavered and gripped the door for support. He needed help and soon.

"Move," I said to three random strangers sitting on the sofa. Two moved right away, but one stoner lingered.

"What the fuck, man," he said.

I gripped his collar, lifted him off the sofa and tossed him to the floor.

"I said, move."

Sage collapsed into the sofa.

"Stay with him," I instructed Kimberly, Sierra and then faced Sage. "I'll be right back."

"We can't stay here," he said.

"We may not have a choice," I said.

"They're gonna call the cops any second now. Look at'em, they're scared," he said, looking over the faces of a crowd that ranged from maybe as young as 17 to as old as, well, Sage.

I turned back to Brenda.

"Don't let anyone call the police," I said quietly, privately to her, and then at normal volume to the room I continued. "I need towels, tape, scissors, and if anyone knows any first aid, well, that would be great.

"The girls aren't injured, but this is my brother and he's been shot by a mugger."

Whispers raced across the room, person to person, as I took Brenda by the elbow and lead her to the kitchen.

"Listen, both of those girls have been raped," I said. "Now, any comfort you can give them, or any place you can put them away from the crowd would be great."

"This isn't my house, but I'll get them into the master bedroom," she said. "What happened to their clothes?"

"No idea," I said. "I'm gonna try and get the bleeding to stop …"

Lexie, entering the kitchen, tapped me on the shoulder and as I spun, she threw her arms around me, in general greeting and not passion.

"Are you okay? What the fuck is going on?"

I took a deep breathe and thought about how to tell this story. I had rehearsed several versions in my mind, but none worked as well as the truth. Regardless of how strange and unbelievable the truth might be.

"Listen, I need your help. There is no one else at the moment that I can turn to. Do you understand," I asked, she nodded her head.

"We have stumbled into something. My friend, the guy that was with me at the diner that morning. He was killed. Murdered. Now, we don't know who did it, but, well, there is some kind of underground sex slave operation here in Panama City. These guys are using a variety of young girls to get their kicks. And they are very fucking dangerous."

Brenda and Lexie listened as I began to weave part of the tale of how the night had unfolded. I left out bits here, pieces there. They didn't need to know it all. They certainly didn't need to know of my suspicions that perhaps Sage and I were on the wrong path. Suspicions that Sage did not share. I could see anger rising up in Brenda, and shock rising in Lexie. I had two new allies in this fight. Whatever fight this was.

Sage and both girls, Kimberly and Sierra, were moved to the master bedroom at the back of the house. Brenda took out for an all night place she knew that might have first aid items, while Lexie made small talk with the two girls and tried to keep Sage from moving too much. I took the time to go through the towel of items I had gathered from the three dead empty souls back at "his" house.

I placed the two hotel keys into my wallet, counted the money, which tallied six-hundred, eighty dollars, minus the two hundred I'd given the pissed off neighbor — I had four-hundred dollars of my own — I tossed the pack of Marlboros and the Bic lighter to a guy that had helped me get Sage into the master bedroom; it turned out the house was in his name for the next week and he was worried about the blood on the sofa, carpet and now the king size bed in the master bedroom. He kept eying the money as if I was going to offer some up to pay for damages or inconvenience. He can go fuck himself. Inspecting the two wallets more closely, there were two cards, one in each wallet, with the same phone number printed on each. This meant something. Everything else was useless.

I inspected the three guns we now had. Two .9mms and one .357. One bullet in the .357. Useless. Four bullets in one of the 9s, three bullets in the other.

I stood and stretched. I am weary and the adrenaline is gone.

I walked to the window. I am lonesome and lost.

I pulled a Camel from my pack. I am foolish and incomplete.

I need to make a plan. I am adrift and without reason.

I need to call the police. I am uncertain and taken with grief.

I need to call Jilly. I am weary and need sleep.

"Do you have a phone I can use?"

"Yeah, man," said the renter. "You can use the one here or in the kitchen."

"I'll just use this one."

Pulling my wallet from my back pocket, I pulled the number to the Day's Inn and the cards with the new numbers I had lifted from the two dead strangers. I dialed the hotel and asked for my room. It's almost 4 a.m. I hate to wake her.

"Hello," said Jilly's groggy voice.

My face was twisting up in pain and grief and exhaustion and anger and frustration and uncertainty and fury. I can feel the tears and I can taste their saltiness on my lips. Sage's hand is patting me on the back. Fuck off, for God's sake. This was your goddamn idea. Please don't die.

"Jilly," I ask, knowing the answer.

"Yes, baby," she said. "Are you okay?"

"We made so many fucking stupid mistakes," the words are choking in my throat. "I don't know."

"Where are you," she asked.

"A house," I said. "I don't know the address."

"Do you need me?"

"Yes. But don't come here. Please. Okay?"

"Baby, do you need me?"

"Yes. Sage has been shot. Three times. It's pretty bad."

"Fuck you," Sage yells. "I'm fine, you pussy."

"Is he okay," Jilly asked.

"I don't know. He needs a hospital, but ..." my voice drifts. I don't want Jilly to see Lexie. She will know right away. She probably already does, but at least she doesn't know who. And not knowing the who maybe better.

"I'm coming," she said. "Get the address. Okay?"

"Okay," I said.

I got the address, gave it to Jilly and walked into the room Lexie and I had shared just a few nights earlier. She sat on the bed, wearing very short shorts, white, and a white tank. Fuck. Her nipples are hard and her hair is swept. She looked at me, and patted the bed. She seems motherly somehow. Caring. And still there is a desire in her eyes. One I cannot sate.

I crawl into bed and sleep finds me; dreamless and still.

I woke with a start. Jilly was staring down at me. Lexie beside me in the bed. She had her clothes on.

"What's happened," I asked.

"Sage got to the hospital. He's in bad shape, Chaz. Bad shape," she said, hanging her head and sweeping her hair from her face. "The police have Kimberly and Sierra. The one cop, Tilly? He said you're an idiot, but a heroic idiot. I convinced them to let you sleep a little bit, but you have to go downtown and make a statement.

"Kimberly and Sierra probably saved your ass as much as you saved them."

I threw my legs to the floor, let the blood find my head, and then stood. I found my jeans and pulled them up.

"So. The girl from the diner, huh?"

"Ah, yes. Yes, we ran into each other at a bar. I, um, knew she was staying here and thought this place would be safe," I said.

"It is that."

"Jilly …"

She held up a hand and smiled.

"Don't. You don't have to," she said. "This time."

She winked at me.

"Good choice," she added. "I'd do her."

Lexie rolled to her side, but remained in deep sleep.

Jilly giggled to herself, softly.

"What," I asked.

"It's just funny," she said. "You and I. This way that we are. The how we are. I remember when I got home from this trip last year, and I was pissed off at you. Madder than I had been in years. Fuck him, I'm done, I told myself. I did. I said that. I told everyone at work that. So, May comes along and Julia is getting married, right? So, I go with a few girls from the office to this sex toy store. Damn, I can't remember the name. Anyway, we go to the store. Now we buy this huge black dildo for Julia, because she is marrying Richard Ellison …"

"Tiny Dick? Julia married Tiny Dick?" I interrupted suddenly.

"Yes, Tiny Dick. So, I bought myself one of these 'realistic cocks' that the store sells. It's this eight inch thing. Not bad. And I thought with my bullet that, hell, I'm gonna have some fun. You know, get off on those nights I just need to get off. And now, okay, why the fuck I'm telling you this I have no fucking clue, but here's the thing. I can 'fuck' anybody with that thing. Brad Pitt. Johnny Depp. It doesn't matter, right? I mean it's a fucking dildo.

"First night, I break out this bad boy and I get up on my knees and start riding it. I got a pillow underneath me. And I am going to fucking town. And you know who I'm fucking? You. You. The dumbass that I am pissed off at. The dumbass that I am finished with. The dumbass that I don't want to see. So, this happens like for a month. I seriously had a masturbation fetish with this thing. Don't ask. So, your birthday comes, right. Remember we all went to Olive Garden cause you wanted Italian that night. I left my panties at home. I did. You asked where they were, remember? I left them at home on purpose because I was going to fuck you. I had to get you out of my system. I was done. And this was gonna be closure. So, we go back to your place. We kiss. I suck your dick hard. We fuck. All good, right? I am in great shape. I walk out the next morning like a champ. That dildo is still sitting in my drawer. Haven't used it since last June right before I fucked you."

"And you keep saying I'm the dumbass?"

"Yes, well, it worked," she said. "For months. No worries. And then you had to go and take your pants off at Rich's trailer. I thought, goddamn, he still has such a nice fucking ass. So, okay, I don't know. You fucked this girl. Yeah. It's not really top of my mind right now. Because this thing we do, this whatever the fuck it is, it has to get decided someday, right? I mean we either throw in or we have to throw it away. We cannot keep on being each other's consolation prize, Chaz. I cannot be the safe place to fall and you can't be mine. I cannot keep fucking dildos and pretending they are you."

The cigarette was burning against my lip. The smoke burning into my eyes.

"We need to bury Roan," I said. "We need to get back to Georgia and then we need to sit down and talk. Really talk."

Jilly again brushed her hair from her face. She was wearing ripped jeans over boots with a Rolling Stones t-shirt I had given her five or six years earlier. She sat on that bed, and the world washed over us.

"I love you, Jilly," I said.

When I had been 14, I started drinking. Nothing heavy. A beer here; a dare to sip vodka there. Most of the kids I grew up with started around the same time. The drinking age was 18 and anyone with an older sibling had easy access to alcohol, to some degree or another. By 15, nearly every kid I knew had some experience with the stuff. Moonshine, whiskey or a bottle of wine. Standing and swaying one night, projectile vomiting onto a wall after four quick shots of dry gin on an empty stomach I swore off the stuff. For the sway, the circular motion of rooms, the fuzzy nature of all objects and the churning in the belly was enough for me. The sea-like rise and fall of my bed. That lasted for maybe a month. Jack and Sage liked getting Arlo and I drunk. Something to do on those boring Georgia nights when the fireflies have all gone to bed and the games of childhood are long gone. I wasn't a fast learner and the pressure to be cool around my older brothers, and other friends, lessened my critical decision making skills at a time when they weren't very skilled to begin with. Brotherly love.

It was my brothers that brought music into my life. Old 45s on a turntable. Beatles, Bay City Rollers, Rolling Stones, ABBA, KISS, Eagles, Fleetwood Mac and even Sex Pistols found their way into our home. Jack had an 8-track in his car. Sage bought himself a sound system with two turntables and two large speakers; he could listen to the Atlanta rock station on summer nights with a crackle in the air.

The music punctuated with occasional yells from my Dad to "turn that shit down."

My brothers brought sex into my life — or at least a 10-year old's idea of sex. Naked women sprawled across the pages of wrinkled Playboys, Penthouses and Hustlers that they had bought at the gas station at the end of the road. Roan and I started sneaking them out back when we were 12 or so. But we only did that a half dozen times just for the thrill of lifting the magazine. Mostly, we just snuck into Sage's room, dove under his bed and pulled out his beat up, pale greenish suitcase he hid them in. I'm sure our momma knew. She never said too much about it. It was one of those things, one of those fights, she wasn't gonna have with us. My dad ignored it all together.

My brothers brought sports into my life. Football was the game; although we played everything. But football, with its crashes and collisions, its controlled violence, drew us in. Jack and Sage went easy on us when we were real little; but as we got older and bigger, they hit us harder and more often. Arlo quit playing sports, drawn to his guitar in his room. He'd been named after my dad's oldest brother, Arlo Evan Wilson, who died in World War II. My brother Arlo liked to tell people he'd been named after the folk singer, but that wasn't true. It sounded cool to girls though and I guess that is what mattered.

The things that held us together as brothers in childhood were not strong enough to hold us together as we entered adulthood and began to find more difference than commonality. It's harder to find ground we all share. The days of hide-and-seek were gone. The days of pick up football games in backyards were gone. The days of sharing Playboys in the hopes of unlocking some great mystery of women were gone. We shared a last name and memories, but could find little now that drew us together, save a holiday or birthday.

All four of us with different jobs, living in different parts of the state. Jack with three kids, from two marriages, whose names I don't think I could recall if I tried — although the oldest was named, Austin. Sage with his two marriages; and I worried his second wife was a full-tilt drunk. Arlo, the most withdrawn, the most un-Wilson kid of the bunch.

And the jobs. The jobs we held, the things we had done to get there, to rise to whatever occupational level we held were all so different. Sharing stories over a turkey was never easy, because none of the other three could relate to whatever item, event, or nuance of the job the one was or might be sharing.

Different as day and night was a pale metaphor; we were as different as water, fire, earth and air. And yet, my love, my deep love, for the three men, now, that I shared a last name with was unwavering, even if I didn't know them as people like I should. Even if I liked them less.

I stared down now at the tubes running in and out of Sage's body, the ride from Lexie's to the hospital a blur, and the only wish I now held or wanted was for him to rise, to live, to run with me once more. Hell, I'd even let him slap the shit out of me if he'd just wake up.

Jilly stroked my hair, and rose, "I'm getting coffee. Do you want anything?"

"Coffee," I said softly. "That would be great. Thank you."

The hospital room was cold, the painting above the bed an image of the sea, with a lone seagull floating above some softly brushed sailboat, tranquil, while the hum and buzz of modern medicine provided a soundtrack for my brother's greatest fight. I'd always bet on Sage, but this was an opponent I couldn't size up, couldn't see. Pale still, and older around the eyes, he labored in his breathing; but still he drew breathe. His hands lay by his side, his face peaceful. It may be hard to win a fight in such a position. I needed him to win this fight. I needed him.

CHAPTER 20

Detective Wilton Tilly sat staring at me, with a cigarette burning between his fingers, as I laid out our tale of vengeance, death and stupidity. He studied my face, fixed on my eyes, looking for deception or lie; and seemed a mixture of stunned, satisfied and bewildered by the tale. In all his years of police work, I felt certain he never heard quite a story.

"You are either the dumbest person in the world," he began. "Or something else ... and I don't know what the something else would be."

"Sir, I don't know what else to say."

"Oh, I think you have said more than enough," Tilly said, rubbing his temples. "Look. Okay. None of this was recorded. Alright? This was just you and I talking. And I don't even know what to say to you at this point. Damn. You know, I thought maybe this was just some freakish coincidence. Some absolutely bizarre set of ... fuck, I don't even know.

"I got five dead bodies ... and best I can figure, hell, maybe six, if your brother dies. Now, how in the hell do you expect me to write this up? Yes, the first two, yeah, your brother is right, that would pass off as a murder-suicide. But ... fuck me. Kid, you dropped the biggest fuck storm into my life."

"Sorry."

The sun came blazing through the blinds of the small conference room on the second floor of the hospital where Tilly and I sat. He rubbed his temples again. He was using a discarded coffee cup for an ashtray, a no smoking sign displayed, prominently, behind his back on the wall beside the only door to the room. I lit up as well. It was my fifth cigarette in probably twenty minutes. I was using an old Coke can.

Tilly wore a tan sports coat over a pale blue shirt, no tie and a pair of Dockers slacks. His shoes were at least two years old, maybe more. Black leather. They'd been nice once. Probably spent two-hundred dollars on those shoes. He liked them. A lot.

I looked down at my faded, ripped jeans and cheap Walmart cowboy boots and felt severely under-dressed. My t-shirt still had blood on it. Just specks of brown here and there. I needed a shower. I needed a different life.

"I, um, I love my brother, detective," I said. "I do. And I loved my friend, Roan. He, um, didn't deserve ... all of this. He was a good guy, ya know? He was quick-witted and always smooth. He had a way, ya know, this way of making people feel at ease. He made you comfortable. He had a joke, or a story, or just a way. He was always good with a room full of girls and it bothers me that I have to talk about the was, the what he was."

"Son, I see bodies, lives ended," Tilly said. "I don't know the living. The 'was' ... I never know the 'was.' I know the 'is.' I know the dead and they all tell the same story. Death. And I am left figuring out how they got there. Choices, decisions and, maybe, destiny; it all boils down to the same thing ... dead is dead, son.

214

"I caught a 14 year old girl once. Her step-father had beaten her to death with a tire iron because she wouldn't suck his dick. I almost killed him. Swear to God, it's the closest I ever came to pulling out my gun and killing someone. Her face was ... mangled. It is unforgettable and etched in my mind. He did eight years in Jacksonville and got killed one night. Three men stomped the life out of him. I don't even know why; and I never asked. I felt ... Jesus, I felt good. I did. I'd never been as happy to hear a man was dead as I was this piece of human shit. The world is filled with fucks. The world has its share of absolute trash. And it serves no purpose. It falls here and there and fucks up everything in its path. Now, I have spent some three decades throwing cuffs on this kind of shit. Reading rights to the unrighteous and the filthy and the losers and the truly miserable sacks of shit that God Himself in His infinite wisdom decides to place here and test us. And you know, I have no answers. No greater moral to sell. Death. It comes and comes and comes again ... and the 'was,' I never get to meet. Just the 'is.'"

The silence stretched between us. This proud black man, with a calling, and me. What? A twenty-something full of himself reporter. Maybe. Is that what I am? Am I, really? We sat, two very different souls, from very different worlds, he and I. He was pre-Civil Rights, pre-Hip Hop, pre-baggy jeans and dreadlocks. In so many ways, he was probably far, far more conservative than I would ever be. He was jazz, baseball, not basketball, and Richard Pryor. He probably owned records and nothing else, and he probably drank a single beer while watching a ball game. A man of moderation, and limits. He was proud. In the best way. He'd earned his place, case-by-case, person-by-person in a world that had been, and in many ways still was, stacked against him. And he never once cried about it. I envied him. To be so clear in who one was. To have purpose and poise and a steely resolve. I was timid and pale by comparison. Yes, I envied him. He was a good man to envy.

"How are the girls," I asked.

"Their parents are on the way," Tilly said. "The FBI is talking with them now. Downtown. CNN is flying in, so I hear. Were you looking for a new job?" he laughed at his own joke and continued. "You opened Pandora's Box with this one. You wanta laugh? I got a guy, now I swear this guy is CIA, I do, and he was wanting to speak with you about Columbians of all things. You know any Columbians? And for the love of God, don't answer that. The CIA, under law, can't work in America. Can't, well, spy on you, you know that? And this guy, whoever the fuck he is, he wants to talk with you about Columbians. You scarred somebody, kid. You shook some tree and all the nuts are falling out."

"Did anybody from The Grunge kill Roan?"

"How the fuck should I know," Tilly said with a laugh. "I have no idea who killed him. I don't. Feel better or worse?"

"The same, I guess."

"Dead is dead, kid," Tilly said. He pulled a cigarette from his pack, lit it and again rubbed his temple. "Hell, you may get a medal. Or, you may get blown up in your car one morning. I have no idea what the fuck stone you and your brother managed to kick over; what hornets' nest you pissed off. But I seriously doubt these fuckers killed your friend. Is that what you want to hear, or no?"

"No. Not really."

"I didn't think so."

Tilly dragged hard at his cigarette.

"Ever hear the name, Escalardo?"

"No, why?"

"He's a Mexican drug lord. He makes extra income off of the sex trade. Probably a side business for him. He makes billions off of marijuana and guns, but I guess enough is never enough for those guys. So, he runs a black market girls network. At least that is what the one FBI guy from Jacksonville said on the phone," Tilly said, dragging again on his cigarette. "Now, I imagine that 'The Grunge' is some kind of off-the-books underground sex club and that this Escalardo is maybe one of the suppliers of young girls.

"Now, okay, I think you and your brother are gonna get a major pass on any charges filed. But I don't know if you pissed off a really big, fucking hornet in the process or not."

I wanted to get back to my brother's room here at the hospital. Jilly was waiting, along with Rich and Dallas. I had no answers for Tilly; and he was still trying to figure out what to do with me.

"The problem we have, the reason I am getting phone calls from every three initial agency in the country, is that book you found," Tilly's eyes fixed on me, a suggestion formed early in his mind, again came from his lips. "Now, you found that book at Mr. Wise's, correct?"

I knew the answer to that now. I knew exactly where he was going; we had been here before. If I hung to the truth and said we had discovered the book in the possession of Moffitt, well, that placed Sage and I in a dead man's house. A dead man, who had not even been discovered by the police yet according to Tilly. He hadn't yet dispatched officers to Moffitt's and the horror scene they would discover there. Sage's carefully woven tale of murder-suicide was going to play out the longer that crime scene sat, according to Tilly, who had already asked the same question now three times. The first time, I had delivered him the truth. The second time and now the third time, I delivered the answer Tilly suggested I make. Moffitt's own name in the book was as curious to Tilly has it had been to me. Why put your own name in that book? It still made no sense. But the existence of Moffitt's name might lend itself to further the murder-suicide story. My answer was easy.

"Yes," I spoke the lie, softly. "We found that in a drawer at Mr. Wise's house."

It was the first time I had spoken the name Mr. Wise since his death. The girls, Kimberly and Sierra, didn't know about the book, not really, at least not enough to declare where it had been found, when or by whom. Their state of mind would only serve to reinforce that it was simply chaos and the pain, torture and sexual assault they had endured would further back the tall tale Sage and I had laid out of stumbling into the freak show. Tilly was simply the ghost writer. A willing ghost writer at that. He wanted this story to have a happy ending.

"Can I get back to my brother? My parents are on the way down."

"Yes, of course," Tilly said. "Kid? Listen to me carefully. From here on out, you talk to no one without a lawyer. You understand me? I mean no one. The FBI will be getting to you soon, and I don't know who else may come around asking questions. You need to dumb up and lawyer up. Okay?"

"Yes, sir."

We shook hands and parted ways. I felt I'd being seeing Tilly again soon, and didn't offer any goodbyes, but rather a casual, "I'll see you later."

I had come clean with Tilly about nearly everything — except for the phone number printed on the two business cards I'd taken off the heavy hitters back at Wise's place, and the hotel keys that each had possessed. Why I held back on that, I wasn't sure. It was probably misplaced loyalty to my brother, or something else. Something unfinished.

I took the staircase down to the lobby and went out a side door to a smoking area next to the hospital to have another cigarette. I needed to clear my mind. An elderly woman in a wheelchair and a woman who appeared to be her daughter were the only other people on the paved area set aside for smokers.

"You have to have the tests," the younger woman was saying to the older.

"Why? Why do I need to be tested for anything?" the older woman responded, with what sounded like a rhetorical question to me.

"Because the doctor needs to rule out some possibilities before deciding on surgery," the younger woman said sounding more than frustrated with the older woman. "We talked about this already."

"I don't understand any of it. At my age, what can they test me for? I am old. What more do they need to know?"

The younger woman took a draw on her cigarette and looked down towards the ground. The older woman, who held a cigarette in one hand, worked the folds of a blanket across her lap with the other.

She looked up and smiled at me.

"Are you here for tests," the older woman asked of me.

"Aunt Vicky!"

"No, ma'am. No tests for me," I said. I smiled at the younger woman and then tried to reassure her that it was quite alright. Her Aunt Vicky reminded me of my grandmother. My paternal grandmother.

"What brings you here, young man? Do you have an ill person in your family."

219

"My brother was shot." I tried to state it as matter-of-factly as possible, but it still sounded dramatic. It is impossible to say someone has been shot without it sounding dramatic.

"I honestly do not understand what is wrong with this country," Aunt Vicky said. "How is your brother doing?"

"Not very well," I said. "He has an infection and fluid in the lungs. At least that is what I can understand from the doctors."

"They do love their medical jargon, don't they," she said.

"Yes, that and tests."

She giggled softly, but the younger woman didn't look that amused.

"Are you married," Aunt Vicky asked. "This is my niece, Elizabeth. She's not married and she's 31 now."

Elizabeth looked mortified.

"It is nice to meet you, Elizabeth, and no, I am not married," I said. "And, I also have to get back upstairs to check on my brother. So, if you'll both excuse me."

I could hear Elizabeth giving her Aunt Vicky a hard time about sharing personal business, and Aunt Vicky giving it right back.

Back in Room 413, Sage's breathing was labored; his chest rising and falling in a slow, choppy rhythm. There were some eight to ten tubes running into him at various points and his yellowish skin seemed almost bruised, tender to the touch even, like the Play-Doh we had played with as small children, it seemed as if one could shove, twist and churn his skin. His face looked worse. He seemed another decade older than he was and, even in this mostly sedated stage the doctors, nurses were keeping him in, pained. His eyes would flutter open from time to time, and he appeared to size up the room, to take an inventory of those present, and they would flutter closed again.

Jilly sat on the arm of the chair I occupied and rubbed my shoulders. Across the room, in two separate chairs, Dallas and Rich sat quiet. Rich seemed numb, as if he had been sedated by the doctors as well. Dallas gave off an air of deep concern. But I couldn't place who the concern was for. It certainly wasn't for Rich. They seemed like two people whose relationship was over, forced into the same room and carrying their nice face, and manners.

My mind was on the what next of it all; the next step. Why did I keep those cards secret? I need to visit that hotel. I need to see the next part. I need to know.

"Jilly, come into the hall with me," I said, softly.

"Sure, babe."

We walked into the pale eggshell white hallway, which was filled with the usual muffled noise of a buzzing hospital; the sound just below the surface. Like a library shushed, with a coffee shop bustle just in another room, we stood in that isolated controlled chaos and I looked into her deep blue eyes. Her hair cascaded down over her soft shoulders and fell on her breasts. She wore a pale blue tank top, with her white bikini top underneath; just the strings of the bikini visible at the shoulders. The hospital was cool, but she seemed warm and somehow more beautiful because of that warmth in this cold place of constant death and pain. I hated to lie to her again. I hated to feel another lie leave my mouth when she of all the people in the world deserved constant truth from me. But I would lie and lie again. The lies protecting a love that truth has a way of dulling.

"I need to get out for a while. I need some air," I said.

"Chaz, your parents are going to be here any time now," Jilly said.

"I know, I know," I said. "I won't be too long. I just need to clear my head is all."

"Please tell me you're not going to do anything more stupid," Jilly said.

"No, no more stupid," I said.

Jilly pushed my hair across my forehead, over my right eye. She leaned up and kissed my forehead.

"Don't be a dumbass," she said with a grin.

"I think time will have to tell on that one."

CHAPTER 21

The Ambassador Motel was down Front, the Miracle Mile, roughly five miles from where we were staying at the Days Inn. It spoke to 1950s Florida cool. Plastered white, with lines designed to convey the image of the ocean rolling in; good times await. It reminded me of the Sinatra records in my parents record collection; all that 1950s and 1960s faux hipster crap. Rat Packs and mob bosses. Guys singing songs about fucking, cleverly disguised as 'holding you tight,' or whatever other then socially acceptable lines were installed to disguise the hidden themes of forbidden, out-of-wedlock or extramarital pleasures; all of which the singers themselves were actually engaged in anyway. Hypocrisy at its finest. I chuckled to myself at the underlying irony of two would-be hitmen staying here, of all the places in Panama City and Panama City Beach.

The traffic hadn't been too bad, and I'd found a parking place across the street from the motel, in the back lot of a seafood restaurant. It was suppertime anyway and I just blended in with the dinner rush at Shuckums Oyster Pub. I took a seat outside, ordered two dozen oysters and a beer, and tried to look like a guy hanging out, waiting for friends.

The back and forth debate that been ongoing in my mind to determine my next step continued as I sipped my beer and slowly ate oysters, one after another. I had covered the entire plate in fresh lemon juice and Tabasco, and fixed my eyes on the Ambassador. Nothing struck me as odd, or out of place. The road, of course, held the normal Spring Break traffic, as did the sidewalks. The few people who came and went from the motel seemed to be the usual collection of vacationers. Certainly, I didn't expect any law enforcement, but I was now, thanks to Detective Tilly, a little bit paranoid that a secret agent man might be lurking behind every telephone pole and hubcap between here and the motel. I was more concerned as to who else may show up looking to collect items from the two dead strangers, or worse, waiting to see if anyone else showed up for them.

I made it through two beers and twenty of the oysters before I made up my mind to cross the street and take a look around. It was closing in on 7 p.m., and I felt certain my parents must be at the hospital with Sage by now. I was certain Dallas and Rich had probably left to meet with Roan's parents and fill them in on all that had happened over the last 24 hours or so.

"Can I get you anything else?" I heard the waitress ask.

"No, just a check please," I replied.

"You sure? We're giving a special on blow jobs tonight."

I spun my head around to see Lexie standing behind me with a sly, little grin on her face.

"How in the hell did you find me?"

"That is like my superhero power and I can't tell you how it works," she replied with a wink.

The paranoia must have been easy to read on my face, and Lexie quickly dropped into the chair beside me, stroked my arm once and spilled the truth of her discovery.

"Relax, relax," she said. "Okay, yes, this is gonna sound a little freaky, but I mean well. I went to the hospital to see you and your brother. I debated it most of the day in my mind, and finally decided to drive over.

"Well, as I got there I saw you heading for your car and I kind of followed you here. I actually lost you, in a way, and I doubled back and figured you must have turned down and come in behind the restaurant. I have been sitting at the bar for about half an hour or so, just debating whether or not to speak with you at all … and I am now really embarrassed about the blow job line."

The sea breeze picked up strands of her pixie hair and tossed it about, furiously, over her eyes and face. She tried to sweep it back, but the nature of the hair cut gave the wind the upper hand. She had too little hair for a ponytail, and just enough hair for the wind to play havoc with it. She had recently applied more purple to the one side and added pink to the back. Her eyes were dazzling. They simply reflected all the available light and burst radiance; her soul shined.

"Do you want a beer," I asked.

"I'd love a drink," she replied. "Okay, so, why are you sitting in Shuckums all by yourself?"

I flagged the waitress and Lexie ordered a Margarita, extra olives. I had a quick internal debate over how to answer her question. The waitress departed, sooner than I would have liked, with drink orders for Lexie and I, and I realized I needed her support, her help.

"The house where we found the girls," I began. "There were two guys, who came in. I don't know. They showed up and the guy, that Mr. Wise person I told you about, well, he had called them. When they were … dead, I went through their pockets. I found two business cards with the same phone number on each and two hotel keys. Both hotel keys go to the Ambassador."

"Did you tell the police?"

"No. No, that is why I am sitting here," I said. "I am going in first. I think my thoughts are to see if I find anything else. I guess if I find nothing, well, I can at least then tell the detective that I'd forgotten or something in all the confusion. He may believe me. He may not. Either way, well, I will have turned up nothing new. If I find something, well, then I have a tougher decision to make."

"Can I ask you something?"

"Yeah, of course."

"What's the point? I mean, I know you have to be turned all kinds of sideways. And I get that. When my daddy was murdered in New Orleans, I was eleven, and I wanted to kill the guy who did it. I wanted to see him in pain. But, well, I was eleven," Lexie said, opening her purse and pulling out her pack of Marlboros. She lit one and put her pack and lighter back into her bag. "I guess what I want to know from you is what happens when you find this person? Are you gonna be able to prove they killed your friend."

"Roan."

"What?"

"Roan. That was his name. And I have known him for twenty years. He was my best friend," I said. "And it dawns on me now that my brothers are and have been my friends as well, even if I couldn't see it. And one of them, the one I disliked the most, drove through the night to come and be by my side. So, my plan is to find who killed Roan and ... well, end it."

"You're willing to go to jail?"

"I don't know."

The music over the bar's PA system suddenly increased in volume and I realized the dinner crowd was being transitioned to the party crowd. It was time to move.

I pulled out my own pack of cigarettes from my shirt pocket, lit one, and blew smoke into the early night air.

"I know that I opened a door and I have to see this through," I said. "When I get to the next part ... I get to the next part. I don't know. I just don't. But I could use an extra set of eyes.

"And I am sorry about your dad. I didn't know that."

"How could you? I just told you. There is a lot you don't know about me, I think. Probably a lot that you had no intention of getting to know," she said. "And, hey, there was a lot about you that I was never going to get to know either. I, no, we both wanted the same thing that night. It was ... it was a good fuck, you know? I was sure you were gone and then suddenly there you were. Covered in blood and sporting the craziest look I think I'd ever seen in another person's eyes.

"I want to help you."

We drank our drinks, paid the bill and made our way to the street. I clasped her hand in mine, better to appear a couple out for a walk I thought, and we made our way across the street; dipping in and out of traffic. We backtracked to the hotel after having walked up the street, roughly a quarter of a mile, and entered the lobby. The hotel had people scurrying to and fro; from middle-aged couples trying to corral various children of various ages, to a group of teenagers giggling in the excitement of a Spring Break night. We made our way down the main hallway and looked at the signage for the room numbers we needed: 213 and 215.

"Let's look at 213 first and then go from there," I said quietly.

"Sounds good to me," Lexie affirmed.

Room 213 of the Ambassador was a spacious loft-style room, which easily could have slept six to eight people. I was a bit surprised at the size of the room, expecting that the two men would have smaller accommodations.

"Take the loft area," I said. "I'll start here by the door and work my way to the back."

"What if I find something?"

"Just put everything of interest, anything you're not sure about together and bring it to this bed," I said. "We'll go through it together and see if any of it is meaningful."

"What am I looking for?"

"I'd look for receipts, messages, phone numbers or addresses," I said. "But really, I think we want anything that just looks unusual or odd."

In a week full of the odd and unusual, I expected something to just leap out at me. I was hoping it wasn't a dead body or a man with a gun.

The first room was a bedroom with two night stands and a dresser. It yielded nothing. I checked beneath the bed, and again found nothing. The room was clean.

A hallway stretched to my left, while the ladder-stairs ran to the right up to the loft. The hallway included a very small kitchenette with a stove, sink and mini-fridge. There was a small bottle of milk in the fridge, two beers and a take out box of Chinese. Nothing.

I continued down the hall and found the living room area, which included a sliding glass door onto the deck and a mixture of furniture, including a sleeper-sofa. The loft area looked down on the living room and I could see Lexie looking through night stands and the lone dresser upstairs. I turned my attention to the two night stands/end tables in the living room area; and again both were empty.

I went into the large closet area, which sat directly behind the kitchenette, and went through four different suits, six pairs of pants, several shirts and two different suitcases. Nothing. And more nothing in the bathroom. And Lexie reported nothing in the loft area. Clean.

We moved quickly to Room 215, and I began to realize I was running out of anything remotely representing a lead. The police now had possession of the black book with the names and code numbers; the biggest and best lead Sage and I had uncovered. I did still hold the business cards with the phone numbers, but I was going to need a well thought out story to make those effective, useful. Room 215 was laid out the same as 213 and this time it wasn't a complete waste of time. I found three receipts at local businesses, including a gun shop. But Lexie made the more disturbing discovery.

A large white envelope was stuffed inside a suitcase with a false shelf. The envelope held twenty-five Polaroid photos of naked, young women ranging in age from what appeared to be 13 to maybe 24 at the oldest. The back of each picture held a single name such as 'Jade,' or 'Eve.'

"Do you think all of these girls are slaves," Lexie asked.

"Maybe," I replied. "Some may be dead. Some may not even be in this country."

Lexie rubbed at the corner of her eye, pushing tears across her face. She laid the pictures down softly on the coffee table, stood up and walked to the sliding glass door.

"What's next? What can we do," she asked back over her shoulder.

"I don't know ... I need to get back to the hospital," I said. "I need to check on Sage, Jilly, and everyone else I guess."

"What are you going to do with these photos," she asked.

"I'm gonna bring them to Detective Tilly. I don't see that I have any other choice," I said. "Lexie, thank you coming up here with me. I won't mention your name to Tilly, or anyone. I don't want to get you into any bullshit that you don't deserve."

"Funny, ya know. How we crossed paths, what, less than a week ago and here I am ... sitting in this room with you now," she pushed her hair back, a single tear was still clinging to her cheek.

I stood, walked to her, and wrapped my arms, gently, around her waist. She shifted her weight, and spun to face me.

"Kiss me," she said. "Please. Just once. Just kiss me."

My lips found hers. Her kiss was incessant, erotic and spoke of invitation to advance to the next stage. In any other environment but this hotel room, that invitation would have been accepted by me.

"Not here," was all I found myself saying.

"I want you again," she softly whispered into my ear.

"Soon," I whispered back.

We walked back into the hallway, I had stuffed the Polaroid shots into my back pocket and our plan was to separate once we got back to the restaurant parking lot.

At the end of the hall, nearest the emergency stairwell, stood a tall dark-skinned man with dark sunglasses, wearing a black suit. I gripped Lexie's arm; and we stood, the three of us caught in uncertain stares. The elevator bell dinged once, doors slide open and a family of four emerged and walked in the direction of the hard-looking man.

"Go," I said to Lexie. "Go now."

CHAPTER 22

Lexie slid into the elevator, the doors closed behind her, and that left the dark man and I staring at each other. The family of four that had emerged from the elevator prior to Lexie's departure disappeared into Room 521. The hallway stood empty, save for the dark man and me. His sunglasses concealed any thought or emotion; he simply stood and stared. I knew there was another staircase roughly 150 feet or more behind me; but making a run was not in my plans. I needed to allow Lexie time to escape and the longer we stared at each other was another moment I bought my new accomplice.

The dark man motioned me towards him, opened the door to the staircase and stood awaiting my decision. With choices few and far between, I walked towards him and the stairs, but stopped just short.

"What do you want?" I asked evenly.

"We need to talk, I do believe," the dark man said.

"I don't know you. What could we have to talk about," I asked, as I tried to remain even, unemotional.

"I think you know the answer to that," he said. "Please, let's move into the stairwell. We can speak there and depart."

Again, my options are limited. I can speak with this man and, perhaps, learn something and move on; or, not. He may want to kill me in the stairwell, I thought. Less potential witnesses and maybe less noise. My mind was racing. I could feel the .9mm tucked into the waistband of my jeans pressing into the small of my back; trying to recall how many bullets I had left. It only takes one, I thought.

I motioned with my hand for him to lead the way; and he stepped through the frame, holding the door for me. His hidden eyes never giving an inch or inkling of plan or thought.

It was my turn to measure my fear; to control, command. The dark man and I were roughly the same physical size; he might be a few pounds heavier. His sports jacket swung open just a bit as he held the door and I could make out just the handle end of an automatic pistol. I couldn't tell the caliber from the brief glance, but I didn't doubt the owner's proficiency with the weapon. Something in the way he carries himself. He is not to be taken lightly. But I will not fear; even in death.

My freshman year of high school, I had either the unbelievable bad luck or brilliant fortune to catch Ms. Bernice Pelham for Freshman English. The five-foot-one, 180 pound bulldog of A hall was a walking legend long before I had even entered elementary school. She had squinty deep brown eyes that in certain lights gave the illusion of being almost black. Her gray stack of hair could seem to sway and almost tilt as her head bobbed and moved during instruction. She was passionate about literature and her status as a never-married woman lead many high schoolers to make cruel jokes about her possible sexual orientation. The young girls seemed more scared of Ms. Pelham, than the young boys in her class. But the young boys often learned to be very afraid, and often learned the hard way. I was one of those.

It wasn't that I was a disruptive, or aggressive student. No, if anything the reverse. I had Ms. Pelham for first period and with football practice in the evenings, chores, odd jobs, homework and the wide range of hormonal changes that lead to sleep issues, I often fell asleep in Ms. Pelham's class. I wouldn't remain asleep for long, however.

She used everything in her power and even things now against the law to wake me or any sleeping teen in her first period. Once dumping a cup of ice water down my back. Once smacking my head, repeatedly, with a ruler — even after waking: "Must keep you awake, Mr. Wilson," I can still recall her saying. Her voice like a buzz saw drunk on helium.

By midterms, I was pulling a D in her class; but by Final Exams, I had passed with an 82, or a low B. She kept me after first period on that final exam day.

"Mr. Wilson, I can only assume that God Himself somehow intervened on your behalf. Regardless, of whatever divine intervention or answered prayers you may have received, you have finished my class with the highest grade that I will award this semester," Ms. Pelham began. I was shocked. I thought I was maybe middle of the pack, and certainly in conversations with classmates, I knew everyone was struggling to pass her class.

"I wanted to say something else however," Ms. Pelham continued. "You show potential and you show grit. I like that in a person. You may go now."

It was, and perhaps is, the greatest compliment I had ever received from someone I had come to respect; even begrudgingly.

The dark man seemed unlikely to offer compliments, and even more unlikely to earn my respect — begrudgingly or otherwise. His suit was fine, cotton and expensive. In the stairwell, with the brighter light bursting through narrow windows at the top of each landing, the suit was a black on black pinstripe, white shirt, and black leather loafers. His shirt was unbuttoned once at the collar. He had paid handsomely for the attire. His posture suggested he was used to fine clothing and very comfortable in it. Once more, I looked like a rube standing next to the sharp dressed-man. I had been standing next to a lot of men in suits on this vacation; more than I imagined when I packed for the trip.

"I do not care to hear your name, and in fact, I simply do not care," he began. I could not place his accent. Like the young woman at Moffitt's house, Milas, his accent seemed to have a hint of French — was it African or South American, I could not be certain; although I had only heard Milas speak three words before her head was ripped from her shoulders. "You asked my name, and you do not want to know that either. What I need from you is a little black book that is missing from Mr. Moffitt's house. And I would ask that you please do not play stupid. It is either in your possession, or the police have it and I must know and know now the truth of it. Do I make myself plain enough for you?"

"Yes," I replied.

He rubbed the black stubble on his chin and cheeks with his left hand and then casually placed both hands on his hips, causing his sports coat to spread open and the handgun under his left arm to be fully displayed. The dark man, with no name, had a thick stock of wild black hair. His hair seemingly combed with nothing more than a good night sleep and a pillow; it flew in countless directions about his head. He had a bulbous nose and three long thin scars that ran from his right eye to his jawbone. The scars each appeared to be a different age, with the one nearest his ear seemingly the freshest; perhaps, as little as ten years old and it was also the thickest scar, the nastiest. He was a man of pure violence. He seemed born to and was probably born into it. This would not end well for one of us. I knew that now.

"The book is gone," I said. "The FBI has it, as I understand it."

"I want to thank you for your honesty," the dark man said. "It is refreshing."

This was it.

I sprang into him as hard as I could across the distance of two to three feet that separated us. I wrapped up as I had been taught in football and drove him down the stairs. We landed, with him underneath me, about six feet down the flight of stairs, and the air briefly escaped from the both of us. He grimaced in pain, his spine hitting the lower step. He was quicker and stronger than I was prepared for and he pulled his right arm up and smashed his open hand into my left ear; a buzz filled the air and my vision went soft briefly. I tried to deliver a series of knees into his groin, but they seemed to bounce off his inner thigh and have little effect on him. He flipped me onto my back, but I rolled and pushed him toward the wall, using my legs for leverage against the stairwell. He brought his head down onto mine and my vision flashed in stars and speckles of light. The dark man stood above me. This was the end.

There was a very small pop sound that rung off the walls of the stairwell, and an odd smile crossed the dark man's lips. He opened his mouth to speak and blood spewed forth, down his chin and onto his nice white shirt. The large hand gun in his right hand fell harmlessly to the floor, as he fell to his knees and then slumbered over onto his face.

At the bottom of the staircase stood Lexie holding a very small pistol. Her face stone.

I had a gash above my left eye where the dark man had crushed his head into my forehead. I felt woozy and uncertain as I tried to stand. There was no time to waste. I climbed onto the dark man and removed his keys, wallet, handgun, three full clips of ammo from his coat pocket and one folded piece of paper. I removed his shoes quickly to see if anything was hidden, and frisked him down one last time. The pop, which sounded like a Black Cat firework that is sold all over the south, had not brought any undue attention to the staircase.

"Come on," I said to Lexie. Tears welled in her eyes and she was still stone solid as she stood.

"He's dead?"

'Yes, Lex, yes," I said. "You saved my life. He would have killed me."

"I killed him," she said that softly to herself, or perhaps to the heavens, as confirmation of what she was seeing and what was now done.

"Lex, there is nothing we can do about it," I said. "We have to move."

I took her gently by the elbow, and turned towards the door leading to the lobby when I realized she was still holding her pistol in her hand. I took the snub-nosed .38 from her hand and put it in her purse. I pulled my shirt down over the Desert Eagle .50 I had lifted off of the dark man, and added the .9mm I had collected at "his" house to Lexie's purse.

"Come," I said, giving her a kiss on the forehead as we headed into the lobby.

I lead the distraught pixie quickly through the lobby, across the road, filled with Spring break traffic, and around Shuckums where roughly an hour earlier we had been drinking. I looked at the clock on my dashboard and it read, 8:20. I had been gone from the hospital for nearly four hours. I needed to call Jilly. I looked up and gently brushed Lexie's face as she sat in my passenger seat.

"Can we leave your car here if we need to," I asked her softly.

"Yes, that is fine."

I opened the dark man's passport, which I had pulled from his coat pocket, and finally had his name, Gabriel Mateus Vasquez. He was Brazilian.

I looked closely at the Desert Eagle he had carried, and there was an inscription on the grip, "O Coração de um Guerreiro." I knew it was Portuguese but was uncertain what it translated to in English. In addition to the powerful handgun, I found a hotel key in his wallet along with twelve hundred dollars in US hundred dollar bills. There was a business card with just a phone number printed on it. I pulled my own wallet and matched the number to the two cards I had lifted from the two dead men in dark suits back at "his" house in Pretty Bayou. I had made up my mind.

"We're going to his hotel room first," I said to Lexie. "From there I can call Jilly and I can call this number. We have some work to do. Are you okay?"

"Yes, I'll be fine," she said. "Put on some music. Please."

I slipped an old Rolling Stones cassette in the player, fired up the engine and headed toward's the hotel Vasquez had been staying at — the Knights Inn, which sat on West Beach Drive, overlooking St. Andrews Bay. It was the same road they had found Roan's body off of just two days ago; laying in shallow water among some rocks in St. Andrews. Two days — it seemed like an eternity to me now. The

Rolling Stones 'Sway' came ripping off the speakers in my car as I sped across the Hathaway Bridge back into Panama City. I lit a cigarette.

I am close. I am very close.

During my last conversation with Detective Tilly, I had gotten a better idea of where Roan was found and I was going to make that my first stop. I needed to see where he had been found. I knew better than to expect some uncovered piece of crucial evidence, the police weren't that incompetent. Especially in a case with a presumed tourist.

"What are you thinking about," Lexie asked. She had curled her legs up underneath her in the front seat, her hair tossing about in the breeze from the open window.

"I'm going to stop at the location where they found Roan, first," I said. "I am starting to wonder more and more about just what Roan was doing that night. That has been itching my brain like crazy the last twenty-four hours. Why did he go back out? He never came and asked me to go with him. He didn't ask to borrow my car. So, why walk out of the hotel? Where was he going to walk to? He sure as hell didn't walk across the Hathaway."

"What do you think," Lexie asked, reaching into her purse for a cigarette and pulling out both the .9mm I had recovered and the .38 that she owned. "Can I put these somewhere?"

"Sure, throw them into the dashboard."

I lit a cigarette and handed it to her once the guns were put away. I had the Desert Eagle underneath the driver's seat and I was trying my best to follow the speed limit. I didn't need to be pulled over with three different guns in the car and at least two of them being used in recent deaths. I was certain the Desert Eagle had caused its share of blood and death as well based on nothing more than my assumptions of the previous owner. I lit my own cigarette and tried to think of an answer to Lexie's second to last question.

"He had a ride," I stated. "Someone picked him up. He wouldn't of walked all the way out here."

I looked out around the myriad of businesses, houses, apartment complexes and condominiums. He wouldn't have walked. Who picked him up? Suddenly, I was angry with myself for not thinking of this question earlier. I had know Roan twenty years and if he didn't have a bicycle, motorcycle, car or truck, he wasn't going. I couldn't recall him going anywhere on foot. Save for short distances.

I turned down the sandy little side road and pulled to a stop.

"Let's look around," I said.

The water lapped softly to the shore here on the banks of the St. Andrews Bay. Peaceful. Quiet. There was a line of police tape that remained behind floating gently in the night breeze. The tape was held down on one end by a rock and tied, loosely, around a nearby tree at the other end. There had been no rain and a patch of dark brown on the sand near a large rock, firmly in the ground, seemed to mark the final resting spot of Roan.

"It's nice here," Lexie said.

"Yes," I replied. "It is. Odd, huh. I mean, why here? Look, there is a sidewalk, what? Maybe, a hundred feet? I wonder if he was dumped here, or wound up here?"

I looked across the expanse of the bay and wondered how long it would take a body to float from one point to another, depending on where it was dropped into the water at.

"Was he shot?"

I turned toward Lexie.

"I don't know," I replied. "The police weren't saying and the final autopsy report is due in the morning, except for the toxicology, which I think they said would take a few weeks. When I saw him, he had an ugly gash on the side of his head, but I couldn't tell you if that was a bullet hole or a rock or something else. He did look swollen, bloated. And I wonder now if he washed up here. And the blood here on the sand ... if he was still bleeding, he was probably alive when he did wash up here. So, was he swimming?"

I looked around one final time, "Let's get over to the hotel."

The Knights Inn was labeled as an 'economy' inn, and the rates were very reasonable, but it was designed for families and Spring Breakers living on a very tight budget. It had a nice location overlooking St. Andrew's Bay, but it was well removed from the action of Spring Break and the Miracle Mile, with its bars, restaurants, clubs and shops.

The doors to each room faced the parking lot and we parked in front of Room 143. I turned off my headlights, turned the engine off and sat for a moment looking at the room, the hotel and our general surroundings.

"We get in and out as quickly as possible," I said. "But I am going to use the phone once we get in there."

"Okay," Lexie said. "I'll take the bathroom, you take the bedroom. Looks small, shouldn't take too long."

We got out, walked to the door and let ourselves in. The bathroom sat to our left, with the double bed sleeping area directly ahead. The two beds were separated by a night stand, all on the left-hand wall. The wall opposite held a dresser and an armoire with a TV on a shelf. Lexie went into the bathroom, while I looked over the closet. Several jackets were hung, along with three full suits and four pairs of slacks. I quickly went through all the pockets and found nothing. I felt a tickle on my face and reached up. Drawing back my hand, I realized my own gash from my fight with Vasquez had reopened. I walked to the dresser, pulling open the top drawer and removed a clean white sock. I looked in the mirror and dabbed the sock against the wound. No one will miss this sock, I was thinking.

"Nothing in the bathroom," Lexie reported. "Any luck?"

"No, not yet," I said. "I had to stop the bleeding again."

"You need to get stitches," Lexie said. "Did you check that case over there?"

"Where?"

"Next to the TV."

I walked to the black case, sitting on the floor next to the armoire, picked it up and placed it on the bed. I tossed the lid open, and Lexie and I both went speechless and cold.

"How much money do you think that is," Lexie asked, when she finally found the words.

"It's got to be over a million dollars," I said.

"I think I just retired," Lexie said.

CHAPTER 23

Two million dollars. It spread across the comforter and I'd never seen anything else as stupefying, dazzling and mind-numbing all at the same time. The case had been heavy to lift from the floor to bed, and I guessed it weighed roughly 40 pounds or more. But despite the weight, I never expected it to be filled with hundred dollar bills wrapped in bundles of $10,000 each. As Lexie and I counted out the bundles, we became like two little kids giddy with Christmas morning, gift-opening excitement.

I recall my first hundred dollar bill. I was 15 at the time and working downtown in the summer of 1984 at Wallace Auto Parts. I got the job through my aunt, my father's sister, who had married Ernie Wallace two years earlier. Wallace, like my aunt, had been widowed and the pair had known each other since high school at Alexander Central. Their marriage surprised and shocked no one.

Mr. Wallace agreed to pay me at the end of July and again near the end of August before school started back. Due to family vacations and 4th of July plans, I didn't start work until July 7th. But by July 31st, true to his word, I received my first payment in cash in a white envelope for the amount of three hundred dollars — in three, one hundred dollar bills. We'd agreed upon $5 an hour, which for a 15 year old was a handsome hourly rate; and two to three days a week, for no more than six hours a day. In July, I ended the pay period with sixty hours, spread out over ten days. The crisp money in my hand with Ben Franklin's face, staring off at only God knows what, left me feeling like the richest kid in Alexander.

Then reality set in.

"This has to be drug money, right," Lexie asked, with a voice sounding hopeful that I might have a creative lie about why a dead man would keep two million dollars in a case.

"Well, not sure what else it could be," I said. "I need to call the hospital. Damn. It's late. I'm gonna call the hotel and then we call this mystery number. I think I have an idea."

Sitting on the bed, opposite the one holding two million dollars, I dialed up the Day's Inn and asked for the room Jilly and I had been sharing. Some vacation, I thought, and let out a little laugh as Jilly answered the phone, sniffing back tears.

"Jilly," I asked.

I heard harder sobs and suddenly Kaelyn's voice on the other end.

"Is this Chaz," Kaelyn asked.

"Yes, Kaelyn. What's going on?"

"Seriously? That's your question. Jesus Fucking H. Christ, Chaz. You do understand that Roan is dead, your brother is in a goddamn coma and you're off on what exactly? A pussy hunt?"

"Hey, slow the fuck up. Put Jilly on the phone."

"She can't talk right now," Kaelyn said, and I knew Jilly was not going to get on the phone. Or at least Kaelyn wasn't going to let her.

"Fine. Fuck it. Is Sarah there?"

"Yes, here."

I heard the phone being exchanged, and Kaelyn's voice in the background saying, "what an asshole," before Sarah's voice came on the line.

"Chaz, what are you doing? Where are you?"

"I am near St. Andrew's Bay. And I think I am beginning to realize why Roan is dead," I said.

"Chaz, your brother slipped into a coma. Your mother is a basket case and your father is going to kick your ass. I mean he's pissed. Arlo is driving down in the morning. And Chaz? Jilly could really use you here. Seriously. She needs to see your face, Chaz," Sarah said sympathetically and diplomatically, two traits she had always possessed.

"Will Jilly speak with me, please."

"I'll ask her Chaz." The phone line went quiet, save for the muffled sound of conversation on the other end of the line. Lexie gently rubbed my shoulders, "I'm going to pee," she said and walked off to the bathroom.

I heard a sniffle and then a "Yes."

"Jilly?"

"Yes, what is it Chaz?"

"Jilly ..." the silence seemed to stretch out. What to say. How to say it.

"Jilly, I am sitting in a hotel at St. Andrews Bay and I am staring at two million dollars in cash."

There was silence on the other end.

"Chaz, what are you doing," Jilly asked softly.

"I am trying to find out who killed Roan, and why Sage is in a coma."

"Baby, you need to ask yourself if that matters."

"Yes, yes, Jilly, a thousand times yes, it fucking matters to me. Roan ..." it was my turn to cry. "I ... I have to know."

"Baby ..."

"I have to know, Jilly. I have to."

"Is she with you?"

Letting out a sigh, I wiped the tears down my face.

"Yes, she is here," I said. "It is not at all what you think."

Lexie, returning from the bathroom, moved to the sliding glass door, peeked through the curtains towards the active swimming pool and then looked down on me. She smiled softly, knowingly.

"I see," Jilly said. "I don't know how this week could be any more fucked up. I have to go Chaz. Do what you need to do, okay. Be safe."

"Jilly, tell my parents I love them," I said. "Do that for me."

"I will," she said, and the line went dead.

"I take it that didn't go well," Lexie asked.

"No, I don't think that went well at all," I said. "My parents are in town, my brother Arlo is on the way down as well. Sage has slipped into a coma."

"I'm sorry," she said.

"None of it is your fault," I said. "None of it."

"You said you had a plan," Lexie started. "And I hope it includes us coming to an agreement on how to split up this money."

"Yes," I said with a laugh. "Yes, it does."

I pulled the black cards with the white digit phone number stamped into the card stock, the mystery number, picked up the phone and dialed. My fate was sealed. This was the only way forward.

"Good evening," said a sultry female voice. "How may I assist you this evening?"

"Yes, I need to speak with Gabriel Vasquez, please."

"I'm sorry?"

"Gabriel Vasquez. I need to speak with him."

"I'm sorry sir, you may have dial a wrong number …"

"No, I have the right number. Let me speak to the person who sent Gabriel to kill me. Can you do that for me?"

There was silence, and suddenly a male voice.

"Who the fuck is this," said the angry voice on the other end of the line.

"The motherfucker who is going to burn your house down," I said, and then hung up the phone.

"We don't have a lot of time," I said to Lexie. I began stacking the money back into the case, layering it as quickly as I could. With the money safe, I walked to the closet and tried sizing up Gabriel's suits. We were roughly the same size and I was tired of being vastly under dressed. I selected two suits, two dress shirts, pulled two pairs of socks, since mine were not fresh, and handed the clothes to Lexie. I lifted the heavy suitcase filled with the money.

"Come on," I said.

We walked to the front office, and I surveyed the map of rooms. A heavy set man with leathery skin and a slight lisp stood behind the counter.

"I'd like room 183, please," I said.

"Let me see ... yeah, sorry, that one is taken," he replied.

"What about room 283?"

"Yeah, I got that one free," he said. "You know it's gonna be ninety-five dollars a night."

I handed him a hundred dollar bill from my wallet.

"Sign here," he instructed.

I wrote down the name, Wilton Tilly.

The attendant never batted an eye and handing over two room keys said, "Have a great night."

I pulled a bag from my trunk that held various items, including clean socks, boxer shorts, and all the bullets from my ever-increasing supply of guns. I pulled all three guns from the car and stuffed them into the bag. We walked across the lot, made our way up to the second story and got into our room.

"I'm gonna grab a shower first thing," I said. "Keep the blinds loose like this, and keep an eye on room 143. If anyone shows up, let me know. I won't be long."

The shower felt like a minor miracle. The water pressure was surprisingly strong for a budget hotel, and the hot water worked. I showered quickly, toweled off and slipped into a pair of boxers. I stepped back into the living/sleeping area and Lexie had her eyes on the parking lot.

"Do you want to take a shower," I asked.

"Yes," she said. "It has been a fucked up day. I wish I had some clean clothes."

"We'll take care of that in the morning, if you can make it through the night okay?"

"Yes, I'll be fine."

"Are you hungry? I notice they have a bar over there. I bet we could grab some food and drinks," I said.

"Should we be seen outside?"

"I don't know. I doubt they know what we look like," I said. "I have a feeling Gabriel just got lucky in finding us ... or someone sent him specifically for us."

"Who?"

"It is possible that if you followed me from the hospital, that he had done the same. But that would have to mean someone told him where I was."

Lexie leaned up, kissed me on the cheek and seemed to pause.

"I'm gonna hit the shower."

I threw on my jeans and t-shirt, again; no need for a suit to cross the parking lot, and go into a bar, I reasoned. I walked to the bar, ordered a 12-pack of beer, and two Philly Cheese Steaks. I felt bad for not asking Lexie what she preferred, but she didn't strike me as a vegetarian. I returned to the hotel to find Lexie wearing a towel and shaking out her pixie hair.

"I got you a Philly Cheese, is that okay?"

"Hell, yes. I love those."

It was nice to guess right.

Lexie reached into the sink and pulled her panties, wet from soaking, wrung them twice and hung them on a coat hanger in the open-faced closet.

"Sorry, I just wanted to feel, um, fresher in the morning when I put those back on," she said with a slight blush in her face.

"No worries," I said, turning to face the parking lot. I opened a beer and the packaging that held my sandwich. Lexie crossed the room, pulled a beer, handed it to me for opening, which I obliged and sat the bottle down in front of her as she opened her own sandwich. She took a huge bite. Nothing girly or feminine about it, stuffing bits and pieces into her mouth, "this is so fucking good."

She was adorable. I was in trouble. I took a large swig from my beer, my own bite of cheese steak and trained my eyes back on the lot. We ate in silence the rest of the way and had made our way through two beers each before either one of us spoke again. There was nothing uncomfortable in the silence. It was as natural as sunlight.

"Do you think someone is going to show up here," Lexie asked, when she finally spoke.

"Yes, I do," I replied. "I might be wrong, of course, but I have a strong feeling that whoever I spoke with knew exactly who Gabriel is, er, was, and that he was staying here."

Lexie ran her hand through her hair and gave it a shake.

"What are we going to do about us," she stated. It wasn't a question. Not in the real sense. It was there hanging in the room and had been hanging between us for some time. Probably since a night spent arguing about the commercialization of Sonic Youth in a loud, obnoxious bar on the other side of the Hathaway.

"What do you want to do about us," I genuinely asked.

"I'm gonna get a little tipsy, first. And then you're going to fuck me," she said, with a twinkle in her eye. "After that, well, we see what kind of stamina you have."

I laughed, but not at her. I laughed at the universe. The madness of finding her. The madness of wanting her. The pain of what that meant. How real I felt with her. How much I was, just was, with her. Comfortable and free.

She leaned back in her chair, lifted her left foot and slide her toes into my boxer shorts, playfully rubbing my member. I grinned; a devilish grin, I am sure and turned to look out the blinds.

A black sedan pulled up behind my Camaro. Four men in black suits exited the car. I strained my eyes to try and make them out. The lot, despite street lights, was still awash in the darkness of night. I was trying to see if any of them were familiar. Were these the same men that at been at Tammy and Tom's house a week earlier? I couldn't tell in the available light. I could see that one held a shotgun, while the other three pulled automatic handguns. They knocked at the door to room 143. They waited. One of the men put his pistol away and pulled something from a pocket. He worked the lock and suddenly the door was open and all four disappeared inside the vacant room.

They were out of sight for maybe five minutes when they reappeared in the dim light of the hotel lot. They seemed far more relaxed than when they had gone inside. They got back into their car and drove off.

I heard Lexie release her breathe. I did the same.

"Do you think we're safe here tonight," Lexie asked, concern etched in her face.

"Yes, I think we are," I said. "I don't think they know what I drive. They never even looked at my car. You know hotels like this, people park wherever they want, so my car being in front of that room doesn't mean anything to them. I think we're okay."

We relaxed as the minutes wore on, drinking beers and talking. This time it was books we'd read or movies we'd seen. Her personal favorite was 'My Own Private Idaho,' on film, and Tom Robbins' *Even Cowgirls Get The Blues*, in paperback. As I listened, I noted what a wonderful storyteller she was. She was incredibly honest, forthright and, in all the right places and ways, funny with a large touch of self-depreciating humor.

It was close to 1 a.m., the beer gone, when we climbed into bed. She dropped her towel and slide up against me; her warm naked skin sending ripples of excitement and passion through my mind, heart and loins. I desired her greatly. Yet, despite that deep desire, or maybe because of it, we continued our conversations in bed. Her head upon my chest, shoulder, we talked about our dreams, aspirations, expectations and disappointments of the lives we had lived and the lives we hoped to live moving forward.

She talked with great passion about the four years she lived with her grandmother in Bay Minette after her father had been murdered. You could feel the deep sadness, remorse as she spoke about her grandmother's death from cancer when Lexie was just 15 years old. Sent to live with her mother and stepfather, she ran away one week after her 16th birthday after the stepfather had tried to force himself upon her. She'd bounced around from friends, cousins and even two different lovers over the next nine years; living currently with an older man of 35, who she didn't love, but was grateful for his kindness. She'd moved between Louisiana, Alabama and Florida through the years before she had landed in the small trailer she shared in Samson, Alabama with Vincent Anders, technically-speaking, her current lover. She claimed that relationship was over. And I had no reason to doubt her.

It was sometime after 2, when we found each other. It was a simple caress of her hair during a lull in conversation that began our free fall into the flames of the other. An inspiring lover; her soft skin and body responding, again and again. Vocal, but not screechy or overly screaming like some phony porn star; her moans guttural, genuinely lifted from her lips as pleasure peaked, ebbed and returned to wash her soul again. Her eyes locking into mine; there seeming fawn shape and light purplish-hue pulling me deeper. Her hands were everywhere, kneading my flesh, pulling and urging.

We tossed and tossed in the flow of eroticism — at times, angry and hard; at others, soft and tender. The pace, the rhythm changing again and again as our chests touched and separated; her small, firm breasts pressing into me, while my masculine chest with its soft tangle of hair that ran between my nipples became matted in the sweat of love. The smell of her sex, sweet and carnal. I wanted to breathe her in, bottle her scent and never let the addiction I now had to it leave my blood. Until finally our bodies, filled with drink and sex, fell into a tangled mess in the destruction that was the sheets, comforter and pillows.

The alarm clock, which I had set for 8 a.m., found us much, much too soon. I woke in love.

CHAPTER 24

The morning sun set St. Andrew's Bay aflame in millions of sparkles, tiny starbursts; each twinkling, rising and falling on the soft rolling waves of the water. I smoked a cigarette on the small balcony while the tiny coffee pot brewed on the bathroom sink. Lexie rose and pulled up her panties, shorts and t-shirt and joined me for a smoke. A month earlier, one of the major cigarette companies had finally admitted what any smoker already knew, that cigarettes were addictive. It was akin to announcing water is wet, or the sun is hot.

Lexie and I jumped into the shower together and once more the nearness, and nakedness, of this woman filled me with longing. I took her as she gripped the shower curtain and the shower head; holding on tight to maintain her balance.

We dried and dressed. I choose one of the white dress shirts, and one of the black suits. The shirt was collarless, with tiny pearl buttons. In the pocket of the coat that went to the suit, I found a beautiful set of gold cuff links. I'd dusted down my boots, my only footwear option, pulled them on, and pulled the slacks down over the boots.

"You look very hot, babe," Lexie said with a smile.

"Let's find you something to wear," I said.

I had dialed a taxi cab company before jumping into the shower and told them to pick us up at 9:15. The driver, a man named, Roberto was a friendly, chatty sort. I handed him five-hundred dollars, "You never picked us up. Do you understand." He smiled and nodded and I knew we had our man.

Roberto took us to one of the women's clothing stores and Lexie picked out a beautiful pink sundress, black combat boots, thigh high stockings, and three matching sets of bras and panties.

"Can't decide on the underwear?"

"No, funny guy, just spending my inheritance," she replied with a wink.

I had Roberto drop us off at a Ford lot in Panama City, and gave him an extra hundred, mostly for insurance policy reasons.

"Welcome to Johnson Ford. We're dealing each and every day. Now, what can I have you drive home in today?" said the salesman named, Jack.

"That one right there," I said.

"Oh, now that is a man truck right there," Jack said, still trying to sell me. "The Ford 350 Dually is an American classic, like Coca-Cola and mommas."

"I'll give you $30,000 cash for it right now," I said.

"Yes, well, um, of course."

Within thirty minutes, paperwork signed, insurance company called, title's stamped, we had our new ride — a black Ford F350 Dually.

It was time to pay Rich a visit.

It took us a little over a half an hour to reach Pretty Bayou, and Rich's trailer park. I slowed down slightly as we passed Rich's trailer and it was obvious something was very wrong. The front door was pulled off the top hinge and there were various items strewn about the yard.

"What the fuck," Lexie said.

"Hang on. We're going around the block."

I drove down to the end of Rich's street, took a left, followed by another left to come up the street parallel to Rich's. I parked two doors down from the trailer that was located directly behind Rich's, pulled the Desert Eagle, checked the clip, and reloaded the gun.

"Stay here, okay? I am going to leave the keys with you. If you hear gunshots or whatever pull up to that trailer right there and I'll hop in. Cool?"

"As cool as it can be, I guess," she said. "Hang on."

Lexie leaned over and kissed me hard, her tongue darting over and around mine.

"For luck, right?"

"Sure, for luck," I replied with a smile.

I hopped from the cab and walked through the yard of one of Rich's unknown neighbors and came up on Rich's trailer through what amounted to his small backyard. The bedroom curtains to the master bedroom were drawn closed and I was unable to see in. I heard nothing coming from inside.

With one last look around the yard, I walked up to the front door and, gently as I could, and as silently, I pulled it open and stepped inside. The trailer was an absolute disaster. Items were broken, smashed and tossed in every direction. The sofa had been ripped open and most of the cabinet doors were missing, with the few remaining doors clinging to the frames. The guest bedroom, the one Jilly and I had had sex in just days earlier, was in equally bad shape. The mattress had been slashed open. Someone was looking for something. I had an odd feeling it was two million somethings.

I turned toward the master bedroom and noticed a woman's bare foot, first. Stepping into the room, Dallas lay naked on the bed, dead. A single bullet hole between her eyes. But it was obvious she had been badly beaten first and possibly raped. The handle of a toilet plunger was shoved into her ass. Her breasts looked like they had been repeatedly punched.

There was no sign of Rich. But this wasn't his doing. I could just feel it in my bones. Rich might have done a lot of things, might be a lot of things. This? No. This was something else. This was a very powerful message. I now wondered if Rich had received the message.

I backed out of the trailer, touching nothing, and walked back to the truck.

"Anything," Lexie asked, as I climbed into the cab.

"Yes," I said. I stared ahead, numb.

"What is it?"

"Rich's girlfriend, you might have seen her, I don't know. Her name was Dallas. She's been murdered. She's dead inside."

"Fucking hell, are you serious?"

"Yes. The place is torn to shit," I said. "Lexie, someone wants that money back and wants it very badly."

"I don't understand, though. Gabriel had the money. Not Rich," Lexie said.

"Yes, but maybe only Gabriel knew that."

"I'm not following you."

"I think Gabriel was thinking of collecting a nice bonus for whacking some southern kids. I mean, if someone thinks Roan and Rich took the money, and they send in a guy like a Gabriel to get it back ... what's to stop him from keeping the money and telling whoever sent him that he never found the cash."

"Where do you think Rich is?"

"I don't know. It's time to visit Tammy and Tom. They are mixed up in this somehow."

I knew where I was heading, but I needed to call Tilly first. Pulling into a Stop-N-Go, I removed his card from my wallet and dropped two quarters into the payphone.

"Detective Tilly here, how may I help you," Tilly's distinctive southern drawl came over the phone.

"Detective, Chaz Wilson."

"Where are you?"

"I can't answer that. How did Roan die?"

"I tell you what, you come down here to the station and I'll tell you all about it."

"I can't do that."

"Can't or just won't?"

"Does it really matter?"

"Yes, yes, it matters. I don't want to zip you into a body bag, son."

"Tilly," I started.

"Son, listen to me. Please listen. Okay? Roan was shot twice, but from two different guns. The coroner believes he took the first bullet to the head at some kind of a funny angle. We recovered no bullet from his head, but the coroner believes it was a .9mm of some kind. The second bullet, however, did the real damage. It was a .50 caliber. Powerful weapon. It hit him in the small of his back, ripped through his liver. Coroner believes your friend had jumped into the water, based on the amount of water in his lungs, and tried to swim to shore. It seems he made it, but then died on the shore. That is how your friend died."

I feel silent. Two guns.

"Now, do I have to tell you how you are going to die? Or, can I talk you into giving up this wild revenge trip you and your brother started?"

"Do you know the Knights Inn, off of West Beach?" I began.

"Yes."

"You'll find my Camaro in front of Room 143, with a passport in the front seat."

"Whose passport?"

"Call the Beach police and ask if they caught an unidentified male in a stairwell at the Ambassador Motel. That's all I can say. I have to go, talk to you later."

I hung up, climbed back into the Ford, and drove to Tammy's.

Four bikers sat around the fire pit in the front yard of Tammy and Tom's house in Pretty Bayou. It was way too early for a party and these four were hardly the festive, party sort. Each looked harder than metal and each held a sawed-off shotgun, or semi-automatic rifle in their laps. They were guarding the home. But for who and why?

I parked in the street across from the house.

"Stay here," I said. "If you have to, you get the fuck out of here."

"Yeah, well, that's not gonna happen, cowboy," Lexie said.

"You're the second person to call me cowboy at this very location," I said with a grin. "What the hell is it about this house."

"Maybe you remind people of Doc Holliday or something," Lexie said, grinning back.

"You're no Big-Nose Kate," I said. "Your nose is too small. Please, if you have to, get out of here. Okay?"

258

"I make no such promise," Lexie said, her face locked. There was no compromise, no negotiation to be had. Her eyes, as uncompromising as they were in this issue, held a deep love. This woman was in love with me. Madly, it seemed.

"Fine."

I climbed from the truck and began to walk up the driveway.

"Where you going, hoss," said one of the bikers.

"To see Tammy. Rich was my friend Roan's cousin," I said.

The front door opened. Tom stood in the frame with his bathrobe hung open, a pair of shorts, pale green t-shirt and flip-flops.

"It's okay boys," hollered Tom to the foursome of bikers. "I was waiting for him. C'mon up, Chaz."

I nodded at the bikers and walked into the house.

Tammy sat at the dining room table, dabbing tissues against her eyes and tear-stained face. She had a deep blue bruise under her right eye. Peter and Rodney, the bikers from the party held a week earlier, sat to either side of Tom, who had reclaimed his spot in his recliner. Rodney sat in a dining room chair he had pulled into the room, while Peter sat on the sofa to Tom's right.

"So, what brings you this way, Chaz? Nice suit by the way," Tom said.

"Thanks, took it from a guy I met in Panama City Beach."

"Nice guy to give you a suit like that."

"Where's Rich?"

Tammy started to speak, and then choked up in tears again. She sat weeping, wiping tears.

"Well, we have had a bit of a bad situation ourselves, Chaz," Tom said. "You know, blood is supposed to be thicker than water, you've heard that, right?"

"Yes, sir."

"Well, Chaz, ahhh, no need to beat around the bush. I run a nice operation, Chaz. Solid, solid business. And you know, I have been bringing Rich along as kind of a vice president of operations," Tom paused, lit a cigarette, and continued. "You try and do right by the one's you love, Chaz. I was paying Rich handsomely. I was. It was good pay, for good work. And, well, Rich was making friends. It seems he made friends with a friend of a close, close friend of mine. So, now there are two old friends who are hurting."

"Who own's The Grunge, Tom?"

"Don't be an impatient lad, Chaz. No one likes to be interrupted in the middle of a story."

"Yes, Chaz. Shut the fuck up," Peter said from the sofa.

I unbuttoned the jacket to reveal the Desert Eagle in my waistband.

Tom's eyes hardened, but Peter and Rodney both laughed.

"What the fuck?" Rodney started. "Dirty Fucking Harry is in the house."

"That gun is gonna get shoved up your lily, white —" Peter never got to finish those words.

I pulled the gun and fired once into his head. The force sent his body back hard against the sofa, while his brains and fragments of bone sprayed the wall behind him. Rodney, caught off guard, fumbled wildly for his pistol.

"Don't," I said as I crossed the distance between he and I. I got behind him as the front door exploded open and two bikers came racing in.

"Stop," Tom yelled, his hand raised. "Stop," he said, softer.

"Who owns The Grunge," I demanded again, the barrel of the Desert Eagle pressed hard into the back of Rodney's head.

Tom let out a sigh.

"There is a group of us. We hold a stake in that operation. It is not a club, per say. It is simply a bi-monthly event held in different locations," Tom said. "Mr. Wise, the one that you and your brother killed the other night? He's a fucking plastic surgeon. Queer as a three dollar bill. But he loves to beat the shit out of women. That's his thing. For a price, we get him his kick. Mr. Moffitt? I understand that he is dead as well, right? He was a fucking war hero. Can they say that about you, college boy? Dillon? I loaned him twenty thousand dollars to start that music shop, what, I think it was fifteen years ago. He came here, you know. Described you and your brother to a tee. He's at a hotel, scared shitless. I give your brother credit. I don't think I scared Dillon as much as your brother did. Hell, you can usually find the fucking location by picking up any swinger's magazine in one of the local smut shops. It's not that hard college boy."

I pulled the trigger and Rodney's head exploded across the carpet. I quickly aimed at Tom. The two bikers in the doorway were frozen. The one held a sawed-off shot gun, the other an M-16. It was serious firepower. Yet, they were unsure what to do next.

The next even caught me off guard.

Two pops, small but distinct, like Black Cats, came from the front yard. The pair turned toward the sound, I swung my gun and I squeezed off two rounds, one for each. They collapsed in a heap on the carpet, reddening with blood. The one nearest the door gasped, choked and finally went silent. The one nearest the hallway died on impact. The bullet tearing through his heart.

I brought the gun back to Tom.

"Where is Rich?"

Tom looked at the carnage in his living room and started to laugh.

"I should have hired you," he said.

"Where's Rich," I repeated.

"I don't know," Tom said. His eyes spoke it; it was the truth. Tammy wept softly behind me.

"That gun," he said, nodding at the Desert Eagle in my hand. "That gun belongs to Gabriel Vasquez. He is Vincente Escalardo's right hand man ... was. Was his right hand man. About four days before you got to town, it seems that Gabriel and Rich decided to make changes at the top of their respective organizations. It seems that Rich was going to take me out, and Gabriel was going to double cross Escalardo.

"I was bringing in a shipment of marijuana and this new speed the kids are all crazy about. They call it Ecstasy. It was a relatively small deal, this month. Two million dollars. Well, it would appear that Rich was going to keep the money, and Gabriel was going to keep the drugs. Gabriel, I assume, had another buyer, willing to pay more. And I have to assume that Rich was going to use my money to bankroll my death. I don't think he acted alone. And I still can't believe he would kill Roan, but at the same time, the death of Roan would have given him good cover to point the finger at Gabriel, while Gabriel could point the finger at Rich. In the meantime, Escalardo and I would have gone to war."

Tom reached slowly for another cigarette and his lighter. Tom exhaled a thick cloud of smoke and looked toward Tammy weeping in the dining room.

"I do believe I have been betrayed by mother and son," Tom said.

"Life's a bitch," I said as I squeezed off four rounds into Tom's gut and chest.

Tammy wailed and choked back vomit, once, before spewing across the dining room table. I pulled a chair, placed my gun on an unmarred part of the table and sat across from her. I let her cry for a solid minute. Lexie stepped into the house, gun drawn, and looked around carefully.

"You okay," she asked.

"I'm fine," I said. "What happened out there."

"The guy grabbed my ass," she said. "The other one was just too ugly."

I smiled at my pixie and turned back to Tammy.

"Where's Rich, Tammy," I said.

"My baby. My baby, they were gonna kill my baby," she sobbed. I stared at this woman. They were crocodile tears. "I needed to make changes, you have to understand. It was my time. It was my time. I wanted Rich to have something. Tom, he always talked down to Rich. But my baby is smart. He's very smart. I never wanted him to kill Roan. Ever. But I am sure Roan did something. He had to have fucked up or something and I bet Rich had no choice. You know Roan, Chaz, he was a smart ass and he probably talked back or something. Or opened his mouth or something. He had to have done something. My Rich is a smart boy. A very smart boy."

"Where's Rich? Don't make me ask again," I said coldly.

CHAPTER 25

The wind came at me from my left to right, and I was wedged into the deer stand between my grandpa and absolute darkness. The rain was thick and it was less falling and more simply hanging and clinging to everything. My clothes felt frozen and every time I needed to move my clothes made a soft crackling sound. We sat twenty feet in the air on the deer stand my grandpa had built on Dr. Milford's property about eight years earlier. The doctor owned about 500 acres adjacent to the Oconee National Forest and allowed my grandfather and his family and friends use whenever grandpa wanted. On this, the last Saturday in November, 1980, just two days after Thanksgiving, while grandpa and I occupied one tree stand, my father and Roan occupied another roughly two hundred yards to our east. Sage and Arlo were camped out in a third stand roughly two hundred yards to our west.

"Want some coffee, boy," my grandpa said, whisper quiet.

"Yes, sir," I replied.

I was thrilled to be in that stand and miserable all at once. It was my first hunt with my grandpa, and my father had begrudgingly agreed to allow Roan to come along. Grandpa claimed me, while Sage and Arlo buddied up, and that left Roan to sit, equally thrilled and miserable I am sure, in a tree stand with my father. Jack, then 18, was off at boot camp.

Grandpa had let me use his .264 Remington with the walnut stock. He'd branded a cross into the handle and had bought the gun in 1964 from a Sears and Roebuck catalog. Remington had extended the barrels that year by two inches on the weapon that Mike Walker and his engineers had created for the company in 1962. My father had mounted a scope onto the rifle sometime in the mid-1970s, much to my grandpa's frustration at the time, "My eyes are just fine. It's not my fault you can't hit shit." Which wasn't exactly true. My grandpa's eyes had been going bad for at least 10 years, and my father could hit anything he aimed at. It was one skill that seemingly passed through the paternal line.

Grandpa placed his 1903 Springfield 30-06 against the trunk of the tree, removed the thermos of coffee, and poured me some into the lid that doubled as a cup. I made sure the safety was locked on my gun, laid the gun across my lap, and took the coffee from him.

"It's cold as the fucking Ardennes out here," he said softly.

I choked on my coffee a little, still not used to hearing him use 'fuck,' in a sentence. Or anyone for that matter. At 11, I mostly heard the 'bad words,' as my mother called them, from my brothers, Jack and Sage. And once when Arlo and I were in a fist fight.

"You okay there boy?"

"Yes sir. What's the Ardennes?"

"Oh, these fucking awful woods in goddamn Europe. I spent the better part of a month in those cold ass trees, up to my nut sack in snow and ice. I was getting paid to kill Nazis at the time, so that was the only upside."

I sipped at my coffee and listened to the rain drip, drop and slap the trees, ground and the few leaves that still clung in late Autumn.

"What was it like, you know, killing somebody," I asked softly.

"I didn't kill any somebodies, Chaz. I killed Nazis. They're not human. I mean, hell, maybe they were once, but something changed them."

"What did they look like?"

"Oh, like you and me, I suppose. Noses, eyes, ears and assholes. Same as anyone. But the hearts. The hearts were different," he looked off into the trees and his eyes seemed to go faraway. "Chaz, there is a time when you have to pull a trigger. I can't tell you. You have to know it. It's no different than sitting out here. If a deer comes along, which I seriously doubt with all your questions and moving about, but if one comes along, perhaps a deaf one, well, you have to know when to pull the trigger.

"It was that way with Nazis. You don't see them the same way as you or me. Do you understand?"

I nodded my head.

My grandpa, Crawford Griffin Wilson was my hero. If he told me the sky was brown, then it was fucking brown and I'd have fought anyone who said differently than my grandpa. Grandpa had started taking my dad and at first just Jack into these trees since 1972 when Jack was 10. Eventually, they added Sage and Arlo to the trip scheduled for the first Saturday after Thanksgiving, each year. Grandpa had volunteered for World War II at the age of 24 after the Japanese bombed Pearl Harbor. He left behind his wife, my grandmother, and three children, including my father, who was just five years old when his father marched off to war. He made marksman and was soon a valuable sniper for the U.S. Army.

My father later followed in his father's footsteps and joined the Army. Jack had recently done the same. At 11, I was certain I would join the Army as well. I never did. Life and dreams shift in the sands of time.

I finished the hot coffee, handed him back the lid and picked up my gun. We sat for sometime, probably another hour in that dark, dreary chill, staring off at trees and waiting for the sun. I fidgeted as little as I could, but sitting still at 11 is a tall order for any boy. Boredom was worse than death, I imagined. At least death brings heaven. Hell must have created boredom.

Grandpa shifted, slightly, and coughed quietly into his gloves. It was then that I heard the faintest of sounds from the ground off to my left; the lightest touch of something on the ground.

I'd been allowed to start shooting real guns when I was eight. Prior to that, it was just shooting my BB gun at old cans and bottles. The first time I had shot a real rifle it kicked into my shoulder and left me with a nasty, purplish bruise that lingered for a week. But I learned. Now at 11, I knew what to do.

I slowly lifted the rifle, pulled it against my right shoulder, and turned the safety off. I looked through the scope my dad had mounted and searched the area where the sound had come from.

My grandfather sat still, saying nothing.

There. I had it. I gently squeezed the trigger. The sound was deafening in what had been nearly two hours of silence, save the rain.

"Damn, did you see something, boy," my grandpa said.

"Yes sir. Buck right through there," I said pointing.

"Did you hit it?"

"Yes."

We climbed down from the tree. By the time we reached the ground (grandpa had insisted on climbing down first, and took his time about it), my dad and Roan were yelling out from our right. "Coming in!" I heard my dad call out.

They met us at the base of the tree, the four wet, cold hunters walked out in the direction of my shot, some 75 feet from our starting point we found him.

I would never again kill one as beautiful, as majestic, as that first one. He was an 8-point buck and a beauty. My dad let out a whistle. My grandpa clamped his hand down on my shoulder and said, "that was a damn fine shot, Chaz."

I had caught the buck in right eye, and the bullet exited underneath his left ear. Straight through the brain.

I would spend the next eight years on the last Saturday in November in those very same woods. In the same tree stand. And over those nine total hunts, I would take 16 deer. None were ever as special as the first. None would ever be as impressive in my mind, or my recollection as that first.

It was in that tree stand in 1987 that Roan and I became friends again after a falling out in June, '87.

We had graduated on June 7, on a blistering hot day. That night we would gather at Sarah Peters' parent's lake house for a blow out keg party. The beer probably played a role in our fight that night.

"Hey, Chaz," Roan hollered at me over the noise. "Deck?"

"Sure, meet you out there," I yelled back. I pulled myself from the sofa and squeezed between the bodies on my way to the hall. The hall was as packed as the living room. Taking a breathe, I shoved past the mix of teens gathered at the Peters' lake house. It was sometime past one in the morning and the outdoor temperature hovered around 85 degrees. The air was thick and heavy. I walked to one of the fifteen kegs placed around the house, yard and refilled my plastic cup and looked for Roan.

The deck like the house was packed. I didn't see Roan anywhere. Then I heard his voice calling me from the backyard and saw his hand wave in the air. Some idiots had actually started a fire. It had to be for the light and not the warmth.

I made my way across the grass, snagged an empty lawn chair and parked next to Roan and Andrea Miller. Andrea was from Putnam High, Class of 85. The now 19-year old was back in town to celebrate with her younger sister, Kimberly, who had also graduated from Putnam on June 5th. Putnam was less a rival high school and simply the closest one to Alexander Central. Often, kids from both schools partied together, slept together and swapped drugs together. Andrea was looking very good in a miniskirt, tank top and nothing else. She had painted her exposed toe nails bright red and her dainty bare feet were propped up in Roan's lap. Her pussy flashed again and again as she shifted and moved. Her skirt barely covering her panty-less ass.

Roan was holding court.

"So, I walked into Sanderson's class, now I'm like fucking 20 minutes late, my hair looks like shit ..."

"Your hair always looks like shit," I tossed at him.

"Fuck you. So I go stumbling in, now it's like the last fucking time I am ever gonna see that asshole, and he is like, no joke, he is like, 'Um, Mr. Bishop, do you or no one in your family own a clock or a watch?' and I'm all like, 'Um, Mr. Sanderson, my nuts were itchy something awful. Have you had your mom checked for crabs?'"

The gathered crowd of twenty to thirty teens, all enthralled by this semi-fictional story, burst into peels of laughter. I smiled at Roan, and then at Andrea, who winked playfully at me.

Jilly came up behind me and threw her arms around my shoulders, kissed my face and then playfully bite my ear.

"I thought it was Chaz who was fucking Sanderson's mom," Jilly asked, jokingly.

"No, babe. That's your mom I'm fucking. She gives better blowjobs," I jabbed back.

She smacked my head, playfully but hard.

"Yeah, you wish," Jilly said.

"I'll give you a really great blowjob, Chaz," Andrea said. She was not joking. "I've always wanted to see this cock of yours that has Jilly chasing you around like a puppy."

"You got a problem with me, bitch?" Jilly started. "Cause, I can kick your cunt up to your ears. Make it easier for guys to find. Oh, wait! They don't have problems finding your cunt, cause it is constantly on display."

Andrea tossed her barefeet to the grass and Roan grabbed her arm before she could get any closer to Jilly. I sat back. I wanted to watch Jilly kick her ass.

"I'll knock your little bitch head off," Andrea screamed angrily.

Someone yelled, "cat fight," and suddenly the crowd seemed to double.

It wasn't really fair, looking back in hindsight. Roan had hold of Andrea's arms and Jilly took full advantage of Andrea's disadvantage and punched her square in the mouth. A real punch. No girl slap. No hair pulling. No swinging wildly. Jilly reared back and threw the straight punch into Andrea's upper lip. Her lip spewed forth in a crimson mix of blood and saliva. Which was soon joined by tears.

"Open that fucking mouth again, cunt," Jilly yelled at her, with her fists balled.

"What the fuck, Chaz," Roan yelled at me. "Get your bitch in line already. Fuck."

I'd started drinking at roughly eight that morning and by the time graduation began at 1 p.m., I was rolling drunk. I threw up into a trash can on the way out of the gym, as did several guys, who'd all been drinking most of the morning. The drinking continued that afternoon and into the night. And hearing Roan call Jilly a bitch set me off. Maybe it was the crowd. Maybe it was Andrea looking at me. Maybe it was just the many maybes all piled on top of one another.

I sprung from the chair and tackled Roan into the grass. It was not my intention to hurt him. But I was going to punch him a couple of times and let it go. I threw two quick jabs at his ribs, rolled over and stood up.

"You don't call her a bitch," I said and started to walk away.

Suddenly, I was on my face in the grass. Roan threw a series of punches into the back of my head. I was able to spin him off of me and throwing a left, caught him just under the chin. I didn't have much on the punch, but it was enough to shake him and it gave me more time to get out from underneath him. His leverage now gone, I rolled to my knees and threw two rights; one into his ear and the second to his temple. The second one was hard. It split the skin to the left of his eye and eyebrow.

"Fuck," he said as he rolled into the grass in obvious pain.

And like that, it was over. I felt bad. Guilty, for hitting him so hard.

"You okay?"

"Fuck off," he said pushing my hand away. "Goddamn. Fuck."

He stood up and snatched a towel someone had handed him to hold against his wounded eye.

271

"Fuck off," he repeated to me and everyone else and he walked away. Andrea, feeling alone and outnumbered, took off after him.

It was two weeks before I saw him again. And even then he refused to speak to me. It wasn't until August that I was able to get him to take my phone call; the week we were both heading to UGA and Athens. We had agreed back in April or May to help each other move and now I wanted to make him keep that promise. I thought it would be our best chance to talk. We talked very little.

It wasn't until Thanksgiving break and a chance meeting on a Monday before Thanksgiving that we began the process to heal the battered friendship.

I'd been sent to the Alexander Post Office by my mom to take a stack of cards she was mailing out for some various relatives with upcoming December birthdays, when I saw Roan emerging from the Army recruiting station next door.

"Roan! Roan," I yelled at him.

He waved and strolled over.

"What you doing man," he asked casually.

"Taking this stuff to the post office for mom," I said. "What are you doing?" I had nodded toward the Army office and he looked back over his shoulder, ran his hand over his hair and looked for an answer.

"Um, exploring options," he said with a bit of a forced laugh.

"What's that mean?"

"Oh, I don't know," he said.

"Everything okay," I asked.

"Yeah, man. Georgia peachy, ya know."

There was a pause in the conversation. Then it hit me.

"Hey, go hunting with me Saturday," I said.

"Um, yeah, okay. I guess so," he said.

That Saturday morning I picked him up at his dad's house at three in the morning. We drove almost an hour to the spot my grandpa had used so often. In November, '87, my grandpa was battling a cold and decided he wasn't going. My father also bowed out, but for no disclosed reason. That left Roan and I alone in the woods for the next five hours.

We hadn't been in the tree stand 20 minutes when I caught the first deer, a doe, through the shoulder. We moved west and an hour later I shot the last deer I was to ever shoot in those woods. A four point buck.

We dragged both deer back to the truck I had borrowed from my grandfather, heaved them into the back and set out for one last trip to sit in the trees. We picked the far eastern stand my grandpa had constructed many years earlier.

For most of the walk into the woods our conversations had centered on deer, UGA football and a wide range of other useless bullshit. This was going to be my last chance to talk about something meaningful and I took it.

"Roan, I am sorry," I said.

"You're gonna spook the deer," he whispered.

"No, man. I am so sorry," I said. "I want to say I was fucked up and drunk and whatever. Truth is I am sorry. Period."

"Can we talk about something else," he said staring into the trees.

"Okay, sure," I said. "Why were you in the Army recruiting station the other day?"

Roan took a deep breathe and let out a sigh.

"I'm failing. Big time," he said. "No surprise, I know. Just Roan fucking up again, so par for the fucking course of my life."

I didn't know what to say and Roan, surprisingly, filled the air and silence all around us.

"You know, that night, I still ended up fucking Andrea," he stated. "I did. I fucked her. She even let me fuck her in the ass. Can you believe that shit? No joke. Never done that before. And the whole time ... I was thinking about how much I hated you. And how you didn't deserve that. You are just you. You are the great Chaz Wilson.

"You want an A, you go get an A. You want to hit a home run, you hit a home run. You want the best looking girl in the whole school, hell, you got her long before she was the best looking girl in school. You are like a blessed son of a bitch and you are as oblivious to that blessing as any one could possibly be.

"I couldn't get a girl like a Jilly in a thousand years."

"What the fuck are you talking about? You just fucked Andrea Miller," I said.

"Yes, and who in a four county area hasn't?"

"I never fucked her."

"You have Jilly. Why would you? Jesus, Chaz, she let me fuck her in the ass not two hours after sitting in my lap for the first time. Not exactly a 'bring home to momma' kind of chick, ya know?"

"She's a sexual young woman. That's not something I would think you would mind," I said with a hint of a smile. I wanted to make a joke, but I could tell Roan was on edge.

"You have a great family, Chaz. Seriously, a great family. I mean, goddamn, you have walking legends for brothers in Jack and Sage. I don't know what is wrong with Arlo."

"No one does," I laughed.

"But your mom and dad are the best. My parents? I was like a breathing footnote in their marriage. I was there for official reasons or something. And I'm gonna say something else to you. That night, you know, I was feeling good. For the first time, I was feeling like the guy everyone wanted to see. I had Andrea in my lap ... it wasn't about you and Jilly for once. And, this is gonna piss you off, but I'm gonna say it any way. You will lose her someday, Chaz. Because deep down, you don't love her. You're not in love with her. And you will tell yourself you are. But you have simply had her. She has been your buddy, your sister, your girlfriend, your lover and she has filled up your time. But you don't want her.

"And the crazy thing is, I'd give my nuts for a girl like Jilly. You have her and she is just an accessory to who you are, man."

I stared into the trees. I didn't have any answer. And ten years later, staring at Roan's aunt across a vomit-stained dining room table, I still didn't have an answer. But I wanted something else answered.

"Tammy, look at me," I said. She stared up, her face bruised from whoever had punched her, tear-stained from perhaps hours of crying, and swollen from the emotional turmoil of it all. "Tell me where Rich went."

"I gave him five thousand dollars," she started. Her voice seemingly cracked, her throat probably raw. "I told him to go west, into Texas."

"Where is he?"

She looked at me, really looked. My eyes hard, cold. I felt like violence, pure and full.

"He called me from Lake Lorraine last night. That's how I got this," she said pointing at her eye. Then she pointed at the corpse of Tom Duncan. "I wasn't gonna tell that motherfucker a damn thing."

"Tammy, did you know Rich killed Roan?"

"Yes, well, he was supposed to kill him. He shot him in the head, he said. But Roan jumped overboard and started to swim toward shore. Gabriel shot him while he was swimming," Tammy said. "That's what Rich told me. That's what he said. We didn't want it this way, but I needed it to look like Rich was innocent. At least until we had everything in place to take care of Tom."

"Thank you, Tammy."

I picked up the gun and shot her once in the head.

"Fuck," Lexie said. "Can you maybe warn a person before you go killing people?"

"C'mon, we have to get to Lake Lorraine," I said.

"How are we going to find him?"

"I have a pretty good idea of where he went," I said. "I'll explain on the way."

CHAPTER 26

Rich's first stepfather, John White had moved Rich and Tammy to Lake Lorraine in 1968 when Rich was just a little over a year old. John had taken the job with Arizona Chemical in Panama City and the trio went to stay with John's older brother, Charles in Lake Lorraine until they could purchase their own home or trailer. Charles White had become a father figure to Rich over the years until John's death in 1979. Tammy bounced in and out of a series of relationships, but Charles tried to maintain contact with the little boy he had come to love as one of his own. When Tammy moved into the home of Tom Duncan in 1989, as Rich turned 22, the relationship went sour. Rich had passed the age of needing a mentor and instead gravitated towards Tom. But if Rich was in a jam, which he surely was, and Tammy said he'd gone to Lake Lorraine, then that left perhaps one person in the world Rich might turn to for help. Charles White.

As badly as I wanted to reach Rich in Lake Lorraine before he moved further west and possibly disappeared into Texas or further, I knew I had to see my brother at the hospital. Even if that meant fending off my mother, father and seeing Jilly. My heart was set now, and no matter what happened over the next 48 hours, I was going to spend the rest of my life and time with Lexie.

We left Tom's house and I drove to the Gulf Coast Medical Center where Sage was clinging to life; comatose and battling infections. I parked across the street from the hospital in the Walmart parking lot, knowing the truck would be well disguised in the economic capital that moved the engine of southern retail. Lexie and I held hands until we got to the hospital's entrance foyer. I had put the Desert Eagle in my waistband, against the small of my back, so that it was covered by the jacket I had lifted from Gabriel.

"Can you stay here," I asked of Lexie.

"Of course," she said. "If you think it is best. I can hang back."

I took the elevator up to the ICU and walked to Sage's room. Jilly sat in a chair in the hallway. Her eyes, soft focused and faraway, seemingly staring at some patch of paint on the wall opposite. Her legs looked tan extending from her chocolate brown shorts to the pink flats on her feet. She was again wearing the Rolling Stones t-shirt I had given her years earlier. Her hand went into her pocket and she pulled a ring. I knew it on sight. It was my class ring. I'd given it to her in 1987. For 10 years she had hung onto the ring as some kind of promise ring or perhaps token of an engagement ring that I'd never purchased. She spun the ring through her fingers twice and held it out to me.

"This is yours," she said softly.

Saying nothing, I took the ring from her outstretched hand.

"I'm flying home," she said. "Kaelyn and Patrick left out this morning for Texas. Sarah and Reggie are leaving in the morning."

"Did they release Roan's body to the Bishops yet?"

"They are supposed to do that later today," Jilly said. "The plan is to fly Roan's body out of Tallahassee in the morning. They are going to hold a funeral at Alexander Methodist on Tuesday morning. Will you be there?"

"I seriously doubt it."

Jilly looked up at me, fury in her face.

"What happened to you, Chaz," Jilly asked, her voice icy and unconcerned with an answer. "What did I do to you?"

"Nothing, Jilly. You never did anything wrong," I said softly. "But we are two small town kids, who were always the biggest fish in our small pond. I want ... I want different water to swim in. I've not been happy, truly happy, my whole life. I move along, Jilly. I go along. I live in the shadows of everything my brothers ever did. The good and the bad."

I leaned back against the wall opposite her.

"I look at you, and see so many beautiful memories, so many beautiful moments. And you cast a large shadow. You are everything I have ever known about love. You taught it to me. You taught me to love. To care. To want. To desire. And I see you and I see this amazing woman. This incredible woman. And I want you to have children and know that kind of love. And I want you to find a man that can give you the house you desire. The vacations, the Christmas mornings, and the Thanksgiving dinners.

"I want you to have a hundred years of smiles and hugs and more memories. And I want to be one of those memories. But I can't be that guy for you. I can't be him."

Jilly wiped tears from her face.

"You remain the biggest dumbass I have ever known," Jilly said softly. "I'll never understand why I am not good enough for you. What mistake I made with you. But I am not going to spend the rest of my life asking myself those questions. I'm not. I'm not waiting on you. I've waited long enough. I'm flying out at 1 p.m., from Tallahassee, and I may be a bigger dumbass than you, but I bought two tickets. So, this is it; my final last ditch attempt to win you. Meet me at the airport and fly home with me and I'll give you one last chance. If you don't show up, then I'll know. And Chaz, if you don't show up ... I never want to see you again. Ever."

"Okay," I said quietly.

I shoved off the wall and walked to the door leading to Sage's room. I looked back over my shoulder at Jilly, who stared at the floor. I said nothing; there was nothing to say.

I opened the door, walked in and found my mother, father and Arlo sitting around Sage in the small room.

Arlo rose, while my parents stared at me. I waved, casually, like a kid whose parents had just seen his poor report card and I had just returned from playing in the yard. I knew I was in trouble. My parents looked like they could chew nails and spit out an airplane. My father's infamous neck vein seemed to grow two sizes larger than I'd ever seen.

"Let's go talk," Arlo said, taking my elbow and spinning me back towards the door, hall.

We stepped back into the hallway, and Jilly had vanished into thin air. Arlo pulled the door behind him and hugged me.

"Are you okay," he asked. Arlo's eyes were the bluest of the three of us that had our mother's blue eyes; a rich blue. His curly blondish locks hung past his shoulders and he was growing what looked like peach fuzz across his face. He was about an inch taller than me, but easily twenty pounds lighter. Maybe thirty. His chin still held the scar that Sage had accidentally given him when he was seven; a toy car that flew from Sage's hand and caught Arlo just right. The scar gave Arlo just a touch of mystery and in the years to come it would give him an added dignified touch. He stood now in Nikes, blue jeans and U2 t-shirt, with the Joshua Tree album cover printed on the front.

"I'm fine," I said.

"Jilly said you and Sage rescued these sex slaves or something from drug dealers," Arlo said. "The newspaper and TV stations have been trying to speak with you. Dad told some guy from the CBS news to fuck off," Arlo and I both chuckled at that before he continued.

"Look, two FBI guys came here about an hour ago. They told dad they need to speak with you today or they are going to issue a warrant for your arrest or something," Arlo said. "Are you in trouble with these drug dealers or something?"

"No, I have that problem pretty much handled," I said, I thought of the collection of bodies back at Tom and Tammy's house and wondered if that had been discovered or reported yet. "I'm going to Lake Lorraine and it is very important you tell no one that, okay. You need to know only for an absolute emergency."

"Of course, man," Arlo said. "Is there anything else you need?"

"Mom and dad pissed?"

"Oh, yeah," Arlo said. "I think dad is wondering if he can still whip your ass, legally."

"Just tell him ..." I started, tell him what? "Tell him I am killing Nazis. He'll understand that."

"Nazis? What the fuck," Arlo said.

"Don't worry," I said. "He'll know what it means. Sage?"

"Doctors think he's gonna make it," Arlo said. "He's fighting off the infection and they think he could come out of the coma at any time."

"If he does. No, when he wakes up tell him that I got the guys who killed Roan," I said. "Make sure he knows that, okay?"

"Sure, man," Arlo said. "Chaz, I love you, little brother. Be safe."

"I love you, too," I said.

I turned and headed for the elevators. I had an almost two hour ride in front of me.

I took the 30A around the outskirts of Panama City Beach until the road ended into US 98 West/FL 30. Lexie sat quietly in the passenger seat, smoking and staring off at the white sands, palms and blue water that seemed to surround. The once vast stretch of lonely road had been filling with luxury condos and four-star hotels, mixed in with the occasional playhouse for those of America's upper crust. In ten years, perhaps less, this area would be forever commercialized and over-populated. It had been the emptiness that had once drawn so many. The isolation and freedom that came from that isolation. It was being packaged and sold in bundles. Like everything in America, it was all for sale. The Clinton years were making a lot of people very rich.

"Is everything okay," I finally said to Lexie, sensing her silence was an uneasy one.

"I talked to her," she said. "Jilly. She came through the lobby and walked right up to me."

"Oh, god. I'm sorry," I said.

"I'm not," Lexie said. "It was a good talk."

I sat perplexed by that.

"What did she say to you?"

Lexie took a deep breathe. She reached into the console that separated the two front seats, pulled a cigarette, lit it and turned to face me in her seat. Her legs tucked underneath her.

"That she has been in love with you and only you since she was eight years old," she said. "And that if I break your heart, she plans on killing me and feeding me to pigs."

That sounded like Jilly.

"And," Lexie continued. "That she is not done with you yet. That I can borrow you, but that she'll have you back."

"I'm sure that she is hurting," I said.

"I have no reason to doubt her," Lexie said.

"Why do you say that?"

"Just a woman's intuition, I think," Lexie said, spinning back to sit forward, she turned her head to the passenger window. Her body language suggesting, strongly, that the conversation was at an end.

We arrived in Lake Lorraine in the late afternoon of a crystal blue day along the Gulf Coast. I found a phone booth with a phone book on a chain and ripped out the page with Charles White listed on Rocket Lane, off of 4th Street. Lake Lorraine was laid out in square blocks with Avenues running east to west, while Streets ran north to south. It didn't take me long to find Charles' trailer. Rich's Nova sat in the driveway.

I parked at the end of the block, checked the Desert Eagle, while Lexie checked her .38.

"Alright, let's finish this," I said to her.

"Sounds good, Doc," she said with a wink.

We walked up the street towards Charles' trailer. Two dogs barked, chained in one of the yards, while a third dog, a large black one, looked up from a shady, grass patch he laid on, blinked twice and put his head back down on his front paws.

Two large, black SUVs passed by Rocket Lane and for a second I froze, fearful that I had been followed by the FBI. The SUVs didn't give any sign of slowing or turning. We walked on.

Charles' trailer was on Lot 3. A white, rusted single wide with a large bay window at the end facing the street. I drew my gun, walked to the front door and knocked.

Charles, now in his late 60s, with a large belly hanging over his sweat pants, opened the door.

"What do you want," he asked, gruffly.

"I'm here to see Rich."

"Well, you can go fuck yourself," Charles said.

I raised the gun to his head.

"Charles, I have come a long way," I said. "Move."

Charles backed slowly into the trailer, and I kept the gun trained against his forehead.

Rich sat to my left, at the kitchen table, with a Bushmaster AR-15. He held the weapon, pointing at the ceiling, and a cigarette burned at his lip. Like our first meeting a week earlier at his trailer in Panama City, he wore only his boxer shorts.

"Well, college boy, I give you an A-plus," Rich said.

I walked Charles back with my gun until he sat in the chair opposite of Rich; I kept my gun on Charles' head, knowing Rich would think twice about firing.

"Do you know this gun," I asked, lifting my hand from the grip just enough for him to make out the inscription on the handle — "O Coração de um Guerreiro."

"That's Gabriel's gun," Rich said, evenly. "Do you know what that says, college boy?"

"No, I don't speak Portuguese."

"Yeah, I don't either," Rich said. "But it says, 'the heart of a warrior.' You got one of those, college boy?"

"I don't know."

"Yes, seems for a college boy that there is an awful lot you don't fucking know."

"I know that Gabriel was dead in a stairwell. I know that," I started. "I know Tom Duncan shit himself when I shot him four times in the gut and chest. I know that. I know there are six bikers that will never again ride. Or breathe for that matter. I know that. I know that I thanked your mom for telling me the truth about you two pieces of shit working together to kill your fucking cousin, you motherfucker. I know that."

I reached into my jacket pocket with my free left hand and pulled the stack of Polaroids of the young, naked women and tossed them on the table.

"I know that Escalardo's Cartel is going to have a hard time kidnapping and raping young women when I am finished. That I fucking know."

"Yeah, yeah, college boy," Rich said. "What else you know."

"I know your mom's brains were every bit as small as I imagined when I blew her fucking head off."

Rich's eyes squeezed tight; fury, rage and grief smashing into him all at once.

Suddenly, the two, large black SUVs screamed into the grass between Lot 1 and Lot 3. Eight Mexican men leapt from the vehicle, all holding automatic M-16 rifles.

"Get down," I screamed at Lexie as I dove for the floor.

The bullets tore through the flimsy metal walls of the trailer. Bullets tore into everything. Miniature explosions as dishes, cups, glass, wooden cabinets, furniture and picture frames were ripped to shreds. The shooting lasting what seemed an eternity, I held my arms over my head, facing an ugly, old sofa with red and black plaid upholstery covering its wooden frame. It was my only protection, as fleeting and pale as it was.

The shooting stopped, and I heard commands shouted in Spanish before the eight men and two SUVs screamed out of the grass and turned up the street, making their escape.

I stood and looked at Rich's bullet-riddled body. He was still sitting, with the Bushmaster now laid at his feet. Charles White had caught two bullets in the head and was slumped over at an odd angle to the table and floor.

I spun to find Lexie.

I found her eyes. So beautiful and blue. A smile crossed her face, she sat in a recliner positioned near the bay window. Her eyes fell to her chest, and my eyes followed. A single bullet hole was in the middle of her chest between her breasts.

"Fuck," I said. "Fuck. Goddamn. Fuck, goddamn. Hang on."

I raced into the kitchen and grabbed the first towel I could find. Racing back into the living room, I put the towel over the wound. I lifted her gently from the chair and laid her on the floor. My mind raced.

"You hang on. You hear me, you hang on," I said, tears falling.

"Well, Doc," she said coughing. "I don't think that went as planned."

"Fuck, you hang on, Lexie," I wept and my words came wrapped in spittle; it was my fury, rage and grief exploding. I had nothing but pure rage to live on, breathe on.

"Chaz, sweetie, listen to me, now," she said. "You go find her. You hear me? You go get her and tell her I said that she deserves you more. You hear me?"

"No, no, Lexie, look this isn't that bad, baby," I said. I pressed down on the wound. Blood was spreading on the thin old, blueish carpet. The bullet had exited from her back. I need to roll her over, I think.

"Baby, listen, you're gonna make it," I started.

Her eyes fixed. I'd seen that look at 11, standing over an 8-point buck in the cold, miserable November rain of north Georgia. I'd seen it again and again this week. It is a doll's eyes; lifeless and unblinking.

Lexie faded into eternity. She was gone.

CHAPTER 27

I am staring at my old boots, sitting in the Tallahassee Regional Airport. There are three specks of blood on the right boot, and one larger blotch of blood on the left. Everything about me is numb, scared and brittle to the bone. I have a plan, I tell myself for what seems the millionth time in the last hour. I have a plan.

Her eyes.

The cold tile of the airport had been freshly waxed and cleaned over night; the light bounces now and images reflect, mirror-like, as people pass to and fro. Flights to catch, flights and friends to receive. It is Saturday in someone's world. Maybe, it just is Saturday. The ballet of life.

Her eyes.

The sun is over my shoulder now, the tall windows reaching from floor to ceiling and light, brilliant sunlight, washing in. The endless blue skies of Florida stretch inside those windows; it is a surreal painting to a walking deadman now. I've lost track of any real sense of time. It was day. It is day. That is as close as I will get to the real time. I need words.

Her eyes.

I am sorry, Lexie. How fucking pale is that? I am sorry. I can offer nothing more. I need to believe that dead Nazis are worth it. What is the line between what is fought for in the name of good or righteousness, and that which is fought from the myriad of grays that evil occupies? At some point, is the violence expelled against fighting the Nazis of the world, corrupting? Does it, did it, seep into my soul?

Her eyes.

"I didn't expect you," Jilly said. She stands to my right, her suitcases pulled behind her on a cart.

"Do you, um, do you still want me," I ask.

"I've never not wanted you," she looks at me and sits down, one chair over. "And I don't know what that says about me."

"There are somethings that you have to know. Things that have to be said," I begin. "Then, you have a choice to make. I can't make this one for you. Do you understand me?"

Jilly nodded.

"I, um, I don't even know where to begin this. I, um, called Edward this morning and resigned. I told him I was unable to come back to work. And, of course, he's a little pissed off at me, but I think he's gonna have to get in line behind my mom and dad, and you, and probably the FBI. So, yeah, I quit my job. I am going to do somethings that you have to understand. And I have done a lot of things already that I don't know if I'll ever be able to explain to you.

"When I was kid, you remember, I thought about joining the Army. You remember, that? I think somewhere in me, I always wanted to feel like I had served something beside myself. Been something larger than just another guy bouncing around from girls and drinks and parties. And the funny thing, I have gone twenty years with the greatest girl in the world on my arm and I never once felt like I deserved you. I always felt like you deserved far, far better than me. That you were settling for me, and I couldn't be sure why you would settle."

"You're such a dumbass," Jilly said with a laugh.

"Let me finish," I said softly.

"Yes, go ahead."

"I have done things to chase you away and every time, you have stuck by me and I couldn't really understand it. I couldn't grasp what you saw in me. What I had that you thought was so special. And in that, in that doubt, I began to wonder. I questioned, what if one day, she sees how un-special, how unremarkable I really am. What if this woman wakes up at thirty-five or forty-five and wonders why she wasted thirty, forty years on this ridiculous guy. And I thought, what if it doesn't take that long. So, every year, for like the last ten, twelve years, I have waited for that. I have kept you at arm's length convinced that you would just walk out the door and I would be crushed. Destroyed. Unable to go on. I couldn't lose you that way and was willing to push you as far away as possible to keep you from ever leaving me broken."

Jilly, turning towards the wall of lockers on the far side of the terminal, took a breathe, pushed her hair past her ears and turned back to me. There was the tiniest of tears in her left eye.

"Do you remember that May day when we were juniors, what, seventeen I think, and we took off for Monteagle, Tennessee? Do you remember that?"

"Yes, I remember. It was a beautiful day. Just the deepest blue sky. We both kept talking about how blue the sky was."

"Yes, exactly. We were so cool skipping school, right? Remember that little area we parked on and we stood and looked over the Tennessee valley and you told me that if we got on the highway we could drive all the way to California? Do you remember?"

"Yes, I do. I was kinda hoping you were going to say, let's go."

"I did. In my heart, I did. I told myself that I will go in whatever direction he points the car. I left it up to you to decide. If you had flown off that fucking mountain, I would have followed you. If you had driven to California, I would have ridden with you. You have been the love of my life. And you deserve me, more than you can even understand. You deserve me, because I deserve you."

Tears went spilling down my cheeks.

"Lexie is dead," the words barely above a breathe; it hurts to hear them in my ears.

"Jesus Fucking Christ, Chaz, are you fucking serious," Jilly's face was pure shock.

"I know who did it, and well, there is more," I said. "Rich and Tammy set Roan up. They killed him. It was all part of some bigger plan they had to take over the drug and sex business that Tom Duncan was running."

"Are you fucking kidding me?"

"No, I wish I was. Really, I keep thinking about how incredibly small and stupid Tammy and Rich had to be to kill Roan. And the reasoning behind it all, if there was any."

"Where's Rich and Tammy?"

"Dead," I said. "And here is where you are going to have to make a decision. Because this time, you can't just get in the car and ride with me in whatever direction I choose to go. I have to hear it from your lips that you want to go in the same direction."

"Okay."

"In that locker over there, I have one point nine million dollars. I have an airplane pilot who is willing to fly us to Rio de

Janeiro within the hour. It's gonna cost us fifty-thousand dollars, but Brazil has no extradition treaty with America. The American dollar is strong there and we can start over. Just you and I," I had laid it all out. Everything.

Jilly plucked at the lint on her skirt, found a stray thread and tugged it off.

"I cried myself to sleep last night," she said matter-of-factly, with no plea or need for sympathy. And she wasn't on the hunt for an apology. She simply wanted it known. "I cried for a lot of reasons. A lot. But the biggest fear I had was two-fold and it was in my mind all night long. One, what if he gets himself killed? And you know what really pissed me off the most? Was that you might get killed over Roan of all people. I know what that sounds like, and how cold and mean that sounds, but I don't care. I didn't want you dead over him.

"And two, what if you don't show up here today? I was actually more scared of the second one. Mostly because when I saw your face at the hospital, I kind of felt sorry for the people that had killed Roan. Because I knew you wouldn't stop going after them until they were dead or you were. It was your baseball face all over again. You get this fixed, determination on your face. It's probably the thing that I love about you the most. Seriously.

"So, when I walked up to you just now and you were sitting here, I was prepared to follow you into hell."

Moving into the chair that separated us and taking her face in both hands, I pulled her lips to mine. Our foreheads came to rest, one on the other.

"Now, I have one condition and it is absolutely non-negotiable. Do you understand 'non-negotiable,' dumbass?" She said wiping soft tears of her own from her eyes.

"Yes."

"When we get to Rio, you marry me on the beach," she said. "And don't tell me you can't afford it, cause I already know how much money you have."

"Yes, yes. I will."

"You will? Don't you have a question to ask me first?"

I climbed down to one knee, put my hands on her knees, and stared into the same eyes that hid with me in a fir tree eighteen years ago.

"Jilly, will you marry me?"

"I'll think about it on the flight to Rio," she said. "But, I'll say yes now, so you don't have to sweat it too bad."

"We have one last thing to do before the flight. Come with me?"

"Yes, of course."

We checked her bags with the pilot, William Clanton and climbed into my new Ford 350 Dually that I was going to leave behind in Tallahassee for the drive over to the Tallahassee Democrat. It was a classy looking building from the outside. Grecian columns ran along the outside of the stoic brick building.

I asked for the reporter on duty, who it turned out was a young kid named, Billy Thurman. He'd graduated from Auburn, but I wasn't gonna hold that against him. I told him a part of my story and told him to call his editor. It took about thirty minutes for the Executive Editor, Malcolm Henderson and Executive News Editor, Pete Willis to show up. The three reps of the Democrat sat on one side of a long Mahogany conference table, while Jilly and I took up two seats across.

I tossed the Polaroid pictures on the table and the three men looked them over, long and hard. Disgust passing both the faces of Henderson and Willis as they saw the obvious condition of the women, especially the younger ones, who were probably no more than 13 years of age.

"Okay, okay," said Henderson. "What do want from us?"

"I'm gonna tell you a story."

Six months later

It is Spring now. The Brazilian winter over, and behind us. Both seasons and time move differently south of the Equator. The people are different as well. Every bit as industrious, hard-working, and dedicated to family as those Jilly and I choose to leave behind; they hold positions, jobs, but seem less defined by them, less consumed with an identity tied to a time clock. We have found them warm, friendly and free-spirited; often we spend our weekends at beach bonfires, singing a wide range of songs, American and Brazilian. In addition to falling deeply in love, all over again with each other, like the teenagers we had been so many years ago, we both quickly fell in love with Brazil and her people.

Jilly is not starting to show yet, and I can't help but smile knowing our child will come in April. There is something cosmic in that. Married life agrees with her and she has quickly made friends with a wide range of neighbors and people in the markets. She often rises early to grab meats, cheeses, breads and vegetables that we love to eat with our fingers while sitting on our deck overlooking the expanse of the city below us.

I am stretched out on the deck chairs Jilly had special ordered from a Chilean company she had read about in a magazine. I hate flying, and I have found this deck, these chairs bring me some measure of small comfort. Jilly's Portuguese is much better than mine and she has taken to reading many Brazilian magazines, newspapers and is even going to work for a construction company that works on many of Brazil's highway and road projects. I have quit the only adult job I ever held, and my business is now also concluded. I will find the next act of myself in time.

We have no plan to ever return to America, nor any desire to do so. There is a buzz in these streets, and at festivals, as 2000 marches closer. People say the world will forget war in the next century. That the old enemies are gone. They laugh and are joyous at the coming new century, millennia. Perhaps, they are too optimistic. They are an optimistic people. Or, maybe the last of my American pessimism clings tight. The cowboy always spoiling for a fight. Perhaps.

Jilly cuts out newspaper clippings from the lone American paper she purchases every day, *The New York Times*. Often, she'll post the clippings in the new scrap book she has begun work on. I think she feels a mixture of convoluted pride in me, the pride of a woman, who is staunchly defended and supported, and uncertainty and confusion and remorse that also eats at me. I feel no victory. There are no parades. No ticker-tape. But it is done.

Escalardo murdered in Matamoros

MEXICO CITY, MEXICO (AP) — Former top general of the Mexican Army, Vincente Javier Rafeal Escalardo was found dead in the streets of Matamoros, a sleepy Mexican town that borders Brownsville, Texas, Wednesday, along with six of his top lieutenants in what authorities believe is an escalation of an ongoing war between rival drug cartels.

Witnesses to the shooting claim a single American-looking gunman fired the fatal shots as the seven men emerged from a pub following the broadcast of a Mexican league soccer game. Authorities dispute the claims of the witnesses and believe the deaths are probably the work of the Durango Cartel, which has been looking to increase its stranglehold over the lucrative Mexican drug trade.

I'll forever be haunted by her eyes. And wonder.

THE END

ABOUT THE AUTHOR

Scott Michael Bowers is originally from Georgia. He has lived across many parts of the United States, preferring the South he knows and has come to love. He has held a myriad of positions including reporter, bartender and a miserable stretch as a repo man.

He is married to wife, Emily, and the couple lives in the foothills of North Carolina with their three children, Fiona, Gideon & Rio.

This is the first of what he hopes will be many novels.

Made in the USA
Lexington, KY
27 January 2015